Hemingway's Reading 1910-1940

Hemingway's Reading
1910-1940

AN INVENTORY

Michael S. Reynolds

PRINCETON UNIVERSITY PRESS
Princeton, New Jersey

IN MEMORY OF PROFESSOR RUDOSLAV TSANOFF

"But what about the soul, Dr. Tsanoff?"
"That, Mr. Reynolds, is metaphysics.
This course does not deal in metaphysics."

Preface

THIS book is not a study of literary influences. Nor is it a compilation of Hemingway's literary allusions. What you will find here is an inventory of those books, periodicals, and newspapers that Hemingway owned or borrowed between 1910 and 1940. The inventory is not complete, but the substantial patterns are far-ranging with frequently obvious implications. Begun as a tool for prying open Hemingway's literary biography, this book should aid scholars on other bents. If nothing else, I hope to deflate the production of absurd source studies, at least temporarily.

Some books so stun us with their brilliance that nothing remains to be said on the subject. These books become classics, but so intimidate the less brilliant that we are speechless. *Hemingway's Reading* will not stun you with its brilliance. Conversely, it is not an end, but a beginning.

Acknowledgments

There are these to be thanked:

Mary Hemingway, whose generosity has made the Hemingway Collection available, and who has graciously permitted me to quote from unpublished material;

Jo August, the archivist who has catalogued the Hemingway papers, and without whose interest, encouragement, and corrections this book could not have been written;

Helen Garrison, my research assistant, whose time, perseverance and ingenuity make her more a joint author than an assistant;

Martha and Robert Brinson, who provided me bed, board, and good company on my many Boston visits.

I also wish to thank:

the Kennedy Library, Yale's Beinecke Library, Princeton's Firestone Library, and the University of Virginia's Alderman Library, and North Carolina State University's D. H. Hill Library.

The computer compilation could not have been accomplished without the superior programming of George Van den Bout and the assistance of the NCSU Computer Center. The travel required could not have been done without the support of the NCSU English Department and the summer grants from the National Endowment for the Humanities and NCSU. My research in Oak Park was made easier by the assistance I received from the Oak Park and River Forest High School, the Oak Park Public Library, and the Village Clerk of Oak Park.

The best help a writer can find is constructive readers, and I have been blessed with several. My wife, who has proofed computer copy these last two years, always kept me humble. Joan Stewart, at NCSU, helped decode Hemingway's misspelled foreign titles. My colleagues at the College of William and Mary gave me encouragement and aid. Julia Epstein corrected the

French entries and translated my letters. Scott Donaldson was particularly helpful in suggesting solutions to several unfound entries and in correcting numerous mistakes.

Thanks are also due my editors at Princeton University Press who found sympathetic and knowledgeable readers whose suggestions and corrections were a blessing.

Finally, I must be grateful to the Cubans for not allowing me a visa, for if they had I would be working on this book for years to come.

Contents

Hemingway's Reading 1910-1940

Hemingway's Bones

Education consists in finding sources obscure enough to imitate so that they will be perfectly safe.

Ernest Hemingway, Ms #489
Kennedy Library

i

THREE years ago, I said that Hemingway's reading was as important to his art as Coleridge's was to his.[1] My conclusion was inductive, based only on what he seemed to be doing in *A Farewell to Arms*. One reviewer somewhat archly allowed that he, for one, was not prepared to accept that statement. His skepticism was just, for no hard evidence supported my guesses. Now, after pursuing that hobbyhorse through dusty pastures, I must revise my original statement: *Hemingway's reading was more important to his art and to his life than Coleridge's was to his*. Here is the hard evidence to prove it.

In a self-portrait, Hemingway wrote that he would rather read than do anything else, except write.[2] His fiction is filled with readers in the midst of the strenuous life. Dr. Adams finds his son Nick under a tree with a book; Jake Barnes, drunk at Pamplona, reads Turgenev. Amid the green hills of Africa, Hemingway reads Tolstoi. That inveterate reader of newspapers, Frederic Henry, quotes Marvell to his pregnant mistress in Milan; Colonel Cantwell quotes Whitman. Robert Jordan, a professor of literature, remembers Quevedo behind enemy lines.

Those are the easy ones—the references one remembers without checking.

Hemingway's fiction and non-fiction, his interviews and his memoir provide lists of great books, critical commentary on authors living and dead, and numerous references to specific reading. In his "Bibliographical Note" appended to *Death in the Afternoon*, he refers us to the 2077 books and pamphlets that were his sources. No one, I think, took him very seriously. Perhaps we should have. Early heed would have led us to a more balanced view of Hemingway, the artist. This book is *not* a compilation of those published references, for they are available to any reader. What follows is a reconstruction of what Hemingway *probably* read between 1910 and 1940. This list is hard data. Books I suspect, but could not prove, he read do not appear. My sources—book orders, book bills, library cards, letters, and inventories—are all public, if somewhat scattered.

During the three years of finding, checking, and double-checking each entry, the hunt has led to Charlottesville, Washington, Princeton, New York, New Haven, Boston, Oak Park, and back again. There were more nights on the road than my wife cares to remember, more pages of holograph than a man should have to read, enough dead ends and zero research to satisfy any masochist. Perhaps, as Hemingway told us, pursuit is happiness.

In the pursuit, this book has changed shape several times. It began with the need for a tool. To start Hemingway's literary biography, we must know what he read. Once I thought the published references enough, but his letters showed them to be only the surface of the matter. Then there was the unpublished fragment, which all of us should memorize. Hemingway said:

> It is not *un-natural* that the best writers are liars. A major part of their trade is to lie or invent and they will lie when they are drunk, or to themselves, or to strangers. They often lie unconsciously and then remember their lies with deep remorse. If they knew all other writers were liars too it would cheer them up.[3]

If not cheering to the scholar, at least it is fair warning.

As geologists know, the relationship between surface terrain and subsurface strata may be slight. A literary biography must get to the subsurface. Not trusting what Hemingway said he had read, I resolved to search out the hard, primary data. In Princeton's Firestone Library, the Sylvia Beach and the Hemingway Collections are rich sources: Hemingway's Paris loan cards from the Shakespeare and Co. bookstore; his correspondence with his Scribner editor, Max Perkins. There I found numerous Hemingway orders for specific books, as well as books Perkins sent him unrequested. Then at the Kennedy Library in Boston, Jo August, the archivist, found a 1940 inventory for twenty-six crates of books that Hemingway took with him to Cuba. Ernest had typed and initialed each page.

The hunt seemed almost too easy, leading to delusions of grandeur. Why not go to the mother lode—Hemingway's library in Cuba? For two years I fished by that obstinate isle: Czech Embassy; Cuban Mission to the U.N.; State Department; Treasury Department; the Cuban Minister of Press Information and Cul-

ture; the Cuban Ministry of Foreign Affairs; Canadian connections; private connections; the CIA. It was a learning experience. I reinvented the wheel.

NOTES FROM A JOURNAL

APRIL 16, 1975

*"Enclosed please find 3 visa application forms which are to be filled in by
you and sent back to this Embassy—together with 3 passport-size photos
and a Money Order for US $5.00, payable to the Czechoslovak Em-
bassy."*

MAY 19, 1975

*The Czech Embassy is on Linnean Avenue, a beige and brownish-pink
building three times larger than necessary. Visitors are confined to a tiny
anteroom. Held there by the lower half of a dutch door, I make contact
with Mr. Hromadka, who speaks excellent English and has been three
years in Cuba. Trying to speed up the visa, I assure him there is nothing
political about my research.*
   "Mr. Reynolds, in Cuba everything is political."
*Were I a political militant or a radical journalist, it might be arranged
in a matter of weeks, perhaps days. But to catalog a library? He shrugs.
The expense to Cuba was great. So many arrangements to be made: a
security man to be with me always; a hotel room; a translator; many arrangements. For what? Cuba would get nothing from my visit. If I could
interest Educational Television in making a film, it might be a different
matter. I should write when I had some offer. No, not directly to Cuba.
Send the letter to the Embassy. He would send it down in a diplomatic
courier pouch.*

JULY 9, 1975

Cuban Mission, U.N

*Señor Pila has yellow-brown skin and speaks softly, smiling. He wishes I
had not come. Where did I get his name? From a friend. I cannot tell
him from a Cuban exile condemned in absentia to die. I should not have
come, for he cannot help me. It is not good even to talk with me. No, he
knows no one in visas. No, he can tell me nothing of conditions or expenses in Havana. We do not go to his office, but speak in the foyer of the
heavily barred brownstone that houses the Mission. Two impassive Cu-*

bans in pointed shoes stare at us from across the room. The security man, sitting beneath a large picture of Che Guevara, makes no attempt to conceal the pistol beneath his coat. Please do not return, *I am told.* It will not help. *It occurs to me that I may have jeopardized Señor Pila's security clearance. I wondered how he would explain me. Outside, I glance instinctively at the dark, empty windows across the street.*

AUGUST 14, 1975

Señor Jose Tabares
Director of Information
Ministry of Foreign Affairs
Havana, Cuba

Dear Señor Tabares,
I am writing you personally on the advice of Mr. Hromadka of the Czechoslovak Embassy in Washington, D.C. In April of this year I made application for a Cuban visa from which I have heard no reply. . . . Richard Hatch, from UNC-TV, and I request permission to film "Hemingway's Cuba" at Finca Vigia. We will. . . .

SEPTEMBER 23, 1975

Thomas J. La Manna from the CIA is in my office. He has a file folder with my name on it. The CIA wants to brief and debrief me if I get the Cuban visa. I insist that there is nothing political involved in my research. With the CIA, everything is political. Castro may talk with me. He does things like that. Talks with some insignificant tourist, giving him a message to take back. The Agency would like to be the first to know. They would ask me to observe certain details: how Castro looked; the color of his skin; his eyes; his speech, was it slurred. As La Manna opens my file, he hurriedly turns the first page. I recognize my signature on the bottom of it. They have copied the Tabares letter I sent to Hromadka. In San Francisco, Patty Hearst has been captured and some crazy has taken a shot at President Ford. My paranoia begins to multiply like a cancer.

NOVEMBER 4, 1975

My Cuban visa application number arrives: 14476-75. It comes via Hromadka.

NOVEMBER 11, 1975

MAILGRAM

Luis Garcia Peraza
Chief Department of Press Information and Cultural Affairs
Ministry of Foreign Affairs
Havana, Cuba

UNABLE TO MAKE PHONE CONNECTION STOP TELEVISION CREW AS
FOLLOWS STOP NEW VISA APPLICATIONS TO FOLLOW STOP

DECEMBER 3, 1975

Over the Thanksgiving break, my office was skillfully broken into. The brass chains on the transom neatly snipped close to the wall. Nothing is missing. Nothing disturbed. The transom was closed after entry. Call campus security. Nothing. No fingerprints on the desk. Not even my own.

JUNE 17, 1976

Still nothing. Called Havana. Mother Bell never severed connections. Probably taping it from both ends. Señor Tabares? There is no Señor Tabares. Comrade Tabares? Oh, certainly, Comrade Tabares is gone for the day. Call again tomorrow.

JUNE 18, 1976

Comrade Tabares will not return for a month. Comrade Garcia will talk. Yes, yes, visas, I understand. A difficult matter. Call back in a week.

JUNE 28, 1976

Comrade Garcia is not in. Call again tomorrow.

JUNE 29, 1976

We do not know of a Comrade Garcia. What is the problem? Visas? Yes, a difficult matter. Comrade Rafael Padilla will discuss visas with you. Call again tomorrow just at this hour.

JUNE 30, 1976

Comrade Padilla is out. He will not return this day. I try to call the Swiss Embassy in Havana. They will not accept any calls from the U.S., not even prepaid. It is not possible. The Swiss Embassy speaks with a Cuban accent.

JULY 12, 1976

Early yesterday morning, Sunday, two men in the back yard with electronic gear. Said they were with Southern Bell Telephone, trying to fix water damage on buried lines.

JULY 18, 1976

Sunday morning. Same men in the back yard. Same story. Said there had been a maintenance call. I walked around the block, but no So. Bell truck anywhere. Men gone when I got back. Ann says she'd made no calls for repairs.

JULY 20, 1976

Phone is doing funny things. Noises we haven't heard before. When did So. Bell ever send out a repair crew on a Sunday morning?

SPRING, 1977

A group of Canadians plans to catalog the Hemingway library in Cuba. Am I interested in going? Yes, but . . . tell me more about it when you get the visas.

SUMMER, 1977

In two years I have not heard a single direct reply from Cuba. Cut the losses and call it "Hemingway's Reading: 1910-1940." Enough is, by God, enough. Let someone else go to Cuba.

Had I gotten to Cuba, I would have grown grey on this book, for every step took three times longer than planned. At the Kennedy Library, Jo August had unearthed another book inventory made at Key West in 1955. By eliminating all post-1940 publications and combining the remainder with the 1940 inventory of Cuban-bound books, the original collection could be reconstructed with reasonable certainty. All it took was time and more patience than I thought I had. Fortunately, my dauntless research assistant, Helen Garrison, never let me take short cuts.

We began with the 1940 inventory.[4] Hemingway had listed the books by title and author's name, frequently only his last one. Most bibliographies list only by author. An entry like *The Writer's Art* by Brown can lead to a nervous breakdown in the *National Union Catalog* where Browns have been unreasonably prolific. Just when the task seemed endless, the computer rescued us. The Ohio College On-Line Catalog contains a data base of over four million book entries. From our local terminal we needed only to punch in the first words of the title and part of the author's last name. Within seconds, a list of possibilities would appear on our screen. The mindless computer loved nothing better than to search for Browns.

If, however, either author or title were the least misspelled, we drew a blank, for computers do not think or guess. Many of the KW-40 titles were foreshortened; many of the authors misspelled. Spanish authors, we discovered, almost always have a triple last name, partly hyphenated. In 1940, Ernest had made no such fine distinctions. Even with all our Browns identified, we still had to check each entry against the *National Union Catalog*, for the computer did not always have the earliest publication date.

The OCLC produced many of the foreign publications, but several obscure ones were not listed. Books published only in England, for example, might not be in the data base. We turned back to the *British Museum Catalogue* only to find that it, also, had curious omissions. The last resort was the *Catalogue of English Books*. Year by year, we thumbed through until we found the entry. Some we never found. Should I ever find a copy of *Immigrants*, for example, I would take great pleasure in burning that book on whose trail we wasted more than a few hours.

Most difficult to find were the continental publications not stored in the computer. For French titles, we began with the *Bibliothèque Nationale* only to discover how useless it was. The first volume was published in 1913; the supplement covers only post-1956 publications. This quaint methodology leaves Jean Cocteau out of the bibliography. We had more luck with French authors in the *British Museum Catalogue*, where Simenon is more completely listed than in his native guide.

Recalcitrant titles we took to the massive card catalog in the Library of Congress reading room. There, at least, one can search by title or author. But even that catalog, I was told, has five percent of its cards missing or misfiled. Every order contains seeds of disorder. Our frontal assault on entropy left me doubting the possibility of accuracy. If this were not to be my life's work, I had to expand my tolerance for error, had to admit that some books could not be verified.

As entries accumulated, we carded each: author, title, date, genre, source, subject and comments. Filing by title, we slowly filled boxes with cards impossible to analyze. The permutations for 2000 titles, each with seven categories of information, are not infinite, but they are formidable. The solution, once more, was the computer.

George Van den Bout wrote a program allowing us to enter, edit, and store the data in TUCC—the massive tri-university computer. Although I never saw TUCC, I became a true believer, capable of punching in the arcane words which moved the dynamo: *myproc clist, filist da(templ5), saveday, ncstat.* The code word, without which the cave would not open, was *inrtomes.* Using a portable terminal with a phone connection, Helen and I began transferring entry cards into electric magic. Neither of us understood the process; it was on-the-job training. In spite of a fool-proof program, we fools erased the first three hundred entries in less than a micro-second. At every turn, we learned humility and patience.

Gradually, George expanded our program to allow sorting the entries by category. Thus, we could recall and print the KW-40 inventory, or all the books ordered from Scribners. We could see the poetry Hemingway read, sorted by year. The computer gave us his reading on Africa, bull-fighting, or American history. Finally, the computer indexed this book. If you have never made an index, the vastness of this statement may escape you. Among those numbers is a treasure hunt.

As we worked through the list, I made periodic attempts to locate more hard data. Charles Fenton, an early biographer, had published some of Hemingway's early reading, but only a fraction.[5] Knowing it impossible to put all into a book, I guessed that his papers at Yale might contain more references. In March of 1977, I went to the Beinecke Library to read through Fenton's meticulous files, where I found another handful of positive identifications. The Stein and Pound Collections were an added bonus: Hemingway letters, some talking about his reading.

The largest blank remained the high-school reading, which the Fenton and Baker biographies only sampled. It seemed unlikely that any undiscovered evidence could still exist in Oak Park sixty years later. Every Hemingway scholar had made that pilgrimage, digging through the high-school newspaper and yearbook, reprinting all the juvenilia. After a year's hesitation, I admitted that I had to go. The other scholars had not been looking for books. The answer is often easy; the difficult part is the question. Without the right question, you never find the answer.

Actually, it was the Fenton files that settled my doubts about going to Oak Park, He, like many scholars, had carried out most of his research by mail. Locating everyone who had known Hemingway in the early years, Fenton sent out form questionnaires and follow-up letters. He had written his book almost exclusively on the basis of what was remembered. Memory, Eliot tells us, can remake the past. Distrusting my own, I distrust the memory of others unless it is supported by primary data. For example, memory has it that Hemingway's 1913 freshman English text was *One Hundred Narrative Poems*,[6] a book not published until 1918. The mind does not remember chronologically.

I went to Oak Park determined to doubt all secondary sources. A good part of the week I wasted just avoiding the Hemingway stories known by every ancient resident, stories told so often that even late-comers had them by rote: Hemingway hated his mother, hated school, hated Oak Park. His mother was large, old fashioned, wore ankle-length dresses, painted pictures, gave voice lessons, had pretensions of grandeur, could not keep a maid, hen-pecked her husband, and was a snob. But few residents remembered their high-school reading: *Actually we weren't in the same class. . . . Shakespeare, we read a lot of Shakespeare. . . . Well, actually we didn't move here until 1920, but nothing had changed.* I did not mention Darwin's answer to that saw.

Hemingway's Oak Park had died a natural death. Streets and houses remained, but little else. When Fenton went there in 1953, he found the town "bigger, shabbier, less genteel and spacious" than when Ernest had lived there. The houses had "become seedy rather than charming in their antiquity, . . . there are boarding houses along North Kenilworth Avenue."[7] By 1977, Oak Park had regenerated: a new village hall, a new library, a downtown mall. At 600 North Kenilworth, the Hemingway house is marked with a bronze plaque. Where apartments had lately cut-up the house, rooms had been restored, creating a two-floor duplex. Al Gini, a philosophy professor, rents the bottom floor, keenly aware of his surroundings. On a warm May evening he and I sipped white wine on Mrs.

Hemingway's front porch, discussing her son Ernest and the mores of Oak Park. On the walls of the living room modern lithographs, prints, and posters had replaced Grace Hemingway's oil landscapes, and a large picture of Ernest looked down on the potted plants. There were no Hemingways left in Oak Park except those in the graveyard. The family mementos, once buried beneath the dated hearthstone, had long since been exhumed by the local historical society. Nothing was left of the Oak Park I needed. All I could hope for were the public records.

In front of Oak Park and River Forest High School, scruffy students lounge about, smoking a last cigarette, waiting for the eight o'clock bell. Inside, students in curious, middle-class, hippie costumes are celebrating Sixties Week; cheap instant nostalgia leaps from bulletin boards. At noon break, live, bad music echoes down halls where once the students knew Cicero. I am not encouraged. Both the enrollment and the physical plant have quadrupled since 1917. Four thousand students do not seem to crowd the maze of hallways. But the old building in which Hemingway studied is still in use, the old lockers still in place.

Most of that day I worked in the school's new library, where hand-written acquisition records, beginning at the turn of the century, have been preserved: author, title, date, number of copies on hand. The year before, in Hemingway's high-school notebooks, I had found reading assignments: *Lecky, 75-79*. Now I was able to match author to text. A large proportion of the holdings had been in multiple copies; perhaps they had been required reading. The ledgers could not tell me.

On the second day, I moved my tape recorder and note-pads into the offices of John Edwards, Business Manager, whose vaults hold the official school records. Proudly, he wanted to show me what others had found: Hemingway stories in the literary magazine, Hemingway journalism, the Hemingway transcript. Here were the relics the pilgrims had come to touch. But what I wanted were records, reports, files, anything left from the Hemingway days, anything and all of it. Somewhat bemused, he began opening file drawers.

That dusty morning produced nothing. Most of the records began in 1920. Various office members thought that the early records had been destroyed or lost. All secretaries and administrators from those early days had long since retired, moved to Florida, died, or all three. Mrs. Nina Grace, a retired teacher working on the school's centennial history, had left me a note:

I doubt there is anything in the English office. I don't know what became of a record of departmental decisions that included some on curriculum. . . . I know that in his freshman year he studied narrative poetry—the "famous" *One Hundred Narrative Poems*, Greek and Roman mythology, and stories from the Old Testament. Of course, there was always grammar study.

In the next three years he would have had *David Copperfield*, Shakespeare (*Merchant of Venice, Macbeth, Hamlet*, perhaps *Midsummernight's Dream, The Tempest, As You Like It*), *Idylls of the King*. For years before I came there had been in the senior year much required collateral reading in 18th- and 19th-century English novels.

There was American Literature, but the emphasis was on English Literature.

I am sorry that I can't produce the evidence.

Mrs. Grace had begun teaching at OPHS after Hemingway had graduated. Like Frank Platt, his freshman English teacher, she too remembered the "famous" book of narrative poems, which could not have been the text.

After lunch, I began reading the only records apparently left from the period: the minutes from the Board of Education meetings, which had been held in the high school. With painful regularity, it met and recorded repairs, additions, purchases, supplies, problems and salaries. Periodically the holograph records recorded the approval for a textbook change, but only changes. Still, it was the first hard evidence of his high school reading; I copied every entry, hoping that the list of texts would appear on the next page. It never did. What did appear was the reason for the library's multiple copies: students had to buy their own texts. In an effort to hold down costs. the library was heavily used in all reading courses, particularly history and English.

There was an obvious corollary: each year a list of required texts had been distributed to a thousand students. I left the school that afternoon with little to show for my day, but I was certain that somewhere one of those lists still existed.

Over an early breakfast next morning, I checked off the possible places where lists might survive. Frank Platt, head of the English department for many years, had died just months before I arrived. Perhaps his papers held a clue. But Fenton and Baker had both questioned Platt, who had incorrectly remembered the *One Hundred Narrative Poems*. I reasoned that if he had kept the lists, he would not have made that mistake. There was John Ghelman, also retired but, as with all who had taught Hemingway, his memory had been so often dredged that new answers were doubtful. What I needed was the list itself. Thinking of my own class records, I would have been hard pressed to tell the texts used five years before. Who would keep such lists? Answer: secretaries.

John Edwards' secretary came early that morning, almost before I did. Her records were filed in a bank of standard grey cabinets. Old records? If they weren't in the cabinets, she didn't know. Sometimes files were consolidated. What did she do with a file cabinet when it filled up? That had never happened. When it did happen, what would she do with it? Probably move it to the attic. The old attic.

The assistant director of the physical plant took me up to the old attic by an equally old elevator. A bare light bulb exposed ancient physics experiments, broken chairs and desks, ground-glass chemistry bottles, faded banners, and three file cabinets—one of them locked. While I began to rifle the open files, a search was made for a key to the third cabinet. An hour later, I had nothing to show but grimy hands and dusty clothes. All the contents pre-dated 1920, but there was nothing on texts. No key could be found for the third file. I said I would wait while the search continued.

Not a little depressed, I poked through the backwash of sixty years. An antique slide projector, bulbless but unrusted, sat on a desk whose last carved date was 1924. Faded orange and blue banners proclaimed championships for teams long forgotten. In a corner, obscured by sealed ballot sacks from municipal elections and covered with a fine coat of dust, books and magazines were stacked waist-high. The foundation of the stack was a four-inch-thick ledger, whose flaking leather spine was labeled in gold—Receipts. Stuck in the attic until the elevator returned, I shuffled through the stack. Some of the magazines were from the twenties, but nothing earlier.

By the time I reached the Receipt ledger, the attic had become uncomfortably warm. Brown dust crumbled from the edges of the thick cover, leaving muddy lines on my shirt and trousers. Inside there were no receipts. Instead, thick scrap-book pages had been inserted, on to which someone had carefully pasted official school memos and announcements. It began before 1910 and ended in the 1920s: graduation programs, school plays and operas, assembly programs and speakers, letters to parents, tardy forms, lists of graduating seniors, rules and regulations, course descriptions and lists of required text books.[8]

The locked cabinet was never opened, but I no longer cared. After recording everything of value, I returned the scrapbook to the bottom of its attic pile.

More than twenty years ago, a technical paper based on secondary sources was returned to me a failure, bearing only the cryptic comment:

"Mr. Reynolds, quite obviously you do not understand the difference between research and *research*."

When I complained that the remark made no sense, I was told that perhaps I had no future in engineering. It took a poem by Auden to clarify the point:

Suppose he'd listened to the erudite committee,
He would have only found where not to look.

The Oak Park attic was our last major find. By July of 1978, we had edited and stored over 2000 verified entries. The computer had printed out pounds of analyses, which were literally strangling my office like kudzu. But what did it all mean? My answers, found in the following sections, are partial, a beginning only. The tool has been made; it now wants sharpening. I have no doubt that more of Hemingway's reading will come to light: perhaps the Scribner bookstore did not throw out all their records; maybe the Germans did not burn the files from Brentano's in Paris; somewhere, someone may have recorded those books the Hemingways donated to the Key West library.[9] Given his reading habits, I suspect the total count for these years may run as high as three thousand books. Should they all be discovered, I think that the significant patterns established by this bibliography will not be measurably altered. Conversely, I do not believe I have seen all of the significant patterns.

ii

In 1940, Hemingway's Cuban library held 800 books. Twenty years later, he and Mary left the Finca shelves jammed. Estimates run between 4000 and 6000 books. Even allowing for unsolicited gifts, he was acquiring 150 and 200 books a year. Now someone is sure to say that owning a book does not mean a man

reads it. No such claims are being made. He may have read none
of them, though that is not probable. For those critics who prefer the "dumb ox" version of Hemingway, no evidence is likely
to change their minds. The rest of us must deal with this list as
our lights guide us. For months I have been sifting the data:
computer printouts, letters, manuscripts, acquisition lists, and
eight years of notes. Stripping speculation from what seems certain, I am left with the obvious. Sometimes it is good to say what
is obvious.

One pattern fairly leaps from the following pages: when
Hemingway liked an author, he read him in depth. Roughly
twenty percent of the entries fall into this category. Some of the
names confirm what we knew: Conrad, Kipling, Turgenev,
Stendhal, Dostoevsky. Others raise interesting questions: Henry
James, Simenon, W. H. Hudson, and T. S. Eliot. What is not so
immediately apparent is the distribution of these authors in time
and place. Half are British, a quarter continental, and a quarter
American. Of the Americans, most are Hemingway's con-
temporaries—friends and competition. Only Twain, James,
Wharton, and perhaps Seton—all of whom were still alive in
1910—could be considered predecessors. The same is not true
for the British and continental writers. Roughly a third of the
British writers precede Hemingway's generation; almost all the
continentals were classics. This is the overall pattern for authors
with multiple entries.

Applying the pattern to the KW-40 inventory confirms the
bias. Of those fiction writers who were his predecessors, he took
with him eighty-eight percent British and continental authors.
The roots of this pattern can be found in Oak Park, where the
high-school curricula failed to recognize an American literary
tradition. England was all. Nothing in the records suggests that
the young Hemingway read any Poe, Hawthorne, Melville,
Emerson, Thoreau, Whitman, Dickinson, Howells, James,
Crane, Norris, or Dreiser. If there was a semester of American
literature, the school did not think it significant enough for a
course description.[10] Nor did the school library recognize
American authors; the only American novel held in significant
multiple copies was Owen Wister's *The Virginian*. Between 1915
and 1917, the only current American authors acquired were
London, O. Henry, Bret Harte, and Hamlin Garland.

The Oak Park public library was not much better. Of the
prominent Americans, only Poe, Hawthorne, Twain, Howells,
James, and Harte were fully represented. Every standard British

author was on the shelves in force, but it was not until 1916 that a single copy of *The Red Badge of Courage* got to Oak Park. All of Horatio Alger was there, but only a little London, nothing of Norris or Dreiser. Small wonder that Hemingway's *Esquire* lists of "great books" left out the Americans. Smaller the wonder at his *de profundis* remarks in *Green Hills of Africa*. As Huck said, "a body that don't get started right when he's little ain't got no show."

During his formative years, none of Hemingway's models of excellence were American. Later he might say that it all started with Huck, but when he began his own picaresque novel (still unpublished), he thought of it in terms of *Tom Jones*.[11] When he wrote his satire, *The Torrents of Spring*, he compared it to *Joseph Andrews* and *Shamela*.[12] He sounds American, but his roots are British. His early concepts of subject matter, structure, and style were influenced by neither the American realists nor the naturalists. For Hemingway, the American writers of the 1890s were a deferred generation. He had to go to Paris to discover Stephen Crane. Twain and James were his only significant contact with the American tradition, and he did not read James until he met Ezra Pound.

The chronological distribution of the reading leads to another obvious remark. For 1920-1925, the crucial years when Hemingway was learning to write, we do not have complete data. Hard evidence from the Chicago-Toronto years is skimpy. We know he met and admired Sherwood Anderson in Chicago. Ernest must have read *Winesburg, Ohio* then, perhaps the earlier Anderson. Later, even after their break, he read each new Anderson as soon as it was published. Very likely Anderson told him to read Stein's *Three Lives*, Turgenev, and George Borrow whom he had recently discovered. In the Chicago milieu, Hemingway could not have avoided *Poetry* magazine. At Y. K. Smith's house, he listened to Carl Sandburg, a *Poetry* favorite, read from new work.[13] Hemingway's unpublished manuscripts from this period contain numerous poems, many of them imitative. Later, from Paris, he published in *Poetry* with the help of Pound.

During the Chicago-Toronto days, Ernest read a good deal of Conrad. Of the nine Conrad books on the list, only *Victory* can be dated from this period. Greg Clark, at the *Toronto Star*, joked with Hemingway about a fellow reporter they called "Lord Jim."[14] Later, Hemingway would say that he was unable to finish that novel. He probably began it in 1920. As for finishing it, you must reach your own conclusions: *It is not un-natural that the best writers are liars.* Carlos Baker has, of course, thoroughly demonstrated Conrad's importance to Hemingway's development. By 1924, Hemingway had read most, if not all, of Conrad.

By 1921, he had also read Havelock Ellis's *Erotic Symbolism* and *The Dance of Life.* D. M. Wright recalls Hemingway using Ellis as a running joke: "I think you'll find your case analyzed on page so and so."[15] Wright also remembers Ernest reading Anatole France in Chicago. Only three France titles show up on the list. There were probably more, for France was a hot literary item; over twenty of his books were available to Ernest in translation.

I have often wondered how proficient a linguist Hemingway was. Could he read the numerous French and Spanish titles that appear in this bibliography? His three years of high-school Latin had helped him pick up a little Italian during the war, but he arrived in Paris (Dec. 1921) speaking little, if any, French. His wife had given him lessons on the boat over. Once in Paris, he was forced to pick up the language quickly. By his own unpublished account, he began with the newspapers. As a working journalist, he compared French accounts with the British counterpart: "They were all written in the same way. You did not have to look up the word. . . . You were familiar with the subject or you easily saw what the dispatch was about and you learned the words." French accounts of sporting events he had seen were also helpful: "You read the story of the fight which was worthless as writing but understandable since you had seen the fight . . . after you had read two blow-by-blow accounts of a twenty round fight you had seen you could read and understand an account of a fight you had not seen."

From the newspapers he progressed to the Payot French editions of war histories, memoirs, and apologies: "There were very many interesting books then about the war in French, most of them translations [into French], and I read them with pleasure happy to find out things I did not know." Another way of learning was to read books in French that he had already read in English. First he read Henri Barbusse, probably *Le Feu.* "It was not quite as bad but it was equally hysterical." He tried the French version of Romain Rolland, whom he had read in English: "It was not much duller than re-reading H. G. Wells in English but it was longer."

Next he read books in French that he "owned in English or could get from Sylvia Beach's library. Stendhal I found had been excellently translated at least Le Rouge et Le Noir and the Charterhouse of Parma which were all the Stendhal I had read then. Madame Bovary was much better in French than in English. . . . Guy de Maupassant's really fine stories were easy to read . . . and I learned what a good writer he was and how he had been cheapened by the translations."[16]

How shall we evaluate this account? We know he read *Madame Bovary* in 1922 and owned a copy by 1923. *Le Rouge et Le Noir* he appears to have read in French by 1927, but much earlier in English. We know he checked *The Charterhouse of Parma* out of Beach's library in 1925. Given the pressure generated by Pound and Ford for him to read *Bovary* in French, Hemingway had more than a tourist's interest in learning the language, and his keen ear, aided by his Latin training, allowed him to learn more quickly than most. As late as 1926, however, Hadley was still translating his letters into French for him. When he packed his working library in 1940, at least twenty percent of the books were in a foreign language. On that sort of trip, a writer does not carry dead weight.

Like that of the Chicago period, the record of his early Paris reading is far from complete. In 1922, Hemingway began borrowing books from the Shakespeare and Co. lending library. Unfortunately, his loan cards for 1922, 1923, and 1924 are not among the Beach records at Princeton. Until those records are found, we have an embarrassingly large hole in the carpet. With more time and resources, I would prolong the search, for I am certain those cards will come to light. Unless shredded or burned, all paper touched by Hemingway has had a remarkable life span. Or perhaps like Borges' archeologist, we will it into existence.

On the basis of his later essays and memoir, one is tempted to extrapolate what Hemingway *might* have read from Sylvia's shop. Noel Fitch has already written an excellent analysis of Hemingway's records there, making some judicious estimates of possible reading.[17] Carlos Baker, the first man on the scene, has provided even more provocative insights, many of which have still to be worked to their conclusions. To whatever ends this bibliography is put, it is well to remember Baker's warning:

Future investigators of Hemingway's literary background are likely to find many resemblances, both profound and superficial, between his work and that of the European masters he used to borrow. . . . But the future investigators are almost certain to discover, before they have gone very far, that

Hemingway's doctrine of "imitation" is of a special kind . . . what he seeks to imitate is not the texture, it is the stature of the great books and the great pictures he admires.[18]

When Ernest walked into Sylvia Beach's in 1922, he was not prepared for the "modern age." He had the foundation but not the framework for dealing with Pound, Joyce, Ford, and Stein. He spoke no French, had no background in French realism, knew none of the Russians, knew none of the modern poets. His only entrée was Conrad. Within two years he had completed a crash reading course that remedied most of these liabilities. In 1924, when the classic Hemingway stories began to explode, he was firmly based in the new tradition: Turgenev, Flaubert, Stendhal, James, and company. He had also read the new masters: Joyce, Pound, Eliot, Ford, Lawrence, and Stein. He had no choice but to read them all. In the literary circle that was Paris, he could not hide his ignorance for long. Making it a virtue, using it as a wedge, he went to Beach, Pound, and Stein asking for education. Among these three mentors and, later, Ford, Hemingway connected immediately with the writers he most needed. They directed him to the essential Flaubert, the important James, the best of the Russians. Along with instruction in the Tradition, they introduced him to the new writers. There was not a single important British, American, or French author then writing who was not known by one of his teachers.

From Sylvia Beach, Hemingway discovered the Russian writers and easy access to the literary magazines, particularly *Dial* and *The Little Review*. At Gertrude Stein's, he learned to listen. Whatever else he got from Stein, she must have directed him to Henry James. She also sent Ernest to Flaubert, whose *Trois Contes* was the model for her *Three Lives*. Given her bent, it is likely she told Hemingway of William James as well. Brooks and Warren entertain such a notion, although they find it unlikely that Hemingway actually read William James.[19] Once the mold is cast, it is difficult to reshape; so too with critics. Hemingway took James's *Psychology* to Cuba years after he had broken with Gertrude. For all the words we have read on his debt to her, the particulars of that debt have still to be worked out.

A deeper debt that has attracted less attention is the one he owed Ezra Pound. When he met Pound in 1922, the poet had recently finished his editorial work on Eliot's *Waste Land* and was helping Beach get Joyce's *Ulysses* published. At no other point in the twentieth century could a novice have found a more current master. Although Hemingway would later make disparaging remarks about Eliot, he took Pound's advice: he read all of Eliot, including the essays. Reading *The Waste Land* with Ezra at your elbow is no bad way to pick up a thing or two. Considering Pound's own *Cantos* of the period, he just might have been helpful with *Ulysses*, which Hemingway called "a most wonderful goddamn book." Pound's enthusiasm became Hemingway's. In the unpublished coda to "Big Two-Hearted River," Nick says: "Joyce was so damn romantic and intellectual about him [Stephen]. He'd made Bloom up. Bloom was wonderful. He'd made Mrs. Bloom up. She was the greatest in the world."[20] Molly's closing soliloquy would echo through Hemingway for years to come.

Pound probably gave Hemingway the same advice he gave the rest of the world:

> I would seize this chance . . . to reaffirm my belief in Wyndham Lewis's genius, . . . And I would name an out of the way prose book, the *Scenes and Portraits* of Frederic Manning, as well as James Joyce's short stories and novel, "Dubliners" and the now well known "Portrait of the Artist" as well as Lewis's "Tarr," if that is, I may treat my strange reader as if he were a new friend come into the room, intent on ransacking my bookshelf.[21]

If ever there was a new friend ransacking Pound's bookshelf, it was Hemingway. All the writers mentioned were to appear in the list of his post-1925 reading. Frederic Manning's *The Middle Parts of Fortune* would receive Hemingway's extravagant praise;[22] he would read enough Lewis to be disappointed by *Time and Man* in 1928. Pound said he would not take responsibility for that book: "You shd nevvuh trust appearances. When gents become phylosophers and write about 'Time and Man' and similar subjeks the strongest ties of friendship are put to excessive strain."[23]

Although Lewis failed Hemingway, Joyce never disappointed him. By 1924 he had read all the Joyce in print. *Dubliners* he would later call the twentieth century's one sure bet for immortality. Look again at the early Hemingway stories and you will see the impact of *Dubliners* in his low key endings, if nowhere else. *Ah, Madame, it is years since I added the wow to the end of a story.*[24]

"The minimum basis for a sound and liberal education," according to Pound, included:

Confucius, *Homer*, Ovid, Catullus, Propertius, *Dante*, *Villon*, *Voltaire, Stendhal, Flaubert,* the Goncourts, *Gautier*, Corbiere, and *Rimbaud*

"This would not overburden the three-or-four-year student. After this inoculation he could be 'safely exposed' to modernity or anything else in literature. . . . He would have axes of reference and . . . would find them dependable."[25] Hemingway completed the course in three years, graduating at the head of his class.

Pound's most important advice may have been directing Hemingway to Henry James. God knows Ernest was getting hit with James from all sides. His first two wives both admired him. Ford Madox Ford regaled Hemingway with James anecodes and Gertrude Stein thought of herself as a female James.[26] The question is not whether he read James, but which James he read.

In 1926, Hemingway sent Pound "An Alpine Idyll" for the new magazine *Exile*. Eventually Pound printed the story but not before forcing Hemingway to rewrite it. In the exchange of letters, he sent Ernest the following advice:

ANYTHING put on top of the subject is BAD. Licherchure is mostly blanketing up a subject. Too much MAKINGS. The subject is always interesting enough without the blankets.

An he sez, sez he, following in the wake of H. J. "It is my the so beautiful form that I am after, I am the ahtist, the american has a techniqueal mind."

An he sez: vot, you tinking?

"Aidnt tinkin nodink."

"I know vot you tinkin: tdamn your vater, dots vot you tinkin."[27]

Pound is tweaking Hemingway for over-writing a story that will not bear the freight, accusing him of trying to out-James James.

Two years later, Hemingway complained to Pound about the endless drawing rooms in *The Awkward Age*. Pound replied:

I never suggested that you read the Awkward Age. I made a nice little map of Henry, the high spots and the low spots, but ov course no one cd. be expected to follow the map, and THEN argue.[28]

A week later, Pound continued:

> My feelings were not injured by your illusions to H. J. Do you
> want the list of vols. I recommended or wd. you rather bore
> yourself with the others so as to know at furst hand.[29]

Pound's map of James had appeared in the *Little Review* ten
years earlier. "People," he said, "ask me what James to read. He
is a very uneven author; not all of his collected edition has marks
of permanence." Ezra highly recommended *The American, Daisy
Miller, Washington Square, Portrait of a Lady, The Pupil*, and *The
Finer Grain*.[30] If we wanted to guess which James the young
Hemingway was reading, these titles would be good bets. A
closer reading of the Pound essays and letters will probably give
us even better information. Left, once more, with the obvious, I
can say only that, under excellent tutelage, Hemingway read
more Henry James than we have credited him with.

Trying to reweave my carpet-hole, I have spun out more
speculations than I intended. But hard data it shall be, starting
with the index, which is no better than the bias of its maker. Be
warned: there are patterns I have not yet dreamed of, patterns
that may blossom to the knowing eye. I do not pretend to be
familiar with each of these entries. In coding the subject matter,
I relied heavily on standard reference works. For the most part,
fiction was not included in the subject code. Moreover, many of
the books subject-coded may be only partly complete, only partly
correct. This book is a tool. Like all tools, it may not reach into
every corner; it may need adaptation for left-handed use; it will
certainly require periodic honing. And like all tools it will be no
better than the craftsman wielding it.

Computer-counting the entire list by genre, patterns appear:

Biography	297
Literary History/Criticism	163
Description & Travel	161
Short Story	136
Poetry	136
Military History/Espionage	131
History	126
Murder Mystery	67
Reference	62
Drama	56
Essays	42
Letters	14

We did not count the novels for two reasons: 1) they were too numerous, and 2) they are sometimes impossible to identify in reference works. Hemingway read a lot of contemporary novels—keeping up with the competition. He read almost all the Scribners' authors, frequently making caustic remarks about them to Perkins.[31] When his editor wondered when Hemingway found time for so much reading, Ernest told him that a sleepless night might consume as much as two books. Mary Hemingway has said that he would sometimes have two or three books going simultaneously, that he read trash and classics.[32] A murder mystery is only about a two-hour read.

Were this book complete, there would be more murder mysteries on the list. Ernest began reading them in Paris; probably Stein sent him to Marie Belloc Lowndes. Jake Barnes was reading a Mason mystery while fishing at Burgette. No A.E.W. Mason shows up on the list. When they were through with books, Ernest and Pauline habitually donated them to the Key West library. No records were kept. However trivial the mystery may seem, one should note that by 1931 he had read Dashiell Hammett, whose style may have implications for *To Have and Have Not*. Between 1933 and 1938 the Hemingways read almost all of Georges Simenon in French. Three Simenons made the trip to Cuba.

Biography, Ernest read early and late. Twenty-five percent of the biographies and letters were of literary figures. The breakdown reveals a familiar pattern: American (17), British (41), continental (25). One of the more interesting possibilities raised by these literary biographies is role-playing. When Hemingway arrived in Paris, he did not know how an author should live, how he should appear in public. The only model he had observed was Sherwood Anderson. The only approved American models were James and Twain, neither of whom could be imitated. With the same care he lavished on his style, the young Hemingway shrewdly developed a distinctive public role. It was, he learned, not enough to write well; one must also act like a writer. In Paris he was surrounded by living examples: Pound had his eccentricities, his clothes; Joyce, his eyes, his cane, his erudition, and Dublin; Stein, her salon, her pictures, her little friend.

Just as he was to do with his fiction, Hemingway supplemented experience by reading the lives of artists and their letters. The three who got the most attention were not American, but British: D. H. Lawrence, T. E. Lawrence, and Byron. Romantics all, these men had led monumental public lives, which, as Hemingway should have noted, eventually dwarfed their writing. Foreign travel, sexual extravagance, beards, costumes, public secrets, adopted countries, bizarre behavior, heroism, isolation, the grand gesture—it wasn't their literature but their lives that Hemingway absorbed. Of course, they do come out in his writing as well. Think of Robert Jordan and then think of Lawrence and his Arabs. Byron had his Greece, Hemingway his Spain. . . . I find myself on the verge of a usual mistake. This is an introduction, not a biography. To those who follow, I give indications only.

The compulsive reading of literary criticism may surprise the "dumb ox" school, but not the reader of the Hemingway-Perkins letters. Ernest might despair of the critics, but he read them religiously. His clipping service sent him reviews for each new publication. He subscribed to most of the literary journals. His letters to Perkins show him acutely aware of published criticism. To what degree this reading influenced his writing is for scholars to ponder, but the task should not be taken lightly. For example, in his 1948 introduction to the illustrated *Farewell to Arms*, he refers to the novel as his "Romeo and Juliet." This analysis has misled more than a few critics. I suspect that he got the idea from the critics after the fact. After *The Sun Also Rises* reviews were in, he called Stein's quote on the "lost generation" splendid bombast, indicating that he had never taken it seriously. The manuscript indicates otherwise. I think his response may have come from the reviews. In the early 1950s, Hemingway read in manuscript three critical works: Baker's *Hemingway: The Writer As Artist*, Fenton's *Apprenticeship of Ernest Hemingway*, and Young's *Ernest Hemingway*. Any study of his later work should take this reading into account.

The history and travel books confirm much of what we knew: war, Africa, Spain, the bull fights. On World War I, he read everything: histories, memoirs, fiction. Elsewhere I have demonstrated the fictional uses to which he put his reading when he wrote *A Farewell to Arms*.[33] During the thirties he began to study the American Civil War, an interest that appears when Robert Jordan is sustained by memories of his grandfather, and reappears in *Across the River and Into the Trees*. The Napoleonic wars were another love, of which we have known all along. Led to them perhaps by Stendhal, he fastened on Marbot, whose memoirs he read first in translation and later in French.

The importance of war to Hemingway's fiction has been thoroughly defined by Baker, Young, *et al.*, not only as a setting but also as the testing-ground for values. The warrior or his surrogate: the boxer, the matador, the white hunter, live by a code of values which sustain them at their trade. The true test of the values comes in defeat: they must hold through death itself—winner take nothing. Hemingway's interest in Marbot, Grant, and T. E. Lawrence reaffirms the critics. Here are the warriors, the men on horseback, who lived by the code.

The reading reveals one other warrior, little connected with Hemingway, whom we should have suspected long ago: the medieval knight. Baker called our attention to Col. Cantwell's "chivalric code,"[34] but no one followed his lead. When Fitzgerald's letters were published, bemused critics did not take seriously his 1934 letter to Perkins:

> Needless to say I am highly curious about the setting of his [Hemingway's] novel. I hope to God it isn't the crusading story he once had in mind, for I would hate like hell for my 9th century novel to compete with *that*.[35]

Nothing in the unpublished manuscripts suggests that Ernest ever began such a novel. His reading, however, suggests that Fitzgerald was not being paranoid.

The last time the two authors were in close contact was during the spring and summer of 1929. Hemingway was drafting and redrafting the closing pages of *A Farewell to Arms*. He was also reading *Chronicles of Crusaders, Decisive Wars of History*, the *Iliad*, and *Life in the Middle Ages*. It was not the first time he had been interested in medieval times; it would not be the last. In 1939, he drafted a "medieval" epigraph for Martha Gellhorn's novel *A Stricken Field*. He did not let her use a title from "Twa Corbies," which he had long been saving: "A New Slain Knight." Try as he might, he never found the book for it.[36]

His interest in chivalry began in high school where he read the first two books of *The Faerie Queene*, Chaucer's *"Knight's Tale,"* and, perhaps most important, Tennyson's *Idylls of the King*. Closer study will show the influence of this reading, but it will not be found on the fiction's surface. There will be few allusions. But it will be there, ironically used perhaps, supporting the value systems of his lonely men. Chaucer's Knight and Colonel Cantwell are of closer kin than is readily apparent.

His known medieval reading began in high school and finished in the summer of 1929. About that time, his fiction began to change. The Hemingway characters from the twenties—Jake Barnes, Nick Adams, Frederic Henry—do not love well and do little heroic but survive. It is in the thirties, just after the last spate of medieval reading, that his characters begin behaving like heroes. Harry Morgan, Robert Jordan, and Col. Cantwell, who love truly, end up heroically dead. And the narrator of *Green Hills of Africa*, pursuing beauty personified in the greater kudu, is on a knight's quest.

Another obvious pattern is one that I suggested but could not absolutely prove in *Hemingway's First War*: first-hand experience was supplemented by research. For *Death in the Afternoon*, he told us he had done the reading. Here we will find many of the books he used. We will also find the reading basis for his Spanish Civil War. Those multiple copies of *Doy Fe* that he took to Cuba had a purpose. His African reading also had its purpose. In the foreword to *Green Hills of Africa*, he told us: "The writer has attempted to write an absolutely true book to see whether the shape of a country and the pattern of a month's action can, if truly presented, compete with a work of fiction."

Fair enough, an African *Walden*. He brought back the heads and horns, wrote the *Esquire* "Letters" to prove it. But what he did not tell us in that disingenuous foreword was that he had also read a whole shelf of books on African hunting.

His African interest began early in Oak Park and continued to the very end. Africa was Hemingway's west. The Marxists could not understand his safari extravagance, could not believe he could waste money so lightly when men were in breadlines. But the African dream was stronger for Ernest than economics. In *The Sun Also Rises*, when Robert Cohn asks Jake Barnes to take a South American trip, Jake refuses. Instead, he suggests:

"Did you ever think about going to East Africa to shoot?"

. . . .

"No; that doesn't interest me."

"That's because you never read a book about it."

(*SAR*, p. 10)

Hemingway read the books, including, I'm sure, Theodore Roosevelt's African adventures. Look at the pictures: Ernest with his Teddy mustache posed next to the trophies. His guide is Percival, the hunter who had led Roosevelt on to the Serengeti Plain thirty years earlier. Hardly a coincidence.

When Ernest returned from safari to Key West, he took with him twenty-one books ordered from Brentano's in Paris. All were about Africa: guides, memoirs, hunting, encyclopedias, and travel books. He read them after the experience and before he wrote *Green Hills*. I think that there is no obvious reference to any of his research in that book, but there, beneath the surface, it supports the exposed tip. We have been taking the iceberg metaphor too much at face value. There are more things to be left out of a story than we have suspected.

We too have left a good deal out. Blinded by scandals and feuds, by memoirs and hearsay, we have not looked beneath the surface, have not pursued the difficult questions. Let us declare a moratorium on nostalgia: on the Hemingway-Callaghan fight, the Dôme cafe, Duff Twysden, on all that public parade. I am sated with drinking stories, bored with gossip. I am particularly bored with psychoanalysis. We must resume the practice of the trade for which we were trained. At the Kennedy Library the treasure-trove is waiting. At the University of Virginia, the *Green Hills* manuscript goes largely unstudied. We have the letters, juvenilia, manuscripts, galleys; we have the Baker biography, the Hanneman bibliography, and, now, the main outline of Hemingway's reading. Let us put aside those burning questions of Margot Macomber's marksmanship, of symbolism at Kilimanjaro, and earn our pay the hard way. We have the territory and a few good maps, which still have blank spaces: unexplored regions. Starting from the measured benchmarks, we, like Eliot's old men, must become explorers.

iii

A warm afternoon in Key West, 1940.

A man is cutting the last filaments that bind him to his wife. No more secret bank accounts to hide his adultery, no more arguments. Pauline keeps the house; Ernest boxes his life for the last time. First to be packed are his books. The crates are labeled *Cuba*. Through the humid day, he carefully types the inventory—titles and authors—on his old portable. The names call up twenty years of memory.

First off the shelf is *Big Game Angler's Paradise*. The crate fills, is numbered and sealed. Twenty-four crates later, he stuffs in what seems to be the last book. There had been this to do. First, the books, then twenty crates of possessions: no inventory needed. At the end, he comes back to the books to fill up the last two half-empty crates. The last book in: *Angling in British Art*.

When the crates arrived in Cuba, Hemingway wrote "OK" on each typed page, but he did not destroy the inventory, maybe because of the writer's feeling for the typed page. Maybe a good

Protestant never destroys the product of hard work. But why take the time to list both title and author? Perhaps for a laugh when future researchers stumbled on it. He built enough jokes into the inventory to suggest that possibility. Whatever the reasons, the inventory is a record, a statement of values, a list of provisions to sustain him in the new country.

Forty years later we must make some sense of the puzzle. When I was younger, the compulsive rationalist in me would have found a reason for every book, but now I am more open to whim. For example, I have looked through the table of contents for the *Cornhill Magazine* of 1867. Certain articles would have caught Hemingway's interest: "Breech Loading Rifles," or "Don Quixote's Country." But would it have been worth it, after all, to crate such a large volume for the sake of dated essays? Could it be the serialized Trollope novel? Unlikely. Reason wants a literary answer, but maybe he just liked the cover. Maybe Pauline wanted it out of the house. The patterns are there in the carpet, but this is no machine-tooled rug.

So let me tell you what I do see, make a few safe guesses, and leave plenty after me. He took almost every book on the Spanish Civil War. With two-thirds of *For Whom the Bell Tolls* already in draft, there were still details to check.

He took everything on bull fights: books, magazines, newspapers. Pauline would have had little use for them, and in taking them Ernest was packing a vestige of the good place, the good times. He had not given up on the bull ring, although it would be almost twenty years before he could return. He still had unpublished matador stories in the trunk—"A Lack of Passion," for one—and there might be more to write.

The same for Africa: culture, hunting, geography, travels, Swahili dictionaries—he took them all. He had only scratched the surface of that possibility. Taking the books was like making a promise—a promise most cruelly fulfilled in his near-fatal African plane crashes in 1954.

He packed a lot of literary memoirs, for he knew that he would write his own. Some he took because they were classics; others, for reference. In 1933 he had promised Janet Flanner he would one day tell the true story of those Paris years. In 1940 he had not forgotten his promise.

Much of what he took was predictable: hunting and fishing books, travel books, reference books, histories. Reliable friends were there: Marbot, George Moore, Liddell Hart, the two Lawrences, and Byron's life. He selected books on European politics,

but few on communism. He left Marx's *Manifesto*. Political
idealism had floundered on the Ebro River in Spain.

Twenty-six crates of books. He was not traveling light into the
new country, but neither had Nick on Big Two-Hearted River.
Emptying a can of spaghetti and a can of pork and beans into his
skillet, Nick had said: "I've got a right to eat this kind of stuff, if
I'm willing to carry it." How else explain *The Romance of Perfume,
Tom Brown's School Days,* or eight copies of *Doy Fe*? But to leave
Anna Karenina and *Madame Bovary*? An adulterer in more than
one country, he may not have wanted blatant reminders. But he
also left *The Adventures of Huckleberry Finn*, which only a few years
before he had called the beginning of American literature.
"There is nothing before. There had been nothing as good
since."[37] Along with Huck, he left Frederic Manning's *The Middle Parts of Fortune*. Two years later, Ernest would say he reread
that book every year to remember his own war wound.[38]
Another copy? The book was out of print.

A lot of old friends got left behind. Some he thought he was
through with: Turgenev and Conrad. He was wrong, of course,
but the choice is a clue, a self-evaluation. Other old friends were
no longer friends: Dos Passos and MacLeish. But political dif-
ferences did not keep him from packing *Three Soldiers* and *Conquistador*. The forties would be a banner decade for war—just his
meat.

The masters, of course, went with him: Pound, Joyce, Eliot,
and James. Does James surprise you? Does Eliot? Ernest packed
the poems and all the criticism—even the Dante essay. In
another crate, he took *The Divine Comedy*. Maybe, just maybe,
Hemingway knew more Dante than most of us. Maybe Cantwell
was serious when he told Renata: "I am Mister Dante. For the
moment" (*ARIT*, p. 246).

It is a bad book, the critics say, a transition piece not worth our
attention. A cheap answer, I say. I have been told by old men
that after *A Farewell to Arms*, Hemingway is all downhill. Suppose, for the sake of argument, the charge were true. When a
professional politician fails in office, social scientists savor the
causes. When a successful general fails in battle, historians
hunger for the reasons. To ignore the so-called failures is to ignore data any archeologist would prize. But these books, they
say, burn with no gem-like flame; they are not Art. Perhaps we
have become too precious. When Eliot died, Ezra could not
speak of art: *Who is there now for me to share a joke with*?[39] The art is
in maker; Art is metaphysics. This book does not deal with
metaphysics.

The artists, of course, are a different matter. Dante, Villon, Baudelaire, Voltaire, Stendhal, Flaubert, Shakespeare, Tolstoi, Dostoevsky—they all got crated for Cuba. Ernest had not sat at Pound's knee for many a year, but much of his advice still tested true. If he did not take the precise volumes once recommended, perhaps his needs had changed.

Some of the books had been with him a long time: Borrow's *The Bible in Spain*, George Moore's *Heloise and Abelard*, Franklin's *Autobiography*. I don't think he took them for sentimental reasons. Borrow is a puzzle until you read him. Skip past the evangelism to the narratives, where he tells a fascinating story. He knows his gypsies. Borrow's *Lavengro* made the trip across; it also made its way into *For Whom the Bell Tolls*. Ernest left *Don Quixote*, but packed Cervantes' *Numancia*: Spaniards holding a fortified hill against superior Roman legions. Hemingway left Homer's *Odyssey*, knowing that Pound and Joyce had squatters' rights, but he took the *Iliad* and *War and Peace*. Once he told Perkins that he would never compete with Tolstoi.

Some of the Key West collections got split: a division of property. Some collections didn't interest Hemingway at all: Edith Wharton, Anatole France, Seton, most of Proust, all of Maurois but one, Nathaniel Hawthorne.

Some of Hemingway's Key West choices run true to form: *Winesburg, Ohio*, Clausewitz *On War*, *Tom Jones*, and Kipling. Some are ironic: *Rule a Wife and Have a Wife*. Some, a little perverse: he took Swinburne and Rossetti, but left Browning. He took books on prostitutes, war, murder, and travel.

It is interesting to speculate — yes, speculate. I have said that writers were untrustworthy. It is interesting to speculate, on the basis of the shipment, where he thought he was going next. Aside from his "Tom Jones" novel, begun and put away in the twenties, he had at hand no significant manuscripts. After finishing *For Whom the Bell Tolls*, which way would he turn? The next six years would be the driest of his entire career: one introduction and a small bag of journalism. In letters and elsewhere, Hemingway made dark comments about truth's being unprintable in wartime. I think that fails to explain the hiatus. He could have written without publishing; he knew subjects other than war. A writer, not writing, feels guilty, and guilt is a great provider of rationale. There was the war effort: chasing subs in his homemade Q-boat. The real problem, I think, was how to follow his giant novel? Where would he find the subject to match that mountain?

The inventory suggests several possibilities. A significant

number of the books deal with wartime espionage. A jaded genre in our time, perhaps, but not without virtue. Inside information, violence, expertise, secrets, isolation, self-reliance: we can see how it fits. With his band of gypsies, Robert Jordan practices that trade. Thomas Hudson, with his band of Cubans, works for Naval Intelligence. The settings are turned inside out: the mountains of Spain become the Gulf Stream. The situations are corollaries: a secret band behind enemy lines; a secret band inside neutral lines. Sabotage becomes counterintelligence. (Don't forget, he took Auden's poetry.) And in the end, the very end, he would be haunted by paranoid fears of the IRS and the FBI secretly trailing him westward.[40]

The American Civil War and the Old West were more fertile possibilities for fiction. During the thirties, Hemingway- had come to realize that these were the two great American myths: *the* war and *the* last frontier, where self-reliance was still a virtue. He took biographies of Davy Crockett, Custer, Grant, Quantrell, Wyatt Earp; histories of western expeditions: lost causes, fast guns, guerrilla warfare, dead and deadly Indians. Robert Jordan, a self-reliant western intellectual, calls upon his grandfather's Civil War memory to sustain him at the moment of truth. Cantwell, in Venice, thinks on Custer. Those moments are as close as Hemingway came to overt use of this reading. There should have been more.

He never wrote the marlin book to complement *Death in the Afternoon*. He never wrote the Civil War book, which could have been a beauty, for he could read terrain maps better than most people see hills first-hand. His last twenty years gave us precious little. Some will say that after the African plane crashes of 1954 he never recovered his form. The manuscript for *A Moveable Feast* belies that cliché. Part of what he never wrote may have been the publisher's fault by omission.

Somehow Perkins never gave Ernest the kind of suggestions he lavished on Marjorie Rawlings, never labored with him as he did with Wolfe. Max was always a little in awe of Ernest, a little diffident. Few and far between are the editor's marks on the typescripts and galleys. Maybe he thought Hemingway would resent suggestions. He probably would have. But Perkins could have encouraged him to do more nonfiction, to do a travel book. What Max wanted was fiction. He never really understood that Hemingway wanted to be a *man of letters*. How could he understand? Men of letters looked like Edmund Wilson, or at least like Dos Passos. Men of letters did not lead outrageous lives. No matter how much Ernest assured Perkins that he really worked hard at his trade, Perkins was left wide-eyed by the legendary life. Hemingway was a novelist, not a thinker, not an intellectual. By the time Perkins died in 1947, the mold was set.

But Hemingway knew all about the man-of-letters tradition. He had studied Ford and Pound. He had read the lives of the artists: Lawrence, Byron. He had watched Huxley, Maurois, and Gide practice it well. A man of letters wrote not just fiction, but essays, nonfiction, travel pieces; he wrote poems and plays; he published his memoirs and perhaps his letters. Then, in his dotage, his publishers issued a fine standard edition of the works, with authorial introductions. Scribners had lavished such care on Henry James, on Ellen Glasgow. But Hemingway did not fit their image. When he wanted Scribners to collect and publish his *Esquire* essays, Perkins dissuaded him. They did publish his play, *The Fifth Column*, but not with enthusiasm. Perkins gently urged Ernest back to the fiction. Only after Hemingway's death would the essays be selectively collected. Three years after Mary Hemingway gave permission, Hemingway's poetry is finally to be published, but not by Scribners. Eventually the entire iceberg will surface; eventually we will see him whole.

Packing his books that day in Key West, he laid in provisions against an uncertain future. Leaving Pauline, who had supported him through the thirties when royalties had not covered expenses, he was cutting loose for another country, another woman. He did not calculate all the risks. *The Theory of the Leisure Class* remained on the shelf, just when he most needed it. With him he took those writers upon whom he had come to rely, just as a hunter favors particular cartridges with particular loads, effective at various ranges. He took some writers for reference, some for style, others as classics. His book crates outnumbered all other possessions. Not planning to return, he could not take unnecessary chances. Some writers, he knew, were "born only to help another writer to write one sentence."[41]

For sheer intensity, there is nothing like a convert, or a self-educated man. After those early Paris years, Hemingway was never again to be embarrassed by ignorance. Books, he once told a friend, were his ammunition. An apt metaphor: the professional hunter never stalks the beast underpowered, and we, the viewers, see only the trophy, never the bullet that killed. The reading habits he developed to compensate for his lack of formal education became an invisible, but crucial, part of his technique. Eliot forces his readers back to the library to retool: art as cryptogram, as crossword puzzle. Find just one more allusion and all will come clear. Of course, that was foolish, but the game interested us. With Hemingway, the meaning does not rest on allusion. On that point, Baker gave us ample warning.

Nothing in this book will radically alter our reading of Hemingway. What eventually will change is our understanding of the artist and the representative man. To know him more clearly is to understand what we have been. He merits our attention because he left us records in his time, records public and private, records which are a barometric gauge of that day's weather. No doubt there will be new interpretations of the novels; no doubt each age will find what it needs in his art. But some of us must become archeologists, sifting the dusty dig through a fine sieve. If, as some would have it, Hemingway self-destructs as an artist, that failure is not unique but symptomatic, an American failure. The point of our study is to arrive where we began and know the place for the first time.

Raleigh, North Carolina 1975

Williamsburg, Virginia 1979

Notes

1. *Hemingway's First War* (Princeton Univ. Press, 1976), p. 283.

2. Kennedy Library, MS #661.

3. Kennedy Library, MS #845.

4. Referred to hereafter as KW-40. A facsimile of this inventory is reproduced in Appendix-4.

5. Charles Fenton, *The Apprenticeship of Ernest Hemingway* (New York: Farrar, Straus & Young, 1954).

6. Fenton, p. 5. The text was edited by G. E. Teter.

7. Fenton, pp. 2-3.

8. Course descriptions and required texts are reproduced in Appendix-2.

9. These dead ends are "zero research." To pursue them further will require more than writing letters.

10. See Appendix-2.

11. Hemingway letters to Max Perkins, Sept. 15, Oct. 15, and Nov. 24, 1927.

12. Hemingway letter to Horace Liveright, Dec. 7, 1925.

13. Fenton Papers, Beinecke Library, Letter from Maude Barret to Fenton, June 29, 1952. Donald M. Wright to Fenton, March 9, 1953.

14. Greg Clark to Hemingway, May 27, 1920.

15. Fenton Papers, Interview with Donald M. Wright, June 28, 1952.

16. Kennedy Library, MS #409.

17. Two versions of Hemingway's reading at Beach's bookshop have been published: Richard Layman, "Hemingway's Library Cards at Shakespeare and Company," *Fitzgerald/Hemingway Annual 1975*, pp. 191-207; Noel Fitch, "Ernest Hemingway -c/o Shakespeare and Company," *F/H Annual 1977*, pp. 157-81. Fitch's work is far superior and most reliable. Before her publication, I had gone through the Beach records twice, finding one or two entries not on the Fitch list. I am particularly indebted to Fitch for checking ambiguous entries against Beach's acquisition lists. Between 1925-27, Hemingway checked out roughly thirty books a year. On this basis, we are probably sixty to eighty entries short for the missing years 1922-25.

18. Carlos Baker, *Hemingway: The Writer as Artist*, 4th ed. (Princeton: Princeton Univ. Press, 1972), pp. 185-86.

19. *American Literature: The Makers and the Making*, Cleanth Brooks, R.W.B. Lewis, Robert Penn Warren, eds. (New York: St. Martin's Press, 1973), p. 2260.

20. Reprinted in Carlos Baker, *Ernest Hemingway: A Life Story* (New York: Charles Scribner's Sons, 1969), pp. 131-32.

21. Ezra Pound, "A Retrospect," *Literary Essays of Ezra Pound*, edited by T. S. Eliot (New York: New Directions, 1968), pp. 13-14. Earliest version of this essay is 1918.

22. See Hemingway's introduction to *Men and War* (New York: Crown Publishers, 1942).

23. Pound to Hemingway, Jan. 7, 1928.

24. Ernest Hemingway, *Death in the Afternoon* (New York: Charles Scribner's Sons, 1932), p. 182.

25. Ezra Pound, "How to Read," op. cit., p. 38. Authors in italics all appear on the post-1925 reading.

26. See Stein's *Four in America*, written in 1933.

27. Pound to Hemingway, Dec. 21, 1926.

28. Pound to Hemingway, Jan. 7, 1928.

29. Pound to Hemingway, Jan. 11, 1928.

30. Ezra Pound, "Henry James," op. cit., pp. 295-338. First published in 1918.

31. Hemingway read heavily in Scribner's publishing list. Perkins frequently sent him free copies of new books they were bringing out. Many of the missing entries in this bibliography were probably Scribner authors. For example, I feel sure that Hemingway read S. S. Van Dine, the mystery writer, but could find no real evidence to support the guess.

32. Author's interview with Mary Hemingway, July 7, 1975.

33. See *Hemingway's First War: The Making of* A Farewell to Arms.

34. Carlos Baker, *Hemingway: The Writer as Artist*, p. 273.

35. Fitzgerald to Perkins, Nov. 20, 1934, in *Dear Scott/Dear Max*, edited by John Kuehl and Jackson R. Bryer (New York: Scribner's Sons, 1971).

36. Carlos Baker, *EH: A Life Story*, pp. 166, 474.

37. Ernest Hemingway, *Green Hills of Africa* (New York: Charles Scribner's Sons, 1935), p. 22.

38. See Hemingway's introduction to *Men at War*.

39. "For T.S.E.," *Sewanee Review*, 74 (Jan.-Mar., 1966), 109.

40. Mary Hemingway, *How It Was* (New York: Alfred Knopf, 1976), p. 491 ff.

41. *Green Hills of Africa*, p. 21.

Appendices

Hemingway's High-School Courses

DURING his four years at Oak Park High School, Hemingway took the following courses. My source of information is his official transcript in the school archives, which has been reproduced in *Fitzgerald/ Hemingway Annual 1972*.

English I, II, III, IV, VI
Latin I, II, III
Ancient History in junior year   (year course)
American History in senior year   (year course)
Applied Music in freshman year   (year course)
Ensemble in freshman year   (year course)
Algebra I in sophomore year   (year course)
Plane Geometry in senior year   (year course)
Biology in freshman year   (year course)
Zoology in sophomore year   (year course)
Chemistry in junior year   (year course)
Commercial Law in senior year   (half-year course)
Manual Training in freshman year   (year course)
Orchestra   (two years)
Gymnastics in freshman year   (year course)

Course Descriptions

REPRODUCED below are the course descriptions that accompanied transcripts sent out from Oak Park High School while Hemingway was enrolled.

ENGLISH I—The emphasis is placed upon oral and written composition, with the definite aim of producing freedom and spontaneity of expression. The classics read during the year furnish the basis for the introduction of the principles of narration and description. Special attention is given to sentence structure. Late in the year the principles of exposition are introduced.

Syllabus for English I

Classic Myths, Gayley	8 weeks
Idylls of the King	9 weeks
Old English Ballads	3 weeks
Rime of the Ancient Mariner	3 weeks
Bible Stories	3 weeks
Franklin's *Autobiography*	2 weeks
Exposition	3 weeks
Ivanhoe	5 weeks

ENGLISH II—In this course three lines of work are emphasized:
1. the history of the language
2. the study of classics
3. the study and and practice of rhetorical principles

Syllabus for English II

History of the Language	10 weeks
Chaucer's *General Prologue*	3 weeks
Twelfth Night	5 weeks
Pilgrim's Progress	2 weeks
The DeCoverly Papers	4 weeks
Macaulay's Essay on Addison	3 weeks
Carlyle's Essay on Burns	4 weeks
Formal Rhetoric Work	3 weeks
Silas Marner	4 weeks
David Copperfield	

Text for History of the Language: Anderson's *A Study of English Words*. Constant reference is made to the following works:

Henry Bradley, *The Making of English*
O. F. Emerson, *The History of the English Language*
Greenough and Kittredge, *Words and Their Ways in English Speech*
Matthews, *Words: Their Use and Abuse*
H. Sweet, *New English Grammar*
Skeat, *Etymological Dictionary*
F. A. Ward, *A Thesaurus Dictionary*
The New Oxford Dictionary

ENGLISH III—(five recitations per week for a half year) This course places special emphasis on the technique of English composition, a thorough review of the principles of narration and description and of exposition is made.

Syllabus for English III

Rhetoric	4 weeks
Burke's *Speech on Conciliation*	6 weeks
Formal Debate Work	3 weeks
Macbeth	5 weeks

Text: Thomas and Howe, *Composition and Rhetoric*

ENGLISH IV—The aim of this course is to present to the students a history of the development of national ideas as reflected in English literature.

Texts
Long, *History of English Literature*
Chaucer, *General Prologue and Knight's Tale*
Spenser, *Faerie Queene, Books I & II*
Shakespeare, *Much Ado About Nothing*
Shakespeare, *King Lear*
Milton, Minor Poems
Milton, *Paradise Lost, Books I & II*
Pope, *The Rape of the Lock*
One 18th-century comedy
Selections from Wordsworth, Shelley, Keats, Browning, and Matthew Arnold

ENGLISH VI—(elective) This is also a theme course. Daily practices given in review of the four forms of English prose composition. The work is based upon Bartlett Wendell's *English Prose Composition*, and *Selected Masterpieces of English Prose*.

High-School Acquisition Records

THIS list was compiled from the Oak Park High School library acquisition records. Because of the multiple copies, it is likely that these books were assigned collateral reading. Most of them do not appear in the bibliography, but Hemingway may have been required to read any or all of them.

Author	Title	No. of Copies
Arnold, Matthew	*Essays in Criticism*	9
Austen, Jane	*Pride and Prejudice*	10
Bennett, E. A.	*Buried Alive*	10
Botsford, G.W.	*Source Book of Ancient History*	10
Botsford, G. W.	*The Story of Rome*	30
Brewer, D. J.	*The World's Best Orations*	10
Brontë, Charlotte	*Jane Eyre*	10
Channing, Edward	*Student's History of United States*	13
Dickens, Charles	*A Tale of Two Cities*	10
Elson, H.W.	*History of the United States*	18
Esenwein, J. B.	*Writing the Short Story*	11
Fiske, John	*The Critical Period of American History*	16
Fiske, John	*The War of Independence*	20
Fling, F. M.	*Source Book of Greek History*	22
Gleason, C. W.	*A Term of Ovid*	29
Green, J. R.	*Short History of the English People*	20
Guerber, H. A.	*Myths of Greece and Rome*	11
Gulick, C. B.	*Life of the Ancient Greeks*	32

Halsey, F. W.	*Great Epochs in American History*, 10 vols.	10 each
Johnston, H. W.	*The Private Life of the Romans*	29
Mitford, William	*History of Greece*	10
Morey, W. C.	*Outlines of Greek History*	22
Muzzey, D. S.	*An American History*	15
Myers, P.V.N.	*History of Greece*	21
Ogg, F. A.	*Source Book of Medieval History*	11
Perry, Bliss	*Study of Prose Fiction*	13
Plutarch	*Lives*	11
Reade, Charles	*The Cloister and the Hearth*	15
Robert, H. M.	*Robert's Rules of Order*	12
Scott, Sir Walter	*Kenilworth*	10
Stevenson, R. L.	*Treasure Island*	10
Thackeray, W. M.	*Vanity Fair*	14
Toller, T. N.	*History of the English Language*	16
West, W. M.	*American History and Government*	24
Winchester, C. T.	*Principles of Literary Criticism*	12
Wister, Owen	*The Virginian*	10
Woodbridge, Elizabeth	*The Drama*	16

Facsimile of the Key West
Book Inventory, 1940

THE following facsimile reproduction of Hemingway's 1940 Key West inventory appears with the permission of the Kennedy Library, to whom I am grateful. Many of the entries present interesting problems in bibliography. Although I have solved most of them to my own satisfaction, not every reader may agree with my solutions. For this reason, I am giving the inventory itself. Every misspelling belongs to Ernest. All the jokes are his own.

```
                         CRATE NUMBER  I
BIG GAME ANGLERS PARIDISE                   MOISE KAPLAN
                            xxx

CASE OF ANTI SOVIET ETC.                    VERBATIM REPORT
SMALL TALK                                  HAROLD NICOLSON
SHERLOCK HOLMES                             DOYLE
TORRENTS OF SPRING                          HEMINGWAY
2 VOL. FAREWELL TO ARMS (RUSS)                  "
HAVE AND HAVE NOT              "                 "
2 VOLS. DEATHIN  FTERNOON   "                    "
5 VOLS.  HAVE AND HAVE NOT(NORW.)               "
2 VOLS.   "    "    "    " (GER.)
WAITING FOR NOTHING                         TOM KROMER
SHOOTING BY MOOR AND FIELD AND SHORE        LOND'ALE LIBRARY
TRAILING THE GIANT PANDA                    T. ROOSEVELT
ELEMENTS OF SHOOTING                        ERIC PARKER
HARDY'S ANGLERS GUIDE
HORSES,JOCKEYS AND CROOKS                   SARL
DEATH IN AFTERNOON (FR.)                     HEMINGWAY
FISH AND FISHING                            FRANK FORRESTER
BATTLES WITH GIANT FISH                     HEDGES
DEEP SEAS AND LONELY SHORES                 PUXLEY
GAMEFISH OF THE SOUTH                       L.S.CRAINE
THE COMPLETE SHOT                           BUCHELL
SEA FISHING                                 A.E. COOPER
TELLING ON THE TROUT                         HEWITT
THIS QUARTER #4                             M OORHEAD
IN OUR TIME (GER.)                          HEMINGWAY
A HISTORY OF SKIING                         LUNN
PRIVATE MFGR OF ARNAMENTS                   N OEL-BAKER
BEHIND THE SPANISH BARRACADES               LANGDON DAVEES
THE CRONICLES OF A GAY GORDON               BR. GEN. J.M.GORDON
GUIDE TO KUTCHRX  KULCHUR                   EZRA POUND
THROUGH TH FOG OF WAR                       LIDELL HART
THE GENERAL                                 FORRESTER
```

Havana

```
                CRATE NUMBER   2
ALSACE LORRAINE                       VOSGES
ESPAGNE                               GUIDE
CAPTAIN HORNBLOWER                    CRAMER ??
BIBLE
NORTH AMERICA                         ANTHONY THORPE
THE GUN                               FORRESTER
2 VOLS. MEMIORS U.S. GRANT            WEBSTER
VUS PAR UN SCRIVIN                    ILYA EHRENBOURG
HISTORIE DE L'ESPIONNAGE             OSCAR RAY
L'CONTE DEVANT VERDUN                 H. MORIN.
LA NOUVELLE GUERRE                    HELMUT KLOTZ
FARVEL TEL VAABENE                    HEMINGWAY
HISTORY OF BRITISH INDIA              HUGH MURREY
LETTERS OF T.E.LAWERENCE              DAVID GANNETT
UNFORGIVING MINUTES                   RAWDEN MALET
BIG GAME HUNTING AND ADVENTURE        MARCUS DALY
GREAT BASIN OF THE NILE                BAKER
JOHN GULLY AND HIS TIMES              BERNARD DARWIN
EDUCATION BEFORE VERDUN              ARNOLD ZWIEG
DANTE'S INFERNO                       LONGFELLOW
SHAKE HANDS AND COME OUT FIGHTING     STRONG
SPANISH ARENA                         FOSS & GERHTY
NOUVELLES PAGES DE JOURNAL            ANDRE GIDE
3 VOLS. GUERRE DE LA PENNSULAR         1807 -14
GAME MANAGMENT
SEA FISHING                           COOPER
GAME FIS OF PACIFIC                   GEO. C. THOMAS
AMERICAN FISHES                       GOOD & GILL
FLA. SALT WATER FISHERMANS GUIDE
EUROPE IN ARMS                        LIDDELL HART
AMERICAN FIGHTERS IS FOREIGN LEGION   PAUL ROCKWELL
2 VOLS. HAVE AND HAVE NOT (RUSS.)     HEMINGWAY
```

Havana

Crate Number 3

Roundup	Ring Lardner
The Short Story	Mathews
Tom Jones	Henry Fielding
Stephen Crane	Thos. Beer
Treasurers Report	Robt Benchley
My Second Country	Robt Dell
The Habits of Good Society	handbook
Earthenware	Edmonds
Sixty Seconds	Max Bodinhiem
Lord and Labor	Pio Baraja
In the Worst Possible Tasste	Riddell
Birds in Town and Village	Hudson
Towns of Destiny	Hillare Belloc
Principles of Equitation	de Souza
The World in the Making	Keyersling
The Naturalist in La Plata	Hudson
The American World	E.A.Mowrer
Islands of the Med.	Paul Wilstach
Creating the Short Story	Larry Goodman
Doctors Son	John O'Hara
La Guerra Carlista	Inclan
Nearer the Grass Roots	Max Anderson
The New Criterion	Review 1936
Draft of XXX Cntos	Azra Pound
Spanish Crown 1808- 1931	Robt Sencourt
Unknown War	Winston Churchill
Good Soldier Schweik	Hasek
Hampshire Days	Hudson
Poems	Swineburne
The Drassin	Maurice Parijanina
The Melody of Chaos	Peterson
Cornhill Magizine 1867	
The Common Leader	Virginia Woolf
Gentle Art of Making Enemies	Whistler
Avowels	Geo. Moore
Letters	Fran cis Newman
Letters of Byron	Howarth
Mr. Pope and Other Poems	Allen Tate
Le Fleurs de Mal et Complemamt	Bandelaire
Immigrants Guide to Calif.	Joseph Ware
Life Of Henry George	Henry George Jr.
Solders March	Fredenburgh
Pride and prejudice	Austin
Evacuations	Carl Van Vechten
Here are Stone	Inn Dall
Santa Fe Expidition	Jacob Robinson
2 vol. God Rest You Merry Children	
Tobacco Road	E.H. Caldwell
White Monkey	Galsworthy

Crate Number 4

IO Volumes	Stevensons Works
I3 Volumes	Antonio Foresti
2 Volumes First World war	Col. Ripington
Las Carredas de Toros	Garrocha
El Consulator Taurino	Alverez
Belmonte	Frenandez
Anuario Taurino 1918	
Frases Celebres de Toreros	Cxraffa
Toros y Toreros 1920	Don Luis
Sanchez Mejias	Alcazar
Hablando con el Gallo de Passion	
Desde la Garda	Minguet
Paginas Tauromacas	
Los Toros de Bonaparte	Ciria y Nassare
Guerrita	L.R.
KI KIRI KI	Don Pio
Guerrita	Pena y Gobi
Antes Y Depues del Guerra	F.Bleu
Toros y Toreros 1921	Don Luis
Resumen Pitonudo de 1929	Ton Parando
Care nd Feeding of Children	Emmett Hold
Captain Singleton	Daniel Defoe
Against the Grain	Huymans
Racundras First Cruise	Ransome
Plain Tales from the Hills	Kipling
Pout Diviner	Tully
Christmas Carol	Dickens
Fieldbook of Am. wild Flowers	Mathews
The Ugly Duchess	Becker
His tory of Conscript 1813	Gillman
Pride and Prejudice	Austin
Fieldbook of No. Am. Mammals	Anthony
London River	Tomlinson
Dubliners	James Joyce
Stalkey's and Co.	Kipling
Zuleiku Dobson	Beerbahm
Winesburg Ohio	Sherwood Anderson

Havana

Crate Number 5

```
14 Volumes   Sol Y Sombre
I  Volume    Zig Zag
2 Vlms       El Torero
el Maganim  Pittoresque  1836
Dicionario Tauromaco  1893
2 Vlms       Tauranaquia
rutmans Dictionary of Thoughts
2 Trilogia Taurina           Millon
Lagaritjio y rascullo y su tiempo
Monte Carlo                  Beresfords
Distillate                   D.G. Munroe
```

Havana

2 Sheet

```
                        Crate Number  6
Red Dawn                        Pio Baroja
Byron                           Xxrlox Maurois
Voltaire and FredrickII         Henriot
Le Destin tragique              de Maupassant
Doy Fe                          Ruiz Villaplana
Men "ith Out Wemon              E.H.
ADVENTURES OF JOSEPH ANDREWS    FIELDING
VUE VIE                         DE MAUPASSANT
" VOL. HAIL AND FARE WELL       GEORGE MOORE
BIRDS OF EASTERN NO. AM.        CHAPMAN
ANTRICHIE HONGRIE               BAEDEKER
LIFE OF SAMEUL JOHNSON          BOSWELL
ENGLISH VERSE                   OXFORD BOOK
THE STATE                       FRANZ OPPENHEIM
LA GASTRONOMIQUE GUIDE
ANNUAIRE DU RING 1933           XXXXXX  BREYER
IN OUR TIME                     E. HEMINGWAY
FLECHTHEIM GALLERIES  1929
L' ESPAGNE                      SANCHEZ CANTON
LA PIPA DE KIF                  RAMON DEL VALLEINCLAN
LA PORT DU FEU                  CLAUD WINZ
NAUFRAGIOS Y COMENTARIOS        DE VACA
DONOGOS TONKA                   JULES ROMAINS
BYRON                           ANDRE MAUROIS
MALAISIE                        FANCONNIER
L' ATLANTIDE                    XXXXXXXXXXX PIERRE BENOIT
LE TIGRE                        JEAN MARTET
CASLENETTES                     CARLOS REYLES
PEINTURE EN FRANCE I 906        MAURICE RAYNAL
MISTI                           DE MAUPASSANT
EVASIONS D'AVIATEURS            1914-18
FAWCETT                         TEX HARDING
VERLAINE                        SATURNIEN
ALCESTIS                        EURIPIDES
MORAVAGIUE                      B. CENDARS
LE VOYAGER SUR LA TERRE         JULIAN GREENE
CINQUENTE   MILLE DOLLARS       E. HEMINGWAY
LES FRERES BOUQUNQUART          PREVOST
```

Havana

```
        CRTE NUMBER  6              2ND SHEET

LA MASION DU CANAL                      SIMENON
COUP DE LUNE                               ''
BENJIMAN FRANKLIN                       AUTOBIO.
THE GLACIERS OF THE ALPS                TYNDIAL
THE WIFE                                ANTON TCHEHOW
A DOLL HOUSE                            HENRICK ISBAN
FROM DELOMITES TO STELVIS               HELENA WATERS
LES MUEB LES                            EMIELE?BAYARD
TWO YERS BEFORE THE MAST                DANA
DE GIL BLAS DE SANTILLANA        2VOLS.
BLACKMAIL OR WAR                        GENEIVE TABOUIS
LES LECIONS DE GUERRE D'ESPAGNE         DUVAL
HUMPHERY CLINKER                        SMOLLETT
HISTORY OF CHAS XII                     TOD HUNTER
SCHOOL MASTER                           ANTON TCHEHOW
MEMIORS OF A CAVELIER                   DEFOE
XMAS CAROL                              DICKENS
FORTITUDE                               HUGH WALPOLE
ESPEONNGUE IS ESPAGNE                   MAX RIEGER
PECHEZ AU BORD DE LA MAR                JONENNE
DOLLARNTURE                             ELLIS P. BUTLER
RULE A WIFE                             BOUMOND AND FLETCHER
TALES AND POEMS                         BRET HART
VOYAGE AND DISCOVERY                     CAPT. COOK
ITALY                                    BAEDEKERS
NOTRE DAME DE PRASLIN                   PARVIEL
ROMANCE OF MACHINE                      PUPIN
SUN ALSO RISES                          E. HEMINGWAY
CENQUANTE MELLE DOLARS                      ''
THOMAS L' IMPOSTEUR                     JEAN CACTEAU
```

CRATE NUMBER7

AS I LAY DYING	FAULKNER
CITIES OF THE PLAIN	MARCEL PROUST
KRISTIN LABRAUNSDATTER	SIGRID UNDSET
JURJEN	JAMES CABELL
THREE FEVERS	LEO WALMSEY
THE DEER FAMILY	THEO. ROOSEVELT
A NOTE IN MUSIC	LEHMAN
PICTURES FROM ITALY	DICKENS
ROD AND LINE	ARTHUR RANSOME
THE CRUISE OF THE TEDDY	ERLING TAMBS
IN OUR TIME	E. HEMINGWAY
JUD GUB	FEUCHTWANGER
THE SPORTING DOG	GRAHAM
FAREWELL TO ARMS	E. HEMINGWAY
SUN ALSO RISES	"
UPLAND GAME BIRDS	VAN DYKE
PHSYCHOLOGY	JAMES
GOOD SOLDIERS	FORD MADOX HUEFFER
BIG GAME FISH IN U.S.	CHAS. HOLDER
WINNER TAKE NOTHING	E. HEMINGWAY
2 VOL. HIST. EUROPEAN MORALS	LECKY
THREE SOLDIERS	DOS PASSOS
CHAS. W. QUANTRELL	J.P. BURCH
AUTOBIOGRAPHIES	YEATS
FAREWELL TO ARMS	E. HEMINGWAY
BEANY EYE	DAVID GANNETT
WATERFOWEL FAMILY	LEONARD SANFORD
INVITATION TO THE WALTZ	??????
DON'T CALL ME CLEVER	LAWRENCE DRAKE /O.K I WON'T (
THE GRASSHOPPERS COME	DAVID GARNNETT
LOS ASES DEL TORERO	SESGO
IN ALL COUNTRIES	DOS PASSOS
THE VIRGINIAN	WISTER
HALF GODS	HOWARD
HOW TO SKI	V. CAULFEILD
I THOUGHT OF DAISY	EDMOND WILSON
THIS IS OUR EXILE	DAVID BURNHAM
GERMANY TODAY AND TOMORROW	HENRY A . PHILLIPS
BOY	JAMES HANLEY
OLD LOVERS GHOST	LESLIE FORD
SPORTING FIRE ARMS OF TODAY	PAUL CURTIS JR.
NORTHWEST PASSAGE	KENNETH ROBERTS

Havana

OK

CRATE NUMBER   8

THE SECOND EMPIRE	CUEDALLA
THE COMPLETE SKI RUNNER	LUNN
LANDS END	HUDSON
LAVENGRO	GEO. BORROW
MINE OWN PEOPLE	KIPLING
SECOND READER	WOOLCOTT
WINE AND WINE LANDS	FRANK. H. BUTLER
WE OTHERS	HENRI BARBUSSE
HALL J. KELLY ON OREGGON	POWELL
DEATH IN AFTERNOON	E. HEMINGWAY
THE GRASS ROOF	YOUNGHILL KANG
PIKES PEAK GOLD REGION	VILLARD
OLD JUNK 1920	H.M.TOMLINSON
SPARKS FLY UPWARD	O. LAFARGE
THE SPANISH BULL RING	MOORHEAD DOWSETT
PAVANNES AND DIVISOONS	EZRA POUND
WAUGH IN ABYSENIA	WAUGH
DE'TRESSE AMERICAINE	MARTA GELLHORN
THE WILLING HORSE	IAN HAY
NATURE IN DOWNLAND	HUDSON
2 VOLS CUERTA DE LA CRUZ	ALEJ.LUGIN
THIRTY TALES AND SKETCHES	R.B.C.GRAHAM
MANNER	E. HEMINGWAY
BIRDS IN LONDON	HUDSON
POEMS IN PRAISE	SAMUEL HOFFENSTEIN
EARLY AUTUMN	BROMFIELD
FISHES	DAVID S. JORDON
C.Q.F.C.	LEON AMELINE
ZADIG	VOLTAIRE
CEUVERES	VILLON
M. CLEMENCEAU	JEAN MARTET
L' AFFAIRE RECLUREAU	FAITS DIVERS
TALLYRAND	JAQUES SINDRAL
PERVERSITS	FRANCIS CARCO
NEITZOCHE EN ITALIE	GUY DE POETALES
L'EC OLEDES FEMMES	ANDRE GIDE
JOURNEY WITH OUT MAPS	GRAHAM GREENE
DOSTOVISKEY	THE BROTHERS K
SALUD COMMARADA	MATHEW CORMAN
BYRON THE LAST JOURNEY	HAROLD NIC OLSON
SOME PEOPLE	" "
TRIGGERNOMETRY	EUGENE CUNNINGHAM
TIGER TRAILS IN SOUTHERN ASIA	RICHARD SUTTEN

Havana

CRATE NUMBER 9

LISTEN THE WIND	ANN LINDBERBH
AROUND THE WORLD SINGLE HANDED	HARRY PIDGEON
TRISTRAM SHANDY	LAURENCE STERN
THE MANY MIZNERS	ADDISON MISNER
THUS TO ~~RESTST~~ REVISIT	FORD MADOX HUEFFER
ANNALS OF A FORTRESS	VIOLET BE DUC
ONE LIVES TO TELL THE TALE	EDMOND GILLAGAN
SMITHSONIAN REPORT 1901	
WOHLD BEFORE THE DELUGE	LOUIS FIGUIER
WINGS FUR AND SHOT	ROBT. VALE
MODERN ART	E OS. CRAVEN
BEYOND THE STREET	EDGAR CALMER
PORTRAITS AND PRAYERS	GERTRUDE STEIN
3 VOLS. HISTORY OF HUMAN MAIRRAGE	WESTERMARK
TALES FROM THE ARGENTINE	WALDO FRANK
REDISCOVERY OF AMERICA	" "
CLIMBS AND SKI RUNS	F.S.SMITH
MEN OF ART	THOS. CRAVEN
BYRON: THE YEARS OF FAME	PETER QUENNELL
ADVENTURES AMONG BIRDS	HUDSON
SCENERY OF PLAINS MOUNTAINS AND MINES	F. LANGWORTHEY
LETTERS OF GERTRUDE BELL ARABIA	LABY BELL
PURITAINS PROGRESS	ARTHUR TRAIN
PERSONAL HISTORY	VENCENT SHEEAN
TAURINE PROVENCE	ROY CAMPBELL
3 VOLS. ON WAR	CLAUSEWITZ
THE REAL WAR 1914-18	LIDDELL HART
SKIN FOR SKIN	LLEWELYN POWYS

Havana

C RATE NUMBER IO

U.S. ARMY IN WAR AND PEACE	COL. OLIVER SPAULDING
THE AFTERMATH I8 1918-28	WINSTON CHURCHILL
LIFE OF MRS CHATTERTON	MYERSTEIN
TARPOMANIA AND BUCK FEVER	E.R. JOHNSON
SHORT STORIES	KAYBOYLE
DE ADMIRAL VON SPREE	HANS POCHAMMER
LES INFANTS TERRIBLES	JEAN COCTEAU
TRIOS CONTES	GUSTAVE FLAUBERT
THE FRIEN DLY ATCTIC	STEFA'NSSON
2 VOL. SIR HENRY WILSON	C.E. CALDWELL
FEAR AND TREMBLING	GLENWAY WESCOTT
COUR DE TZARSKOIE	ALEX. SPIRIDOVITCH
MEMORIES OF 48YEARS SERVICE	GEN. HORACE SMITH-DORRIEN
THE GANGS OF N.Y.	HERBERT ASBURY
LETTERS OF GERTRUDE BELL	LADY BELL
INCENDIE DU REICHSTAG	LIVRE BRUN
MY LIFE AS AN EXPLORER	SVEN HEDIN
GAME ANIMALS IN AFRICA	R.LYDEKKER
AM. DUCK GOOSE AND BRANT SHOOTING	WM. BRUETTE
SAVAGE SUDAN	ABEL CHAPMAN
LAKE NGAMI	JOHN ANDERSON
AMERICAN CARAVAN	B ALFRED STIEGLETZ
WILD SPORTS OF SOU. AFRICA	CORNWALLIS HARRIS
AFRICAN GAME TRAILS	THEO. ROOSEVELT
WITH RIFLE IN FIVE CONTINENTS	P. NIEDIECK
TWENTY FIVE YEARS BIG GAME HUNTING	PIGOT
MY DAY IN COURT	ARTHUR TRAIN.
RED CAVALRY	I. BABEL

Havana

CRATE NUMBER II

8 VOLS. THE GREVILLE MEMOIRS	
THE CHANTI FLASK	MARIE BELLOC LOWNDES
HEAVENS FOR THE GALLANT	THOS. ROURKE
TO THE PURE	ERNST& SEAGLE
CARE AND FEEDING OF ADULTS	CLENDENING
THE HOGARTH LETTERS	
TWO TALES OF SHEAN AND SHAUN	JAMES JOYCE
DORTHY M. RICHARDSON	JOHN C. POWYS
THE WRITERS ART	BROWN
THE AMERICAN	HENRY JAMES
DANTE	T.S. ELLIOT
THE HEARTLESS LAND	JAMES STEARN
POEMS 1928-31	ALLEN TATE
TALES OF ANG:ERS ELDRADO	ZANE GREY
COLLECTED POEMS	H.D.
PORTRATES IN MINIATURE	LYTTON STRACHY
FIRST PERSON SINGULAR	W.S. MAUGHAM
CHAMBER MUSIC	JAMES JOYCE
POEMS	W .H. AUDIN
REVIEWE FRANCAISE	1933
ICRO	LAURS DE BOSIS
ULTRA MARINE	MALCOLM LOWERY
ARE OF THE NOVEL	HENRY JAMES
WE ACCEPT WITH PLEASURE	BERNARD DE VOTO
THE LAND OF PLENTY	CANTWELL
NINTY TIMES GUILTY	HICKMAN POWELL
THE COMPLETE MANUAL FOR YOUNG SPORT'	F. FORRESTER
ANGLING	OUT OF DOOR LIBRARY
LA BOX E	
SAILORS DON'T CARE	EDWIN LANHAM
POEMS	YEATS
~~DRY FLY AND FAST WATER~~	~~PHILLIP GORDON~~
MODERN SHOT GUN	GERALD BURRARD
SPORT OF MANY LANDS	H.A.L.
EIME	CUMMINGS
SHOOTING TRIPS IN EUROPE&ALGERIA	H.P. HIGHTON
SMALL BORE RIFLE SHOOTING	CROSSMAN
SCOUT AND RANGER	JAMES PIKE
SPORTING RIFLES	CASWELL

Havana

CRATE NUMBER 12

THE GREY PILGRIM	PHILLIP GORDON
2 VOL. POEMS 1909-25	ELIOT
UMBRA	EZRA POUND
2 COPIES DEATH IN AFTERNOON (RUSS)	HEMINGWAY
HOURRA L'OURAL	A RAGON
9 VOLUMES	OWEN WISTER
LES GRANDES PROCES L'ANNEL	GEO. LONDON
QUEVEDO	CASTELLANOS
MORCEAUX CHOISIS	BANDELAIRE
L'EQUIPAGE	KESSEL
SUPERIOR FISHING	ROOSEVELT
EA FOND DE LA MER	SONREL
AUTOBIOGRAPHY	DAVID CROCKETT
PROTRAIT OF ARTIST YOUNG MAN	JAMES JOYCE
SAM SLICK OF SLICKVILLE	DARLEY
LA CONTITIONE HUMANE	MALRAUX
IN OUR TIME	HEMINGWAY
SPORTSMANS HAND BOOK	ROWLAND WARD
SELECTED POEMS	EZRA POUND
2 VOL. ENGLISH SWHILI DICTIONERY	A.C.MADEN
VIVA MAXICO	FLANDRAN
TYPHOON	CONRAD
THE FAIR REWARDS	THOS BEER
LA GRANDE PECHE	SAUVAGE
FR. AND ENGLISH DICTIONERY	
A PORTRAIT OF A LADY	HENRY JAMES
DAWN'S LEFT HAND	DOROTHY RICHARDSON
CRONICLES OF CRUSADERS	BOHN
WINES OF FRANCE	H.W.ALLEN
REVOLT OF THE MASSES	ORTEGA& GASSET
IN BRIGHTEST AFRICA	AKELEY
AMERICAN GAME SHOOTING	CURTIS
SPORT IN ASIA & AFRICA	DANE
CHAMIOS HUNTING	CHAS. BONER
JOHN RIDDELL MURDER MYSTERY	RIDDELL
THE ABYESS OF CASTRO	STENDHAL
WILD SPORTS OF THE WORLD	GREENWOOD
THE GAD TO EN-DOR	E.H.JONES
CLOTHES	ERIC GILL
DIARY OF E.H. (IN AFRICA)	
LONG HUNT	JAMES BOYD
LORD WALSINGHAM	RALPH GALLWEY
3 VOL. ON ICHTHYOLOGY	JORDON-HUBBS
NOT TO BE REPEATED	??????
SAN CRISTOBAL DE LA HABANA	R ALPH HERGESHIMER
BETTER TROUT STREAM	HEWITT
NEW COUNTRY	MICHAEL ROBERTS
ANGLERS CATALOGUE	FARLOWE
THE YEARLING	MARJORI RAWLINGS

Havana

```
                    CRATE NUMBER 13

LA LIDIA REVISTA TAURINA
    "    "    1882 - 86
2 VOL LA LIDIA  1915-16
SANGRE Y ARENA
2 VOL. LEDGERS DE TOROS
DOCTRINAL TAURONACO DE HACHE
BOB WHITE QUAIL                    HERBERT STODDARD
BOOK OF GOOD LOVE                  JEAN RUIZ
PROTRAITS AND SELF PORTRAITS       GEO. SCHREIBER
GAME OF BRIT. EAST AFRICA          CAPT. XXXX C.H. STIGAND
PRIZE RING                         BOHM LYNCH
```

Havana

CRATE NUMBER I4

RCORDS OF BIG GAME IN NO. AM.	PRINTESS N.GRAY
2 VOL. RECORDS (BRANISH)	
3 VOL THE TIMES	
ESTAMPAS DE TOROS	PEDRO VINDEL
TORERIAS I925	
LARGE GAME SHOOTING	COL. KENLOCK
DICTIONNAIRE DES PECHES	
THE HUNTING & SPOOR CEN. AFR. GAME	DENIS LYELL
SPORT IN EUROPE	F.G. AFLABO
2 VOL. TRANSATLANTIC REVIEW	1924
AMERICAN ANGLERS BOOK	NORRIS
LETTERS OF H.D. LAWERENCE	
GAME RANGER ON SAFARI	PERCIVAL
FISHIN G FROM EARLIEST TIMES	WM. RADCLIFFE
DEUTCHLAND	HIELSCHER
LE MAGASIN PITTORESQUE	1871
THE HAPPY FISHERMAN	STEPHEN GWYNN

Havana

CRATE NUMBER 15

9 VOL.	KIPLING
2 VOL. BIG GAME SHOOTING	HUTCHINSON
MILITARY SPORTING RIFLE	CROSSMAN
TIGER MAN	DUGUID
FAREWELL TO 5TH AVE.	CORNELIUS VANDERBILT JR.
BOOK OF THE LION	A.E.PEASE
RECOLLECTIONS OF A BOXING	JOE PALMER
L'ITALIE DANS LA GUERRE 1915-18	TOSTI
USE OF POETRY	ELIOT
SI FAN MYSTERIES	SAX ROHMER
BEST SHORT STORIES 1932	O'BRIEN
SHOOTING	HAWKER
THE TRAGIC ERA	CLAUDE BOWERS
CARSON THE ADVOCATE	ED. MARJORIBANKS
2VOL. HELOISE & ABELARD	GEO. MOORE
BOOKS OF SAINTS	MAYBE JESUS ???
IMMIGRANTS GUIDE TO ORE.& CAL.	HASTINGS
BIG GAME SHOOTING IN AFRICA	MAYDON
ATLANTIC CIRCLE	OUTHWAITE
SPORT IN THE HIGHLANDS OF KASHMIR	ZOUCH DARRAH
HUNTERS WANDERINGS IN AFRICA	SELOUS
BOOK OF THE SPRINGFIELD	CROSSMAN
BOOK OF THE TARPON	DIMOCK
THE COMPANY OF ADVENTURES	BOYES
WHO'S WHO ANIMAL WORLD	GEO. JENNISON
ELEPHANT	BLUNT
THE GUN	GREENER
GAME BIRDS OF KENYA & UGANDA	SIR FRED JACKSON
BELMONTE	HARRY BAERLEINS
HUNTING THE ELEPHANT IN AFRICA	STIGAND
MEN AND MEMORIES	WM. ROTHENSTEIN
BERNARD SHAW	FRANK HARRIS
EXPRESSION IN AMERICA	LUDWIG LEWISHON
EXPRESSION IN AMERICA	
THE INDESCRETE MARQUIS	HERBERT S. GROMAN
SCRIBNERS MAGAZINE BOOK	JULY TO DEC.1887

Havana

CRATE NUMBER 16

The Nile Tributaries of Abyassinia		Baker
Letters of Napoleon	1810-14	Frave
Caoba the Guerilla Chief		Emmerson
Life and Letters of Today	Vol.xviii	
Military Lessons		Helmut Klotz
El Espectacula mas Nacionale		S.G.R.
Look Stranger		W.H.Audin
2 Vol. La Habana 1546		
Propaganda		Sidney Rogerson
Biscayne Bay	1887-1937	
Hoy Fe		Vilaplana
This England		V.S.Prichett
Canciones de las Brigades Int.		
Boxing Record 1938		
Fiesta (Russ)		E. Hemingway
5th Col. "		"
Favorite Flies		Mary O. Marbury
2 Vol. In Wildest Africa		C.G. Schillings
Frascuecs		Hernandez
The Solar Salmon		Henry Williamson
2 Vol R.E.LEE		Freeman
Am.Angler in Australia		Zane Grey
The Hundred Years		Phillip Guedalla
Game Birds		Hugh Pollard
Gun Room Guide		"
Boxing in Art And Lit.		Wm. D. Cox
An Artist Game Bag		Lynn B. Hunt
Revenar		Max Jimenez
Farewell to Arms		E. Hemingway
Les xhaxsxd8 Chasseurs d'espions		Ladoux
In Italy in 1936		Gli Alberghi
We Fight Death		Gusti Jirki
2 Vol Canciones de Guerre	1937-38	
Sons la Foi du Serment		Jean Flory
Description Gen. de la Europe		
Numancia		Raphael Alberti
War and Peace		Count Leo Tolstoy

Havana

```
                    CRATE NUMBER  17
THE HUNTING AND SPOOR OF SOUL AFRI. GAME      DENIS LYELL
BRITISH AGENT                                 BRUCE LOCKHART
LEGAL RIGHTS OF PREFORMING ARTISTS           SPIESER
GAME RANGERS NOTE BOOK                        PERCIVAL
ALL THE BRAVE                                 PAUL& ALLEN
MEN  FISH AND TACKLE                          RALPH BANDANI
PERSONAE                                      EZRA POUND
LES GOLFS DE FRANCE                           REGNY
EAST COAST OF FLORIDA                         W.H. GREGG
MODEERN SHOTGUNS AND LOADS                    CHAS. ASKINS
PAUL DE KOCK                                  JEAN
ROOSEVELT  1880- 1919                         WISTER
NAPOLEON AT ST. HELENA                        FORSYTH
LA BA TAILLE DE JUTLAND                       PAYOT
NATURAL HISTORY ANIMALS                       JENNISON
R.E.LEE                                        FREEMAN
LIFE OF JOHN MYTTON                           NIMROD
41 YEARS IN XERICA INDIA                      LORD ROBERTS
CORNHILL MAGIZINE VOL XLVII
ANGLING IN EASE AFRICA                        HATLY & COPLEY
TUNNY FISHING                                 MITCHELL HENRY
8 COPIES      DOY FE                          VILAPLANA
LIBRESY FALLETES DE TOROS                     ARGUER
EFEMERIDES TAURINAS            JUBY TO DEC.
LA COSCENZA DI ZENO                           ROMANZO
CENQUANTE MILLE DOLLARS                       E. HEMIN GWAY
ENGLISH WORD SND PHRASES                      ROGETS
GARIBALDIS DEFENCE OF ROMAN REPUBLIC
2 VOL A STAFF OFFICERS SCRAP BOOK             IAN HAMILTON
A SPANISH JOURNEY                             MEIER GRAEFE
I DETTI DE GESU
SPORTS AND PASTIMES OF ENGLISH PEOPLE         STRUTT
A. GATTORNO
```

Havana

CRATE NUMBER 18

OK

TALES OF TAHITIAN WATERS	ZANE GREY
AXELS CASTLE	EDMOND WILSON
WILDERNESS TRAIL BOOK	DEEP RIVER JIM
FACT	E. HEMINGWAY
MIROIR DES SPORTS 1928	
PROGRAMA	D.C.DE ESP.
8 VOLS FRENCH GAME AND FISH BOOKS	
DON QUIJOTE DE HOLLY WOOD 1936	
JO BOAT BOYS	COWAN
MAGIC MOUNTAIN	MANN
CAPIJON	SHORT STORIES
A CHINESE MARKET	HENRY HART
MEMORIAL EXIBOTION	GEO. BELLOWS
PIRATES Y CORSARIOS EN CUBA	ULLIVARRI
QUATRE SAISONS	COLETTE
COMMERCE	
AFRICAN HUNTING	BALDWIN
2 VOL. DANTE	LONGFELLOW
HISTORICAL ROMANCES	STANLEY WEYMANE
RUGGLES BUNKER AND MERTON	WILSON
2 VOL BIG GAME SHOOTING	BADMINTON LIBRARY
FIRE AND SWORD IN INDIA	WINEGATE
TRAVELS OF MARCO POLO	MANUEL KOMROFF
HOW I FOUND LIVINGSTON	STANLEY
WINTER CARNIVAL	DECK MORGAN
REVELATION	BARABBAN
THE CROSSING	WINSTON CHURCHILL
NARROW CORNER	MAUGHM
LIBERTY OF CUBA	RUEBENS
CHANCE HAS A WHIP	HOLDEN
AFRICAN HUNTER	VON BLIXON
TOM BROWNS SCHOOL DAYS	SOME OLD BOY
AH KING	MAUGHM
ALECK MAURY	CAROLINE GORDON
SOLDIERS PAY	WM. FAULKNER
THE THIRD NEW YEAR (ESQUIRE)	ARNOLD GINGRICH
CYRANO DE BERGERAC	KUHNE
AMERICAN LIT. 1880-1930	A.C. WARD
RICHARD CARVEL	WINSTON CHURCHILL
OF HUMAN BONDAGE	MAUGHM
ACTIVE ANTHOLOGY	EZRA POUND
VOYAGE AU BOUT DE LA NUIT	ROMAN
THE SPANISH MARRIAGE 1554	HELEN SIMPSON
FRENCH GOVERNMENT	

Havana

CRATE NUMBER 19

A SHORT HISTORY OF SPAIN	HENRY SEDGWICK
UNROMANTIC SPAIN	MARIO DIAZ
SIR HENRY MORGAN	ADOLPH ROBERTS
GUIDE TO FRANCE 1929	MICHELIN
GREEK MEMORIES	COMPTON MCKENZIE
IN OUR TIME	E . HEMINGWAY
300 TRICKS CAN DO IT	T HURS TON
TAURINE PROVENCE	R OY CAMPBELL
IN DARKEST SPAIN	REV. ALEX STEWART
SPANISH GALICIA	AUBREY BELL
SHALL WE EAT FLESH	(SOME VEGITARIAN)
MAD ANTHONY WAYNNE	THOS. BOYD
REBELS AND RENEGADES	MAX NORMAD
POEMS AND SONNETS	ERNEST WALSH
LE SOLEIL SE LEVE AUSSI	E. HEMINGWAY
TERRES HOSLITES DE L'ETHIOPIE	MONFREID
MEN OF GOOD WILL	ROMAINS
THE ROAD TO NOWHERE	WALSH
THE BIBLE IN SPAIN	GEO. BORROW
SPAIN	S. DE MADARIGA
STUDIES IN SUBLIME FAILURE	SHANE LESLIE
WIFE OF ROSSETTI	VIOLET HUNT
GREAT SEA STORIES OF ALL NATIONS	H.M. TOMLINSON
GRAIN RACE	ALLEN VILLIERS
HENRY VIII	FRANCIS HACKETT
WYALL EARP	STEWERT LAKE
GOETHE	NEVINSON
EPIC OF AMERICA	J.T. ADAMS
BIBLIOGRAPHY OF E.H.	COHN
IT WAS THE NIGHTENGALES	FORD MADDOX FORD
ISSIONE	CARLO LINATI
IS 5	E.E.C.
BATTLING NELSON	BATTLING NELSON
ABC OF ECONOMICS	EZRA POUND
FIRST ATHENIAN MEMORIES	COMPTON MACKINZIE
REN EE SINTERNIS	
AVES INSECTIVORAS	PENA MARTIN
THE SMALL DARK MAN	M AURICE WALSH
THE ROMANTIC NINTIES	LE GALLIENNE
AMERICAN EARTH	ERSKIN CAULDWELL
POCAHONTAS	DAVID GARNETT
JUAN GRIS	KUNST
POEMS OF GERARD HOPKINS	BOBT. BRIDGES
FONTAMARA	SILONE

Havana

```
                    CRATE NUMBER  20
BLURPINGTON OF BLURP                    H.G.WELLS
AFTER STRANGE GODS                      T.S.ELIOT
GATHERINGS FROM SPAIN                   RICHARD FORD
TO THE LIGHTHOUSE                       VERGINIA WOOLF
AM. RED CROSS IN ITALY                  BAKEWELL
DREAMY RIVERS                           HENRY BAERLIEN
GOOD BYE WIS.                           GLENWAY WESCOTT
LUCY CHURC H AMIABLY                    GERTRUDE STEIN
WAY OF ALL FLESH                        SAMEUL BUTLER
THE ILLIAD OF HOMER                     LANG LEAF& MYERS
LIBRO DE GALLITO                        QUERRITA
THE MAN WHO LOST HIMSELF                OSBERT SITWELL
CREATIVE CRITICISM                      SPINGARN
POETICAL WORKS                           ROSSETTIS
GOOD OLD ANNA                           MRS BELLOC LOWNDES
FEISTA(GER.)                            E. HEMINGWAY
PETER EBBETSON                          DU MAURIER
MAGGIE                                  STEPHEN CRANE
THE DEVIL IN THE FLESH                  RAYMON RADIGUETA
BEYOND DES IRE                          SHERWOOD ANDERSON
2COPIES FARVEL TEL VABNENE              E E. HEMINGWAY
LIFES HANDICAP                          KIPLING
CATHOLIC ANTHOLOGY             1914-15
IMM IGRANTS                             CHAS.  BONE
MR. MIDSHOPMAN EASY                     CAPT. MARRYAT
JESTING PILATE                          HUXLEY
GERMAN SHORT STORIES
LES COMPAGANONS DE JEHU                 DUMAS
HAPPY TRAVELER                          FRANK TATCHELL
JOURNEL OF LEO TOLSTOI         1895-99
ROXANA                                  DEFOE
MANY THOUSANDS GONE                     BISHOP
POEMS  FOR HARRY CROSBY                 C.C.
MUSIC AT NIGHT                          HUXLEY
SAVAGE PILGRIMAGE                       D.H.LAWERENCE
PUMPKIN COACH                           LOUIS PAUL
42 YEARS IN THE WHITE HOUSE             I.H. HOOVER
SPY & COUNTER SPY                       RICHARD ROWAN
ONES COMPANY                            PETER FLEMING
HISTORY OF AN AFRICAN CHIEF             PRINCE NYABONGA
TIME AND THE RIMER                      THOS. WOLFE
AMERICA                                 ALFRED STIEGLITZ
PICTURES OF WAR                          STEPHEN CRANE
INSIDE EUROPE                           JOHN GUNTHER
LAUGHTER IN THE DARK                    VLADIMIR NABOKOFF
THE OLD MANS PLACE                      JOHN SANFORD
```

Havana

CRATE NUMBER 2I

FLIGHT SOUTH	CHAS. GRAWSON
HAVING CROSSED THE CHANNELL	MARCEL BOUELSTON
AM. DEPLOMATIC GAME	PEARSON & BROWN
REDDER THAN THE ROSE	ROBT. FORSYTHE
THE FURYS	JAS. HANLEY
5 COPIES SPANISH EARTH	E. HEMINGWAY
THE MAN WHO SAW THROUGH HEAVEN	WILBUR STEELE
BETWEEN MURDERS	SHERRY KING
MOON AND SIXPEN CE	MAUGHM
NEXT TIME WE LIVE	URSULA PAROTT
TWO WARS AND MORE TO COME	HERBERT MATHEWS
PRISON LIFE	WORK BURR THOMPSON
SAINT AND MARY KATE	FRANK O'CONNER
NATURAL HISTORY	WHITE
THE MONTEBANK	WM. LOCKE
STUDS LONIGAN	JAS. FARRELL
FISHING AND SHOOTING	EARL BUXTON
WORLD WAR	LIDELL HART
HUNTERS WANDERINGS IN AFRICA	SELOUS
DELAY IN THE SUN	ANTHONY THORNE
ROAD TO WAR	WALTER MILLIS
DOWN THE GREAT RIVER	GLAZIER
FOR AUTHORS ONLY	KENNETH ROBERTS
CHARLOTTE LOWENSKOLD	SELMER LAGERLOF
PERMIT ME VOYAGE	JAMES AGEE
THE SHADOWS BEFORE	WM. ROLLINS JR.
PROFILE	EZRA POUND
RETREAT FROM GLORY	BRUCE LOCKHART
MEN AND MEMORIES	WM. ROTHERSTEIN
BEYOND THE MEXIQUE BAY	HUXLEY
SECOND COMMON READER	VIRGINIA WOOLF
DRAMATIS PERSONAE	YEATS
FREE FORESTER	HORATIO COLONY
NINTEENTH CENTURY PAMPHLETS	CARTER & POLLARD
OXFORD COMPANION TO ENGLISH	PAUL HARVEY
DAYS OF WRATH	ANDRE MALRAUX
ENGLISH VERSES	OXFORD BOOK
FIELD BOOK OF MARINE FISHE	CHAS. BREDER JR.
LIFE OF JOHNSON	BOSWELL
THINGS SEEN IN NORWAY	S.C. HAMMER
SHADOWS BEFORE BOOK III	

Havana

```
                    CRATE NUMBER 22
JUST FISHING TALK                    CLIFFORD PINCHOT
TENTING ON THE PLAINS                MRS. E.B.CUSTER
I'M ALONE                            CAPT. RANDELL
TAHARA                               HAROLD SHERMAN
AFRICAN ADVENTURE                    DENIS LYELL
TOPPER                               THORNE SMITH
ABC MURDERS                          AGATHA CRISTIE
CONFESSIONS OF ANOTHER YOUNG MAN     BRAVIG IMBS
JUNGLE GAINTS                        NEWELL BRENT JR.
THE WAY OF THE TRANSGRESSER          NEGLEY FARSON
INNOCENTS ABROAD                     ??????
DECISIVE WARS OF HISTORY             LIDELL HART
EL JIMMY                             HERBERT CHILDS
TUNNY FISHING                        HENRY
MARK TWAINS AMERICA                  BERNARD DEVOTO
RIDING THE MUSTANG TRAIL             ROERESTER   BLAKE
COMMON READER                        VIRGINIA WOOLF
UNDER THE AX OF FACISM               GAETANO SILVERMMI
FLIGHTS OF THE LEAST PETREL          GRIFFING BANCROFT
ATLANTIC GAME FISHING                KIP FARRINGTON
FIRST WORLD WAR                      LAWRENCE STALLINGS
BOWSTRING MURDERS                    CARTER DICKSON
OVERTURE TO DEATH                     NGAIO MARSH
BORN TO TROUBLE                      PATRICK MEADE
YOUNG GRIFFO
MILITARY HISTORY OF WORLD WAR        GERALD MACENTEE
MEN OF NESS                          ERIC LINKLATER
CHEMISTRY IN MEDICINE                STIEGLITZ
ANALES TAURINGS              1900
kkaxbx
THE VOYAGE OUT                       VIRGINIA WOOLF
WORLD ALMANAC    1935
PRIDE AND PREJUDICE                  AUSTIN
LES COMPAGNANS DE JEHU               DUMAS
WHILE THE BILLY BOIES                HENRY LAWSON
MR MIDSHIPMAN EASY                   CAPT. MARRYAT
2 VOL ADVENTURES OF A YOUNGER SON    TRELAWNY
FROM THE CAPE TOCAIRO                CROGAN & SHARP
```

Havana

```
                          CRATE NUMBER 2 ₿
     #2 ₿
3 VOL. SHAKESPERARE
REVOLUTION                1870-71           J. CLARETIE
PITTORESQUE               1856-65
AN ANGLERS ANTHOLOGY                        A.B. AUSTIN
73 VOLS. ASSORTED FRENCH PAPER BOUND BOOKS
THIRTY CLOCKS STRIKE THE HOUR               SACKVILLE-WEST
POINT COUNTER POINT                         HUXLEY
BLACK TULIP                                 DUMAS
REVOLUTION '69                              Belda
```

Havana

```
                    CRATE NUMBER    24
#24
BOXING RECORD  1929-30-31-33
LOVE IN USA.                              JOSEPH HERGESHEIMER
POST ADOLESENCE                           W.C.ALMON
AM. REVIEW
THEN AND NOW  1921-'36
THE FIGHT                                 HAZLIT
IO COPIES LES VERTES COLLINES D'AFRICA    HEMINGWAY
AM. SHORT STORIES                         ALBATROSS
PEGRE ET POLICE INT.                      DE HAUTECLOGUE
I2 COPIES INT. LIT.
LE PASSAGER DU POLARLYS                   SIMIONON
LA COMEDIE DE CHARLEROI                   ROCHELLE
27 COPIES ON SPAIN AND BULL FIGHTING
I5 COPIES HORO DE ESPANA
JOSE MARTI
BOUND  YEWYORKER
IO NOVELS IN FRENCH
2 COPIES CLOSE UP
I CAN DIDATE FOR GOVERNOR                 UPTON SINCLAIR
THE EXILE                                 EZRA POUND
MER MARINES MARINS                        VALERY
CATALOGUE CURIOS Y ANTIQUES
EL FEROZ CABRILLA                           MUNOZ
SPANISH DICTIONERY
4 ARMY MANUELS
MR. DOOLY IN PEACE AND WAR
TRILBY                                      DU MAURIER
REEDS SEAMANSHIP
SO RED THE NOSE
PHOTOGRAPHS                   I839-I937
BOOK ON ANGLING                           FRANCIS
FEISTAS DE TOTOS
FIFTH COL.                                HEMINGWAY
HARDY'S ANGLERS GUIDE
THE DAUGHTER (BOUND GALLEY)               BESSIE BREWER
ROMANCE OF PERFUME                        RICHA RD LE GALERENE
```

Havana

```
            CRATE   44

HAPPILY FORE EVERAFTER              ARNOLD GINGRICH
HARRMAN                             EUGENE QUINCHE
NATURALIST OF THE AMOZON           BATES
MODERN AM. PROSE                   CARL VAN DOREN
RETURN TO YESTERDAY                FORD MADDOX FORD
THE EXILE                          EZRA POUND
JANE EYRE                          CHARLOTTE BRONTE
AND EVEN NOW                       MAX BEERBAUM
SHADOWS IN THE SUN                 SIDNEY FRANKLIN
EXTRAITS D'M JOURNEL               CARLOS DU BOS
TROUT FISHING FROM ALL ANGLES      TAVERNER
LA NOUVELLE REVUE FRANCAISE        1929
CONQUESTIDOR                       ARCHIE MCLEISH
THE COMPLEAT GOGGLER               GUY KILPATRICK
LUSTRA                             EZ RA POUND
BIG GAME FISHES OF THE U.S.        HOLDER
SIGNIFICENT CONTEMPORARY STORIES   MORRIELESS
AFRICA DANCES                      GEOFFREY GORER
```

CRATE # 45

THE OPPENHEIM OMNIBUS
THIS TIME A BETTER EARTH   TED ALLEN
COMRADE OF THE STORM   PETER B. KYNE
MARCH OF A NATION   H.G.CARDOZA
GREAT BASIN OF THE NILE   ALBERT NYANZA
A RIFLEMAN WENT TO WAR   MCBRIDE
3 VOL. TRANSITION
ANGLING IN BRITISH ART   W.SHAW SPARROW

Havana

Hemingway's Recommended Reading List

DURING the thirties, Hemingway made a number of public statements about great literature. Like his mentor, Pound, he defined art by example, recommending a number of books that no author should ignore, books that were his literary forebears. In the *Paris Review* interview and later in *A Moveable Feast*, he reconfirmed most of those selections. In the same instructional spirit in which he made the lists, I give you a comparison based on the KW-40 inventory.

BOOKS TAKEN	BOOKS LEFT	BOOKS NOT THERE
War and Peace	*Anna Karenina*	*The Red and the Black*
Dubliners	*Madame Bovary*	*Ulysses**
Portrait of the Artist	*Huck Finn*	*Buddenbrooks*
Tom Jones	*Fathers and Sons*	*Red Badge of Courage*
Joseph Andrews	*Remembrance of*	*Turn of the Screw*
Portrait of a Lady	*Things Past*	*Sportsman's Sketches*
The American	Balzac	*Sons and Lovers*
Cpt. Marryat		*Sentimental Education*
Autobiographies		*Far Away and Long Ago*
Kipling		
Brothers Karamazov		
Hail and Farewell		

*He owned an edition of *Ulysses*, but it was not in Key West.

User's Guide and Inventory

AUTHOR, TITLE

Any author or title that could not be verified in a standard reference work is indicated by a double asterisk. (E.g. *Battling Nelson***) In some cases, what we have mistaken for the title may merely be the subject matter of the book. In other cases, the problem may be one of misspelling in the source. Some of the unverified entries may have been privately printed in such limited editions that they were never cataloged.

Items #1-245 have no authors noted. Most of these entries are periodicals and newspapers.

DATES

A date in parentheses indicates the first publication date of a book that Hemingway owned. Most of these dates are found with books coming from the two Key West inventories. He may have gotten the book any time between the publication date and 1940. For books published in the 1930s, it seems safe to assume that he got his copy soon after publication. Dates prior to 1910 have been included for consistency.

Dates without parentheses indicate when the books first came into Hemingway's possession. Some books he may have read earlier than the date indicated, but we have no hard proof.

No date means that the precise issue or edition could not be proven, nor could it be verified from the source.

SOURCES

Following is the key to the less obvious source abbreviations. A source entry such as EH-MP indicates a letter, in this case from Hemingway to Max Perkins. All titles come from the sources. All dates without parentheses also come from the sources. Books with KW-40 and KW-55 sources appeared on both inventories.

AH	Audre Hanneman, *Ernest Hemingway, A Comprehensive Bibliography*
AH-2	Supplement to Hanneman bibliography
Anderson	Sherwood Anderson
ATH	M. H. Sanford, *At the Hemingways*
Baker	Carlos Baker, *EH: A Life Story*
CH	Clarence Hemingway, father
Dos Passos	John Dos Passos
EH	Ernest Hemingway
"Emily"	Emily Goetsmann
EP	Ezra Pound
Fenton	Charles Fenton files, Beinecke Library, Yale
FSF	F. Scott Fitzgerald
G. Clark	Gregory Clark
GH	Grace Hemingway, mother
GHH	Variant of GH
GP	Gus Pfeiffer
GQ	Grace Quinlan
GS	Gertrude Stein
HH	Hadley Hemingway, first wife
I Godolphin	Isabelle Simmons Godolphin
KL	Kennedy Library
KL:Brentanos	Book bill from Brentano's bookstore, Paris
KL:Cape	Book bill, Jonathan Cape, publishers
KL:EH Collection	Books owned by EH at the Kennedy
KL:Farrar and Rinehart	Publisher's book bill
KL:Simon and Schuster	Publisher's book bill
KW-40	Key West inventory done by EH in 1940
KW-55	Key West inventory done in 1955
Liveright	Horace Liveright, publisher
MacLeish	Archibald MacLeish
MP	Max Perkins
"Mr. Gud"	Unknown correspondent
"Mr. Reed"	Unknown correspondent
OPBE	Oak Park Board of Education, minutes

OPHS	Oak Park High School
Paris Tribune	Paris edition of Chicago *Tribune*
PH	Pauline Hemingway, second wife
SB	Sylvia Beach: when alone indicates records from Paris bookstore. Otherwise, indicates a letter.
SCRBNR	Publisher's book bill
Taggard	Genevieve Taggard

All my sources are reliable; however, the KW-55 inventory must be qualified. Any book with KW-55 as its only source was probably in the Key West library in 1940 when Hemingway packed for Cuba. He may have left it there for a number of reasons. Perhaps he had read it and had no further use for it. Or it may have been a book of Pauline's which he had never read.

COMMENTS

All comments beginning with EH are Hemingway's own, either in print or in a letter. Any other comments are authorial.

Because Helen Garrison and I spent two years loading the computer, certain anomalies appear. For example, magazine subscriptions may appear as: *subscrp, subscript,* or *subscription.* Forgive us these lapses. Forgive also the computer its idiosyncrasies. For reasons not clear, TUCC printers do not recognize the exclamation point. Perhaps this shortcoming is best explained as the computer's lack of emotion. Whatever the reason, the results are curious. See, for example, Item #325.

1. Aero Digest, 1938,Oct.14.
        SOURCE: Brentanos
2. Almanach du Chasseur, 1930.
        SOURCE: KL:EH Collection
3. Alsace-Lorraine.
        SOURCE: KW-40
        COMMENT: Vosges, Guide Blue.
4. American Magazine, 1918,Nov.
        SOURCE: CH-EH
        COMMENT: CH: sent the last issue.
5. American Mercury, 1938,Oct.
        SOURCE: Brentanos
        COMMENT: Oct.10 and Oct.31 bought issues.
6. American Review.
        SOURCE: KW-40
        COMMENT: Owned bound vol. dates unknown. Mag. pub.
            1933-37.
7. American Rifleman, 1936,July.
        SOURCE: SCRBNR
        COMMENT: Vol,83.
8. American Rifleman, 1936, July.
        SOURCE: SCRBNR
        COMMENT: Vol.82.
9. Angling, (1897).
        SOURCE: KW-40
        COMMENT: The Out of Door Library.
10. Annuaire du Ring 1933, (1933).
        SOURCE: KW-40
        COMMENT: Boxing yearbook.
11. Anuario Taurino 1918, (1918).
        SOURCE: KW-40
12. Appleton's New Spanish Dictionary.
        SOURCE: KW-55
13. Atlantic Monthly, 1936, July.
        SOURCE: SCRBNR
14. Atlantic Monthly, 1933,Aug.
        SOURCE: EH-MP; KL:EH Collection
        COMMENT: EH: Stein has lost all sense of taste.
15. Battling Nelson **.
        SOURCE: KW-40
        COMMENT: Probably "Life, Battles and Career of
            Battling Nelson" by Oscar B.M.Nelson (1909).
16. The Bible, 1912.
        SOURCE: ATH; KW-40
17. Bifur, 1929,Sept.
        SOURCE: KL:EH Collection
18. Biscayne Bay 1887-1937 **.
        SOURCE: KW-40
19. Bookman, 1929,Nov.
        SOURCE: KL:EH Collection
20. La Boxe et les Boxeurs, 1925.
        SOURCE: KW-40
        COMMENT: Issued May-August 1925.

21.   Boxing Record, 1929.
          SOURCE: KW-40
          COMMENT: Annual.
22.   Boxing Record, 1933.
          SOURCE: KW-40
          COMMENT: Annual.
23.   Boxing Record, 1931.
          SOURCE: KW-40
          COMMENT: Annual.
24.   Boxing Record, 1930.
          SOURCE: KW-40
          COMMENT: Annual.
25.   Boxing Record, 1938.
          SOURCE: KW-40
          COMMENT: Annual.
26.   Brentano's Book Chat, 1928,Autumn.
          SOURCE: KL:EH Collection
27.   Burke's Peerage, 1926.
          SOURCE: EH-MP
          COMMENT: EH: costs 900 francs and weighs 5
              pounds.
28.   Canciones de Guerra 1937-38, 2 vols. **.
          SOURCE: KW-40
29.   Il Carroccio, 1919.
          SOURCE: KL:EH Collection
          COMMENT: Revista di coltura, propaganda e difesa
              italiana in America.
30.   Carteles **, 1929,Mar.
          SOURCE: EH-MP
          COMMENT: May be Carteles, Combines and Trusts in
              Post-War Germany by R.K.Michels.
31.   Case of Anti Soviet **.
          SOURCE: KW-40
          COMMENT: "Verbatim Report".
32.   Catalogue Curios y Antiques**.
          SOURCE: KW-40
33.   Cavalcade, 1938,Oct.8.
          SOURCE: Brentanos
34.   Cavalcade, 1937,Sept.
          SOURCE: KL:Brentanos
          COMMENT: EH received Sept.11-Oct.30.
35.   El Clarin, 1930.
          SOURCE: GP-EH; KL
          COMMENT: EH received July,1930-Dec.,1932.
36.   Colliers, 1938,Oct.
          SOURCE: Brentanos
          COMMENT: Oct.20 bought three copies, probably back
              issues.
37.   Commerce, 1925,Autumn.
          SOURCE: KW-40; KL:EH Collection
38.   Contact, 1932,May.
          SOURCE: KL:EH Collection

39. Il Convento, 1925.
      SOURCE: KL:EH Collection
      COMMENT: Owned issues June-July.
40. The Cooperative Commonwealth, 1921,Oct.1.
      SOURCE: KL:EH Collection
41. Cornhill Magazine, (1867).
      SOURCE: KW-40
42. Cornhill Magazine, (1883).
      SOURCE: KW-40
43. Coronet, 1937,Feb.
      SOURCE: KL:EH Collection
44. Las Corridas de Toros **, (1873) **.
      SOURCE: KW-40
      COMMENT: May be this date. "Su origen, sus
          progresos y sus vicisitudes, por D.F.S. de A."
45. Cosmopolitan, 1938,Oct.
      SOURCE: Brentanos
      COMMENT: Bought issue on 28 October.
46. Description Gen. de la Europe **.
      SOURCE: KW-40
47. Dial, 1929,Jan.
      SOURCE: SB
48. Dial, 1927,Nov.
      SOURCE: SB
49. Dial, 1922.
      SOURCE: EH-Sherwood Anderson
      COMMENT: EH read throughout 20s.
50. Dial, 1928.
      SOURCE: SB; KL:EH Collection
      COMMENT: Read Jan.and Dec. issues. Owned April
          issue.
51. Dictionnaire des Peches **.
      SOURCE: KW-40
52. Don Quijote de Hollywood **, (1936).
      SOURCE: KW-40
      COMMENT: Date on inventory.
53. The Double Dealer, 1922,May.
      SOURCE: KL:EH Collection
54. El Eco Taurino, 1930.
      SOURCE: GP-EH; KL
      COMMENT: EH received July,1930-Dec.,1932.
55. Efemerides Taurinas, 1931.
      SOURCE: KW-40
      COMMENT: Probably July,1931-Dec.,1932.
56. Escape**, 1933,Dec.
      SOURCE: Brentanos
      COMMENT: Numerous books with this title in 1933.
57. Esquire, 1935,Dec.
      SOURCE: KL:EH Collection
58. Esquire, 1936,Aug.
      SOURCE: KL:EH Collection
59. Esquire, 1933,Autumn.
      SOURCE: KL:EH Collection

60. Esquire, 1934.
       SOURCE: KL:EH Collection
       COMMENT: Jan-Nov.,1934.
61. Esquire, 1937,Oct.
       SOURCE: KL:Brentanos
       COMMENT: EH received Oct-Nov.,1937. Read
           throughout 1930s.
62. Europaische Revue, 1929,Nov.
       SOURCE: KL:EH Collection
63. Everyman, 1929,Dec.12.
       SOURCE: KL:EH Collection
       COMMENT: Periodical.
64. Ex Libris, 1924,Jan.
       SOURCE: KL:EH Collection
65. Experiment, 1929,May.
       SOURCE: KL:EH Collection
       COMMENT: Periodical.
66. Field and Stream, 1938,Oct.
       SOURCE: Brentanos
       COMMENT: Bought issue on 28 October.
67. Field and Stream, 1925.
       SOURCE: CH-EH; EH-CH
       COMMENT: Father mailed copies.
68. Field and Stream, 1937.
       SOURCE: KL:Brentanos
       COMMENT: EH ordered.
69. Field**, 1938.
       SOURCE: Brentanos
       COMMENT: May be Field and Stream. Subscribed
           Oct.,1938-Sept.,1939.
70. La Fiesta Brava, 1930.
       SOURCE: GP-EH; KL
       COMMENT: EH received July,1930-Dec.,1932.
71. Fiestas de Toros **.
       SOURCE: KW-40
72. Florida Salt Water Fisherman's Guide **.
       SOURCE: KW-40
73. French and English Dictionary **.
       SOURCE: KW-40
74. French Game and Fish Books **.
       SOURCE: KW-40
       COMMENT: 8 vols.
75. French Government **.
       SOURCE: KW-40
76. Game Birds**, 1938,Oct.
       SOURCE: Brentanos
       COMMENT: May be Hugh Pollard book. See below.
77. Gamoma**, 1938,Oct.
       SOURCE: Brentanos
       COMMENT: May be Gammon and Espionage by N.
           Bentley.
78. German Short Stories, (1920).
       SOURCE: KW-40

79. Golden Book Magazine, 1928.
         SOURCE: Brentanos
         COMMENT: Jan-Dec. subscribed.
80. Great War Intl**, 1938,Oct.
         SOURCE: Brentanos
         COMMENT: Probably a magazine.
81. Le Guide Gastronomique, (1933).
         SOURCE: KW-40
82. La Habana **, (1546).
         SOURCE: KW-40
         COMMENT: Newspaper, periodical? Date on inventory.
83. The Habits of Good Society, (1864).
         SOURCE: KW-40
         COMMENT: Etiquette handbook "the whole
            interspersed with humorous illustrations of
            social predicaments".
84. Hablando con el Gallo de Passion **.
         SOURCE: KW-40
85. Hardy's Anglers' Guide.
         SOURCE: KW-40
         COMMENT: Produced annually by Hardy Bros.,Ltd.,
            Alnwick, England.
86. Harper's Bazaar, 1936,July.
         SOURCE: SCRBNR
87. Harpers, 1936,June.
         SOURCE: SCRBNR
88. Harpers, 1937,June.
         SOURCE: SCRBNR
89. Harpers, 1936,July.
         SOURCE: SCRBNR
90. Horo de Espana**.
         SOURCE: KW-40
         COMMENT: EH took 15 copies to Cuba.
91. Hotels in Italy,1936.
         SOURCE: KW-40
92. Hound and Horn , 1929,Fall.
         SOURCE: KL:EH Collection
93. Hound and Horn, 1932.
         SOURCE: KL:EH Collection
         COMMENT: Oct.1932-Mar.1933.
94. Hound and Horn, 1931,Winter.
         SOURCE: KL:EH Collection
95. I Detti de Gesu **.
         SOURCE: KW-40
         COMMENT: The Sayings of Jesus?.
96. International Book Review, 1924.
         SOURCE: CH-EH; EH-CH
         COMMENT: Nov.,Dec. issues read in Mar.1925.
97. International Book Review, 1925.
         SOURCE: CH-EH; EH-CH
         COMMENT: CH sent throughout year.
98. International Literature, 1935.
         SOURCE: KL:EH Collection
         COMMENT: Nos.5 and 9.

99.   International Literature.
            SOURCE: KW-40
            COMMENT: Literature of the World Revolution: pub.
                in Moscow, 1932. EH took 12 copies.
100.   International Literature, 1934.
            SOURCE: KL:EH Collection
            COMMENT: No.6.
101.   Jose Marti **.
            SOURCE: KW-40
            COMMENT: May be title or author.
102.   Journal of the American Medical Association, 1919.
            SOURCE: ATH
103.   Ken, 1938.
            SOURCE: KL:EH Collection
            COMMENT: April-July owned.
104.   Kikiriki: Espana Taurina, (1918).
            SOURCE: KW-40
105.   Ledgers de Toros, 2 vols. **.
            SOURCE: KW-40
106.   Liberator, 1920,Oct.
            SOURCE: KL:EH Collection
            COMMENT: Max Eastman, editor. Superseded Masses.
107.   Libro de Gallito **.
            SOURCE: KW-40
108.   La Lidia Revista Taurina.
            SOURCE: KW-40
            COMMENT: Vol.1-10, Madrid 1882-1891.
109.   La Lidia, 1930.
            SOURCE: GP-EH; KW-40
            COMMENT: Illustrated bullfight paper. Issues
                1882-1886.
110.   La Lidia, 1930.
            SOURCE: GP-EH; KW-40
            COMMENT: Illustrated bullfight paper. 1915-16, 2
                vols.
111.   Life and Letters of Today, vol.XVIII **.
            SOURCE: KW-40
            COMMENT: May be magazine of this title. Difficult
                to verify date by vol. number.
112.   The Literary Digest, 1918.
            SOURCE: CH-EH
            COMMENT: CH sent to EH in Milan hospital.
113.   The Little Review, 1923,Oct.
            SOURCE: EH-GS
            COMMENT: EH read throughout 1920s.
114.   The Little Review, 1925,Spring.
            SOURCE: KL:EH Collection
115.   The Little Review, 1929,May.
            SOURCE: KL:EH Collection
            COMMENT: Two copies.
116.   The Little Review, 1922.
            SOURCE: KL:EH Collection
            COMMENT: Autumn and Winter issues.

117. The Little Review, 1923.
     SOURCE: KL:EH Collection
     COMMENT: Spring issue and Autumn-Winter issue.
118. The Living Age, 1938,Aug.
     SOURCE: KL:EH Collection
119. London Times Literary Supplement, 1938,Oct.
     SOURCE: Brentanos
     COMMENT: Oct.8 bought 2 issues. Oct.31 bought 1
     issue.
120. Le Magasin Pittoresque 1856-65, (1856).
     SOURCE: KW-40
121. Le Magasin Pittoresque, (1871).
     SOURCE: KW-40
     COMMENT: Owned copy of 1871. May be bound vol.
122. Le Magasin Pittoresque, (1836).
     SOURCE: KW-40
     COMMENT: Owned copy of 1836. May be bound vol.
123. Miroir Des Sports 1928, (1928).
     SOURCE: KW-40
124. Nation, 1937.
     SOURCE: KL:Brentanos
     COMMENT: EH received Sept.25-Oct.30.
125. Nation, 1940.
     SOURCE: EH-MP
     COMMENT: EH ordered three month subscrp. beginning
     in Oct.
126. Nation, 1928,Jan.
     SOURCE: EH-SB
127. Le Navire d'Argent, 1926,Mar.1.
     SOURCE: KL:EH Collection
     COMMENT: Owned two copies.
128. The New Criterion, 1927.
     SOURCE: KW-40
129. New England**, 1938,Oct.
     SOURCE: Brentanos
130. New Masses, 1935,Sept.17.
     SOURCE: KL:EH Collection
131. New Masses, 1926.
     SOURCE: EH-Sherwood Anderson
     COMMENT: May(?) issue. EH read Jolas poems in it.
132. New Masses, 1940.
     SOURCE: EH-MP
     COMMENT: EH ordered three month subscrp. beginning
     Oct.
133. New Masses, 1937.
     SOURCE: SB
134. New Republic, 1938,Oct.
     SOURCE: Brentanos
     COMMENT: Bought issues on Oct.14 and 31.
135. New Republic, 1927,May 18.
     SOURCE: KL:EH Collection

136. New Republic, 1929,Jan.
        SOURCE: EH-MP
        COMMENT: EH: Millay sonnets sound like a lecherous
            cat.
137. New Republic, 1933,June.
        SOURCE: EH-MP
138. The New Republic, 1926.
        SOURCE: SB
        COMMENT: Sept.15th issue.
139. The New Republic, 1937.
        SOURCE: KL:Brentanos
        COMMENT: EH received Sept.29-Oct.30.
140. The New Republic, 1940.
        SOURCE: EH-MP
        COMMENT: EH ordered three month subscrp. beginning
            Oct.
141. New Statesman, 1937.
        SOURCE: KL:Brentanos
        COMMENT: Received Sept.25-Oct.30.
142. New Statesman, 1929,Nov.30.
        SOURCE: KL:EH Collection
143. New Statesman, 1938,Oct.
        SOURCE: Brentanos
        COMMENT: Bought issues on Oct.20,24,31.
144. New York Daily Mirror, 1932.
        SOURCE: EH-MP
        COMMENT: Received two months beginning Aug.8. EH:
            can't miss the Holman case.
145. New York Evening Post, 1940.
        SOURCE: EH-MP
        COMMENT: Three month subscript. beginning Oct.2.
146. New York Evening Sun, 1932.
        SOURCE: EH-MP
        COMMENT: Two month subscript. beginning Aug.8. EH:
            can't miss the Holman case.
147. New York Herald Tribune, 1938,Feb.
        SOURCE: EH-MP
        COMMENT: EH: reading back issues of book section.
148. New York Sun, 1935.
        SOURCE: EH-MP
        COMMENT: Three month subscript. beginning May 1.
            Sent to Bimini.
149. New York Sun, 1939.
        SOURCE: EH-MP
        COMMENT: Ten day subscript. sent to ranch
            beginning Sept.8.
150. New York Times, 1939.
        SOURCE: EH-MP
        COMMENT: Ten day subscript. sent to ranch
            beginning Sept.8.
151. New York Times, 1937.
        SOURCE: KL:Brentanos
        COMMENT: Received Aug.27-Oct.26.

152. New Yorker, 1936.
    SOURCE: SCRBNR
    COMMENT: Billed for subscript. in July, 1936.
153. New Yorker, 1937.
    SOURCE: KL:Brentanos
    COMMENT: Received Sept.9-Oct.25.
154. New Yorker.
    SOURCE: KW-40
    COMMENT: Took bound vol. to Cuba.
155. New Yorker, 1938,Oct.
    SOURCE: Brentanos
    COMMENT: Bought issues on Oct.17,20,28.
156. New Yorker, 1932,Oct.
    SOURCE: EH-MP
157. News Week, 1937.
    SOURCE: KL:Brentanos
    COMMENT: Received Aug.21-Oct.9.
158. Night and Day, 1937.
    SOURCE: KL:Brentanos
    COMMENT: Received Sept.9-Oct.28.
159. La Nouvelle Revue Francaise, (1929).
    SOURCE: KW-40
160. La Nouvelle Revue Francaise, 1931,May.
    SOURCE: KL:EH Collection
161. La Nouvelle Revue Francaise, 1928.
    SOURCE: KL:EH Collection
    COMMENT: Owned Feb. and June.
162. La Nouvelle Revue Francaise, 1927.
    SOURCE: KL:EH Collection
    COMMENT: Owned issues for May,June,July and
        August.
163. Oak Leaves, 1919,Oct.11.
    SOURCE: KL:EH Collection
164. Omnibus, 1931.
    SOURCE: KL:EH Collection
    COMMENT: London.
165. Omnibus, 1932.
    SOURCE: KL:EH Collection
    COMMENT: London.
166. Outdoor Life, 1938,Oct.
    SOURCE: Brentanos
    COMMENT: Bought issue on Oct.20.
167. Outdoor Life, 1937.
    SOURCE: KL:Brentanos
    COMMENT: Received Sept.25-Oct.30.
168. Pagany, 1931.
    SOURCE: SB
    COMMENT: In Sept. EH read March issue.
169. Poetry, 1923,Jan.
    SOURCE: KL:EH Collection
170. Der Querschnitt, 1925,Feb.
    SOURCE: KL:EH Collection

171. Der Querschnitt, 1926.
      SOURCE: KL:EH Collection
      COMMENT: July and Sept.
172. Der Querschnitt, 1927.
      SOURCE: KL:EH Collection
      COMMENT: Feb. and March.
173. Der Querschnitt, 1928,Feb.
      SOURCE: KL:EH Collection
174. Der Querschnitt, 1924,Nov.
      SOURCE: KL:EH Collection
175. Der Querschnitt, 1929,Sept.
      SOURCE: KL:EH Collection
176. Reader's Digest Magazine, 1936, July.
      SOURCE: SCRBNR
177. Records (Spanish), 2 vols. **.
      SOURCE: KW-40
178. La Revue Europeenne, 1930,Jan.1.
      SOURCE: KL:EH Collection
179. Revue Francaise, 1933.
      SOURCE: KW-40
      COMMENT: 1933 was last year of issue.
180. Saturday Evening Post, 1919.
      SOURCE: Bill Smith-EH; EH-Bill Smith
181. Saturday Evening Post, 1918.
      SOURCE: CH-EH
      COMMENT: CH sent to EH in Milan hospital.
182. Saturday Review, 1926.
      SOURCE: SB
      COMMENT: Subscribed Oct.,1926-March,1927.
183. Saturday Review, 1926, Oct.
      SOURCE: SB
      COMMENT: Subscrip. Oct.-Mar.,1927.
184. The Saturday Review of Literature, 1938,Oct.
      SOURCE: SB
      COMMENT: Read Jan.-Oct.
185. The Saturday Review of Literature, 1940.
      SOURCE: EH-MP
      COMMENT: 3 mo. subscript. beginning Oct. 1940.Sent
          to Sun Valley.
186. The Saturday Review of Literature, 1929,Oct.12.
      SOURCE: KL:EH Collection
187. Scientific American, 1918.
      SOURCE: CH-EH
      COMMENT: CH sent to EH in Milan hospital.
188. Scribner's Magazine, 1936,July.
      SOURCE: SCRBNR; EH-MP
      COMMENT: EH read throughout late 20s and all of
          30s.
189. Scribner's Magazine, 1933.
      SOURCE: KL:EH Collection
      COMMENT: Owned March,April,May issues.
190. Scribner's Magazine, 1928,Aug.
      SOURCE: EH-MP

191.   Scribner's Magazine, 1935.
         SOURCE: KL:EH Collection
         COMMENT: Owned May,June,October,November issues.
192.   Scribner's Magazine, 1937,Jan.
         SOURCE: KL:EH Collection
193.   Scribner's Magazine, 1927.
         SOURCE: KL:EH Collection
         COMMENT: Owned two copies Mar. One copy each of
            April,May,June.
194.   Scribner's Magazine, (1909).
         SOURCE: KL:EH Collection
         COMMENT: Owned Dec. issue.
195.   Scribner's Magazine, 1930,Aug.
         SOURCE: KL:EH Collection
         COMMENT: Owned two copies.
196.   Scribner's Magazine, 1929.
         SOURCE: KL:EH Collection
         COMMENT: Owned
            May,June(2),July(2),August(2),October.
197.   Scribner's Magazine, 1934,Nov.
         SOURCE: EH-MP
198.   Scribner's Magazine Book, (1887).
         SOURCE: KW-40
         COMMENT: July-Dec.1887.
199.   Secret Service **, 1937,June.
         SOURCE: SCRBNR
         COMMENT: Multiple possibilities.
200.   Sir Walter Raleigh, 1929,Sept.
         SOURCE: SB
         COMMENT: Author unknown. Perhaps John Buchan,
            Milton Waldman, or Martin A.S. Hume.
201.   Smithsonian Report, 1901, (1901).
         SOURCE: KW-40
         COMMENT: 770pp.
202.   Sol Y Sombra, 1930.
         SOURCE: GP-EH; KW-40
         COMMENT: 14 vols.
203.   The South and East African Yearbook 1933, (1934).
         SOURCE: KW-55
204.   Spain Today, 1937.
         SOURCE: KL:EH Collection
         COMMENT: No.3. Pub. by the Communist Party of
            Spain.
205.   The Sportsman, 1936.
         SOURCE: SCRBNR
         COMMENT: Subscript. beginning July.
206.   The Sportsman, 1930,Dec.
         SOURCE: MP-EH
         COMMENT: MP sent last issue on Dec.5.
207.   The Sportsman, 1931.
         SOURCE: MP-EH
         COMMENT: Subscript. for 1931 beginning in Jan.
208.   The Sportsman, 1938,Oct.
         SOURCE: Brentanos

209. The Spur, 1929,Dec.1.
         SOURCE: KL:EH Collection
210. The Spur, 1936.
         SOURCE: SCRBNR
         COMMENT: Subscript. beginning July. Horses.Sports.
211. St.Nicholas, 1910.
         SOURCE: ATH
         COMMENT: EH read as boy. Subscription at home.
212. St.Nicholas, (1890,Feb.).
         SOURCE: KL:EH Collection
213. Story Magazine, 1936,June.
         SOURCE: SCRBNR
214. Sunset's Complete Gardening Book, (1939).
         SOURCE: KW-55
215. S4N, 1923.
         SOURCE: KL:EH Collection
         COMMENT: Sept.19,1923-Jan.1924.
216. Das Tage Buch, 1929,Dec.14.
         SOURCE: KL:EH Collection
         COMMENT: Berlin.
217. Testimony Against Gertrude Stein, 1935,Feb.
         SOURCE: KL:EH Collection
         COMMENT: Transition magazine Pamphlet No.1.
218. This Quarter, 1929.
         SOURCE: SB
         COMMENT: Sept.19, read No.5.
219. This Quarter, 1927.
         SOURCE: EH-Ernest Walsh; KW-40
         COMMENT: EH assisted in early pub. Took issue #4
             to Cuba.
220. This Quarter, 1930.
         SOURCE: KL:EH Collection
         COMMENT: Owned July-Aug.
221. This Quarter, 1929.
         SOURCE: KL:EH Collection
         COMMENT: Owned Oct.-Dec.
222. This Quarter, 1931,Dec.
         SOURCE: KL:EH Collection
223. This Quarter, 1925,Spring.
         SOURCE: KL:EH Collection
224. Time, 1938,Oct.
         SOURCE: Brentanos
         COMMENT: Bought issue on Oct.8.
225. Time, 1937.
         SOURCE: KL:Brentanos
         COMMENT: Subscript. Sept.9-Oct.25.
226. The Times **.
         SOURCE: KW-40
         COMMENT: 3 vols. May be London Times.
227. Torerias **, (1925).
         SOURCE: KW-40
         COMMENT: Date on inventory. May be an annual or
             periodical bound.

228. El Torero **.
         SOURCE: KW-40
229. Toros y Toreros 1920, (1920).
         SOURCE: KW-40
         COMMENT: Bull fight yearbook.
230. Toros y Toreros 1921, (1921).
         SOURCE: KW-40
         COMMENT: Bull fight yearbook.
231. Town and Country, 1936,July.
         SOURCE: SCRBNR
232. Transatlantic Review, 1924.
         SOURCE: KW-40; KL:EH Collection
         COMMENT: EH sub-editor. Owned
             April,May,July,September issues.
233. Transition, 1928.
         SOURCE: KW-40; KL:EH Collection
         COMMENT: Took three bound vols. to Cuba. Owned
             Feb.1928 issue.
234. Transition, 1927.
         SOURCE: SB; KL:EH Collection
         COMMENT: Read June issue in Paris. Owned
             May,June,July,November,December issues.
235. Vanity Fair, 1928,Jan.
         SOURCE: EH-SB
236. Vanity Fair, 1925,Jan.
         SOURCE: EH-GS
237. The Virginia Quarterly Review, 1934,Jan.
         SOURCE: KL:EH Collection
238. Vogue, 1937.
         SOURCE: KL:Brentanos
         COMMENT: Sept.1-Oct.15, sent to Spain.
239. Vogue, 1936.
         SOURCE: SCRBNR
         COMMENT: June and July issues.
240. Webster's Collegiate Dictionary.
         SOURCE: KW-55
         COMMENT: Four copies.
241. Webster's International Dictionary Unabridged.
         SOURCE: KW-55
         COMMENT: Second edition.
242. Wild Life in Game Sanctuary **, 1939,June.
         SOURCE: EH-MP
         COMMENT: May be title or subject. Ltr. mentions
             Serengeti.
243. World Almanac 1935, (1935).
         SOURCE: KW-40
244. Youth's Companion, 1918.
         SOURCE: GH-EH
         COMMENT: GH sent to EH in Milan hospital.
245. Zig Zag, 1930.
         SOURCE: GP-EH; KW-40
         COMMENT: GP ordered 1923-25 for EH.
246. Adam, George and Pearl. A Book About Paris, (1927).
         SOURCE: KW-55

247. Adamic, Louis. <u>Dynamite:the story of class violence</u>
     <u>in America</u>, (1931).
     SOURCE: KW-55
248. Adams, Edward C.L. <u>Nigger to Nigger</u>, 1928,Oct.
     SOURCE: EH-MP
     COMMENT: EH:very very good. Enjoyed it greatly.
        Thanks for sending it.
249. Adams, James Truslow. <u>The Epic of America</u>, (1931).
     SOURCE: KW-40
250. Adams, James Truslow. <u>The March of Democracy</u>, (1932).
     SOURCE: KW-55
251. Adams, Samuel Hopkins. <u>The Incredible Era</u>, 1939,Oct.
     SOURCE: EH-MP
     COMMENT: Harding administration.
252. Addison, Joseph. <u>The De Coverly Papers</u>, 1914.
     SOURCE: OPHS
253. Affalo, Frederic G. <u>Sport in Europe</u>, 1934,Mar.
     SOURCE: KL:Brentanos; KW-40
     COMMENT: Pub.1900.
254. Agee, James. <u>Permit Me Voyage</u>, (1934).
     SOURCE: KW-40
     COMMENT: Intro. by MacLeish. Yale Younger Poets
        Series.
255. Aiken, Conrad. <u>Costumes by Eros</u>, 1928,Oct.
     SOURCE: EH-MP
     COMMENT: EH read and liked.
256. Akeley, Carl Ethan. <u>In Brightest Africa</u>, (1923).
     SOURCE: KW-40
257. Akins, Zoe. <u>Declassee</u>, 1920,Nov.
     SOURCE: EH-Grace Quinlan
     COMMENT: EH saw play.
258. Albalat, Antoine. <u>Gustave Flaubert et ses Amis</u>,
     (1927).
     SOURCE: KW-55
259. Albatross **. <u>American Short Stories</u> **.
     SOURCE: KW-40
     COMMENT: May be this title ed. by Fred L. Pattee,
        1936.
260. Alcazar, Frederico M. <u>Ignacio Sanchez Mejias</u>, (1922).
     SOURCE: KW-40
261. Alcott, Louisa May. <u>Jo's Boys</u>, (1886).
     SOURCE: KW-55
262. Aldrich, Mildred. <u>A Hilltop on the Marne</u>, (1915).
     SOURCE: KW-55
263. Alexander, Roy. <u>The Cruise of the Raider "Wolf</u>,"
     1939,Oct.
     SOURCE: EH-MP
     COMMENT: EH ordered.
264. Allan, Ted. <u>This Time a Better Earth</u>, (1939).
     SOURCE: KW-40
     COMMENT: Historical fiction.
265. Allen, Herbert Warner. <u>The Wines of France</u>, (1924).
     SOURCE: KW-40
     COMMENT: Wines and wine-making.

266. Allen, Hervey. Toward the Flame, 1926.
     SOURCE: EH-MP
     COMMENT: EH: has heard it is a good book.
267. Allingham, Margery. Black Plumes, 1940.
     SOURCE: EH-MP
     COMMENT: Ordered by EH.
268. Allingham, Margery. Flowers for the Judge, 1936,
     June.
     SOURCE: SCRBNR
269. Alvarez **. El Consultor Taurino **.
     SOURCE: KW-40
     COMMENT: Perhaps Serafin Alvarez Quintero.
270. Ameline, Leon. Ce Qu'il Faut Connaitre de la Police
     de ses Mysteres, (1926).
     SOURCE: KW-40
271. Andersen, Hans Christian. The Wild Swans, (1922).
     SOURCE: KW-55
272. Anderson, Jessie Macmillan. A Study of English Words,
     (1897).
     SOURCE: OPHS
273. Anderson, Karl Johan. Lake Ngami, 1934,Mar.
     SOURCE: KL:Brentanos; EH-MP; KW-40
     COMMENT: Pub.1856. South Western Africa.
274. Anderson, Sherwood. Beyond Desire, (1932).
     SOURCE: KW-40
275. Anderson, Sherwood. Dark Laughter, 1925,Sept.
     SOURCE: Anderson-Liveright; EH-Sherwood Anderson
     COMMENT: Anderson sent EH a copy.
276. Anderson, Sherwood. Many Marriages, 1923.
     SOURCE: EH-Sherwood Anderson; EH-MP; Fenton
277. Anderson, Sherwood. Nearer the Grass Roots, (1929).
     SOURCE: KW-40
     COMMENT: Elizabethton, Tenn.
278. Anderson, Sherwood. Poor White, 1921.
     SOURCE: Baker
279. Anderson, Sherwood. Puzzled America, 1935,Apr.
     SOURCE: EH-MP; KW-55
     COMMENT: EH received and read.
280. Anderson, Sherwood. Sherwood Anderson's Notebook,
     1926,Mar.
     SOURCE: EH-Isidor Schneider
281. Anderson, Sherwood. A Story-Teller's Story, 1925,Mar.
     SOURCE: EH-Sherwood Anderson; AH
     COMMENT: See EH review in "Ex Libris,"II
          (Mar.,1925).
282. Anderson, Sherwood. Winesburg, Ohio, 1921.
     SOURCE: Baker; KW-40
283. Andrews, Roy Chapman. On the Trail of Ancient Man,
     1926, Oct.
     SOURCE: SB
     COMMENT: Borrowed Oct.,1926; returned Feb. 28,
          1927.

284. Annesley, Charles. The Standard Operaglass, (1899).
         SOURCE: KW-55
         COMMENT: Detailed plots of 155 operas.
285. Anon. Abyssinia and Italy, (1935).
         SOURCE: KW-55
         COMMENT: Issued by Royal Inst. for International
             Affairs.
286. Anon. The Allianza Nazionale: Documents of the Second
         Italian Resorgimento, (1931).
         SOURCE: KL:EH Collection
287. Anon. Beowulf, 1916.
         SOURCE: Fenton
         COMMENT: HS reading.
288. Anon. " Deor's Lament," 1916.
         SOURCE: Fenton
         COMMENT: Old English in trans.
289. Anon. Everyman, 1916.
         SOURCE: OPHS
290. Anon. Juan Gris, (1929).
         SOURCE: KW-40
         COMMENT: Pub. by Kunsthaus, Zurich. 16pp.
291. Anon. Kansas City Star Style Book, (1917).
         SOURCE: KL:EH Collection
         COMMENT: Inscribed:"To Ernest Hemingway from Pete
             Wellington with affection.".
292. Anon. Letters Addressed to A.P.Watt 1883-1929,
         (1929).
         SOURCE: KW-55
293. Anon. Not to be Repeated: Merry-go-round of Europe,
         (1932).
         SOURCE: KW-40
294. Anon. " O Western Wind," 1926.
         SOURCE: EH-E.Walsh
         COMMENT: EH quotes, calls ideal poetry. Probably
             read in HS.
295. Anon. Old English Ballads, 1913.
         SOURCE: OPHS
         COMMENT: HS text.
296. Anon. Programa de Espectaculos, (1902).
         SOURCE: KW-40
         COMMENT: Fiestas de Mayo in honor of the coming of
             age of Alphonso XIII.
297. Anon. Report of the Department of Military Affairs,
         Jan.-July 1918, (1918).
         SOURCE: KL:EH Collection
         COMMENT: Red Cross report listing EH and his
             medals for wounding. EH owned.
298. Anon. Shall We Eat Flesh, (1934).
         SOURCE: KW-40
         COMMENT: Rational Living Library.
299. Anon. " Sir Patrick Spens," 1916,May.
         SOURCE: OPHS
         COMMENT: Memorized for HS.

300. Anon. The Song of Roland, 1924,July.
    SOURCE: Eric Dorman Smith-Carlos Baker
    COMMENT: EDS: discussed with EH after Pamplona festival.

301. Anon. Tanganyika Territory Game Preservation Department Annual Report, 1932, (1933).
    SOURCE: KL:EH Collection

302. Anon. Then and Now: 1921-1935, (1935).
    SOURCE: KW-40
    COMMENT: Articles, stories and poems from the magazine "Then And Now."

303. Anon. " Twa Corbies," 1926.
    SOURCE: EH-E.Walsh
    COMMENT: EH quotes three stanzas. Read in HS. A great poem.

304. Anon. The War in Italy, 1918,Sept.
    SOURCE: KL:EH Collection
    COMMENT: No.18, Arms and Ammunition. Soldier's Edition.

305. Anthony, Harold Elmer. Field Book of North American Mammals, (1928).
    SOURCE: KW-40

306. Anthony, Katherine. Catherine the Great, (1925).
    SOURCE: KW-55

307. Antongini, Tommaso. D'Annunzio, 1938,May.
    SOURCE: SCRBNR; KW-55
    COMMENT: EH sent copy to V. Pfeiffer.

308. Aragon, Louis. Les Beaux Quartiers, (1936).
    SOURCE: KW-55

309. Aragon, Louis. Hourra l'Oural, (1934).
    SOURCE: KW-40

310. Archer, William. The Life, Trial and Death of Francisco Ferrer, (1911).
    SOURCE: KW-55

311. Arguer **. Libros y Felletos de Toros **.
    SOURCE: KW-40

312. Arthur, Chester A. Twelve Poems, (1927).
    SOURCE: KL:EH Collection

313. Asbury, Herbert. The Gangs of New York: an Informal History of the Underworld, (1928).
    SOURCE: KW-40

314. Asch, Sholem. Moskau, (1930).
    SOURCE: KW-55

315. Asch, Sholem. The Mother, (1930).
    SOURCE: KW-55

316. Asch, Sholem. The Nazarene, (1939).
    SOURCE: KW-55

317. Askins, Charles and Seth Wiard. Modern Shotguns and Loads, (1929).
    SOURCE: KW-40

318. Asquith, Cynthia, ed. The Black Cap, 1927, Oct.
    SOURCE: SB
    COMMENT: "New Stories of Murder and Mystery".

319.   Atherton, Gertrude. Black Oxen, (1923).
          SOURCE: KW-55
320.   Atholl, Katherine S., Duchess of. Searchlight on
          Spain, (1938).
          SOURCE: KW-55
321.   Atwater, Richard T. Mr. Popper's Penguins, (1938).
          SOURCE: KW-55
          COMMENT: Juv. lit.
322.   Atwood, Wallace W. and Helen Goss Thomas. The
          Americas, (1929).
          SOURCE: KW-55
          COMMENT: Geography.
323.   Atwood, Wallace W. and Helen Goss Thomas. Nations
          Beyond the Seas, (1930).
          SOURCE: KW-55
          COMMENT: Geography.
324.   Atwood, Wallace W. and Helen Gross Thomas. Home Life
          and Faraway Lands, (1928).
          SOURCE: KW-55
          COMMENT: Geography and text book.
325.   Auden, W.H. Look, Stranger!, (1936).
          SOURCE: KW-40
326.   Auden, W.H. The Orators, 1933,Nov.
          SOURCE: SB
327.   Auden, W.H. Poems, (1930).
          SOURCE: KW-40
328.   Auden, W.H. and Christopher Isherwood. Journey to a
          War, (1939).
          SOURCE: KW-55
329.   Audubon, John James. Birds of America, (1827).
          SOURCE: KW-55
330.   Aulnoy, Marie C., Comtesse d'. Travels into Spain,
          (1930).
          SOURCE: KW-55
          COMMENT: Pub. first in 1691.
331.   Austen, Jane. Pride and Prejudice, (1813).
          SOURCE: KW-40
332.   Austin, A.B., comp. An Angler's Anthology, (1931).
          SOURCE: KW-40
333.   Aymar, Gordon C. Bird Flight, (1935).
          SOURCE: KW-55
          COMMENT: Two copies.
334.   Ayme, Marcel. La Jument Verte, (1933).
          SOURCE: KW-55
335.   Babel, Isaak. Red Cavalry, 1929,May.
          SOURCE: Philip Jordan-EH; KW-40
          COMMENT: Trans. from Russian by Nadia Helstein.
336.   Bacon, Francis. " Of Studies," 1915,Sept.
          SOURCE: OPHS
          COMMENT: Memorized first two-thirds for HS.
337.   Baedeker, Karl. Autriche Hongrie, (1905).
          SOURCE: KW-40
          COMMENT: One of the numerous Baedeker guides.

338. Baedeker, Karl. Italy **.
     SOURCE: KW-40
     COMMENT: One of the numerous Baedeker guides.
339. Baedeker, Karl, publ. Spain and Portugal, Handbook
     for Travellers, 1931.
     SOURCE: EH-MP; KW-55
     COMMENT: EH ordered.
340. Baerlein, Henry P.B. Belmonte:the Matador, 1934,
     April.
     SOURCE: EH-MP; KW-40
341. Baerlein, Henry P.B. Dreamy Rivers, (1930).
     SOURCE: KW-40
342. Bagnold, Enid. National Velvet, 1935, July.
     SOURCE: EH-MP
     COMMENT: EH ordered.
343. Bahr, Jerome. All Good Americans, 1936, Oct.
     SOURCE: EH-MP; KL:EH Collection
     COMMENT: EH intro:"a fine honest writer . . .
        writes very good stories full of irony and empty
        of bitterness.".
344. Bailey, Liberty Hyde. Hortus, (1935).
     SOURCE: KW-55
     COMMENT: Gardening dictionary.
345. Baker, Dorothy Dodds. Young Man With a Horn,
     1938,July.
     SOURCE: EH-MP; Brentanos; KW-55
     COMMENT: EH: effectively written.
346. Baker, Samuel White. The Great Basin of the Nile,
     (1866).
     SOURCE: KW-40
     COMMENT: Likely read in 1934.
347. Baker, Samuel White. The Nile Tributaries of
     Abyssinia, (1869).
     SOURCE: KW-40
348. Bakewell, Charles Montague. The Story of the American
     Red Cross in Italy, (1920).
     SOURCE: KW-40
349. Baldwin, William Charles. African Hunting and
     Adventure from Natal to the Zambesi, 1934, March.
     SOURCE: EH-MP; KW-40; KL
     COMMENT: Published 1863.
350. Balfe, Michael William. The Bohemian Girl, 1915.
     SOURCE: OPHS
351. Balfour, Patrick. Grand Tour: Diary of an Eastward
     Journey, 1935, July.
     SOURCE: EH-MP; KW-55
     COMMENT: Ordered by EH.
352. Balzac, Honore de. " Doomed to Live," 1919.
     SOURCE: Grace Quinlan-EH
     COMMENT: EH read story to GQ.
353. Balzac, Honore de. La Femme de Trente Ans, (1832).
     SOURCE: KW-55
354. Balzac, Honore de. Le Lys dans la Vallee.
     SOURCE: KW-55

355. Balzac, Honore de. La Maison Nucingen, (1838).
     SOURCE: KW-55
356. Balzac, Honore de. Sur Catherine de Medicis, (1897).
     SOURCE: KW-55
357. Bancroft, Griffing. Lower California: a Cruise ,
     (1932).
     SOURCE: KW-40
358. Bandini, Ralph and Joseph Coxe. Men Fish and Tackle,
     (1936).
     SOURCE: KW-40
     COMMENT: The story of J.A.Coxe as told to Ralph
        Bandini. Pub. prvt. by Bronson Reel Co.
359. Barbusse, Henri. Under Fire, 1918.
     SOURCE: KL
     COMMENT: Le Feu, trans. by F. Wray.
360. Barbusse, Henri. We Others: the Stories of Fate, Love
     and Pity, (1918).
     SOURCE: KW-40
     COMMENT: Nous Autres trans. from French by
        Fitzwater Wray.
361. Baring, Maurice. Half a Minute's Silence, (1925).
     SOURCE: KW-55
362. Barker, Dodd, Webb. The Story of Our Nation, (1929).
     SOURCE: KW-55
     COMMENT: For young readers.
363. Barlow, Joseph W. Basic Spanish, (1939).
     SOURCE: KW-55
364. Barnes, Djuna. Ryder, (1928).
     SOURCE: KW-55
365. Barnum, P.T. Barnum's Own Story, 1927, Oct.
     SOURCE: SB
366. Baroja y Nessi, Pio. La Busca, (1917).
     SOURCE: KW-55
     COMMENT: From series: La Lucha por la Vida.
367. Baroja y Nessi, Pio. Locuras de Carnaval, (1937).
     SOURCE: KL:EH Collection
     COMMENT: In EH's copy a little highlighting in
        opening chapters. Mostly uncut.
368. Baroja y Nessi, Pio. The Lord of Labraz, (1926).
     SOURCE: KW-40
369. Baroja y Nessi, Pio. Red Dawn, (1924).
     SOURCE: KW-40
     COMMENT: Trans. from Spanish by Isaac Goldberg.
        Struggle for Life series.
370. Barrett, Wendell. William Shakespeare, 1916.
     SOURCE: KL
     COMMENT: HS assigned reading.
371. Barretto de Souza, Joseph M.T. Principles of
     Equitation, (1925).
     SOURCE: KW-40
372. Barry, Philip. War in Heaven, (1938).
     SOURCE: KW-55
     COMMENT: Sci. fi.

373. Bartholoni, Jean. Le Roman de Petrarque et de Laure
         (1927).
         SOURCE: KW-55
374. Barton, Margaret and Osbert Sitwell, eds. Sober
         Truth, 1933,Nov.
         SOURCE: SB
         COMMENT: "Collection of 19th.C. episodes,
             fantastic, grotesque and mysterious.".
375. Bassiere, Rene E. La Crise Mondiale, (1923).
         SOURCE: KW-55
376. Bates, Henry Walter. The Naturalist on the River
         Amazon, (1864).
         SOURCE: KW-40
377. Bates, Ralph. The Olive Field, 1936.
         SOURCE: KL:Cape; KW-55
378. Baudelaire, Charles Pierre. Les Fleurs de Mal et
         Complement.
         SOURCE: KW-40
379. Baudelaire, Charles Pierre. The Intimate Journals of
         Charles Baudelaire, (1930).
         SOURCE: KW-55
         COMMENT: Trans. by C. Isherwood. Intro. by T.S.
             Eliot.
380. Baudelaire, Charles Pierre. Morceaux Choisies,
         (1930).
         SOURCE: KW-40
381. Bayard, Emile. L' Art de Reconnaitre les Meubles
         Anciens, (1920).
         SOURCE: KW-40
382. Bazalgette, Leon. George Grosz: L'Homme et L'Oeuvre,
         (1926).
         SOURCE: KL:EH Collection
383. Beach, Sylvia. Catalogue of a Collection, (1935).
         SOURCE: KL:EH Collection
         COMMENT: Shakespeare and Co. catalogue of MSS and
             rare editions of Joyce, Whitman and Blake.
384. Beard, Charles A. and Mary R. America in Mid-Passage,
         (1939).
         SOURCE: KW-55
385. Beaumont, Francis and John Fletcher. Rule a Wife and
         Have a Wife, (1640).
         SOURCE: KW-40
386. Beaverbrook, William Maxwell Aitken. Politicians and
         the War, 1914-1916, 1929, June.
         SOURCE: SB
387. Becker, Carl Lotus. Modern History (2 vols.), (1931).
         SOURCE: KW-55
         COMMENT: Becker-Duncalf-Magoffin hist. series.
388. Beer, Thomas. The Fair Rewards, (1922).
         SOURCE: KW-40
389. Beer, Thomas. Stephen Crane, (1923).
         SOURCE: KW-40
         COMMENT: "a study in American letters." Intro. by
             Conrad.

390. Beerbohm, Max. <u>And Even Now</u>, (1921).
    SOURCE: KW-40
391. Beerbohm, Max. <u>Seven Men</u>, 1923,Aug.
    SOURCE: EH-William Bird
    COMMENT: EH owned copy. Enoch Soames, Hilary
        Maltby, Stephen Braxton, James Pethel, A.V.
        Laider, and "Savonarola" Brown.
392. Beerbohm, Max. <u>Zuleika Dobson</u>, <u>or</u>, <u>An Oxford Love
    Story</u>, (1911).
    SOURCE: KW-40
393. Belda y Carreras, Joaquin. <u>La Revolucion del 69</u>,
    (1931).
    SOURCE: KW-40
394. Bell, Aubrey. <u>Spanish Galicia</u>, (1922).
    SOURCE: KW-40
395. Bell, Florence Eveleen, ed. <u>The Letters of Gertrude
    Bell</u>, (1927).
    SOURCE: KW-40
396. Bell, Hugh M. <u>Bahamas, Isles of June</u>, 1934.
    SOURCE: EH-MP; MP-EH; SCRBNR
    COMMENT: Ordered by EH.
397. Bellini, Vincenzo. <u>I Puritania</u>, 1914.
    SOURCE: OPHS
    COMMENT: EH saw.
398. Belloc, Hilaire. <u>Towns of Destiny</u>, (1927).
    SOURCE: KW-40
399. Bellows, George W. **. <u>Memorial Exhibition **</u>.
    SOURCE: KW-40
400. Benchley, Robert Charles. <u>My Ten Years in a Quandry</u>,
    (1936).
    SOURCE: KW-55
401. Benchley, Robert Charles. <u>The Treasurer's Report, and
    Other Aspects of Community Singing</u>, (1930).
    SOURCE: KW-40
402. Benda, Julien. <u>La Trahison des Clercs</u>, (1927).
    SOURCE: KW-55
    COMMENT: Philosophy.
403. Benham, William Gurney, comp. <u>Putman's Dictionary of
    Thoughts</u>, (1930).
    SOURCE: KW-40
    COMMENT: Quotations, proverbs.
404. Benjamin, L.S., ed. <u>Great German Short Stories **</u>,
    1930,May.
    SOURCE: EH-MP
    COMMENT: EH ordered German war stories pub. by
        Liveright. Prob. this one.
405. Bennett, Arnold. <u>Journal of Arnold Bennett, Vol.2</u>,
    1932,Oct.
    SOURCE: EH-MP; KW-55
    COMMENT: Covers 1911-1920.
406. Bennett, Arnold. <u>Journal of Arnold Bennett, Vol.3</u>,
    1933,May.
    SOURCE: SCRBNR; KW-55
    COMMENT: Covers 1921-1928.

407. Bennett, Charles Edwin. <u>Latin Grammar</u>, 1914.
     SOURCE: OPHS
     COMMENT: HS text.
408. Bennett, Constance. <u>Blackmail</u>, 1938,Mar.
     SOURCE: SB
409. Benney, Mark. <u>Angels in Undress</u>, 1937, June.
     SOURCE: SCRBNR
     COMMENT: Pseud. of Henry Ernest Degras.
410. Benoit, Pierre. <u>L' Atlantide</u>, (1919).
     SOURCE: KW-40
411. Benson, Edward Frederic. <u>Final Edition</u>, 1940.
     SOURCE: EH-MP
     COMMENT: Ordered by EH.
412. Beraud, Henri. <u>Ce Que J'ai Vu a Rome</u>, (1929).
     SOURCE: KW-55
     COMMENT: Italy and facism.
413. Beresford, S. R. <u>Monte Carlo</u>, (1923).
     SOURCE: KW-40
     COMMENT: Gambling methods.
414. Bergamin, Jose. <u>El Arte de Birlibirloque</u>, (1930).
     SOURCE: KL:EH Collection
     COMMENT: Some highlighting in beginning of EH's
        copy.
415. Bernard, Theos. <u>Penthouse of the Gods</u>, 1939,Mar.
     SOURCE: EH-MP
     COMMENT: Sent to children.
416. Bessand-Massenet, Pierre, ed. <u>Air et Manieres de
        Paris</u>, (1937).
     SOURCE: KW-55
417. Bessie, Alvah Cecil. <u>Men in Battle</u>, 1939,Oct.
     SOURCE: EH-MP
     COMMENT: EH: much of book very fine.
418. Bierce, Ambrose. <u>An Occurrence at Owl Creek Bridge</u>,
        1928.
     SOURCE: EH-MP
     COMMENT: EH indicates he has read story, probably
        earlier than 1928.
419. Birabeau, Andre. <u>Revelation</u>, (1930).
     SOURCE: KW-40
     COMMENT: Trans. of La Debauche by Una, Lady
        Troubridge.
420. Birch, D. Percival Lea. <u>Sea Fishing</u>, 1935,Apr.
     SOURCE: EH-MP; SCRBNR
     COMMENT: EH ordered and received.
421. Bird, William. <u>A Practical Guide to French Wines</u>,
        1924,Aug.
     SOURCE: EH-GS
422. Bishop, John Peale. <u>Act of Darkness</u>, (1935).
     SOURCE: KW-55
423. Bishop, John Peale. <u>Many Thousands Gone</u>, (1931).
     SOURCE: KW-40
     COMMENT: Historical fiction.

424. Black and Davis. <u>Elementary</u> <u>Practical</u> <u>Physics</u>,
        (1938).
        SOURCE: KW-55
425. Blackford, William Willis. <u>War</u> <u>Years</u> <u>with</u> <u>Jeb</u> <u>Stuart</u>,
        1934,Oct.
        SOURCE: EH-MP
426. Blackmore, Richard D. <u>Lorna</u> <u>Doone</u>, (1869).
        SOURCE: KW-55
427. Blake, Forrester. <u>Riding</u> <u>the</u> <u>Mustang</u> <u>Trail</u>, 1935,Apr.
        SOURCE: EH-MP; <u>KW-40</u>
        COMMENT: Trail drive of wild horses from N.M. to
            Okla.
428. Blake, William. <u>The</u> <u>World</u> <u>is</u> <u>Mine</u>, 1938.
        SOURCE: KL:EH Collection
        COMMENT: Advance copy of preview edition for EH.
429. Blasco Ibanez, Vicente. <u>A</u> <u>los</u> <u>Pies</u> <u>de</u> <u>Venus</u>, (1926).
        SOURCE: KW-55
430. Blasco Ibanez, Vicente. <u>Arroz</u> <u>y</u> <u>Tartana</u>, (1894).
        SOURCE: KW-55
431. Blasco Ibanez, Vicente. <u>Blood</u> <u>and</u> <u>Sand</u>, (1919).
        SOURCE: EH-MP
        COMMENT: Trans. by W.A.Gillespie. EH read prior to
            April,1933, probably in late 1920s.
432. Blasco Ibanez, Vicente. <u>La</u> <u>Corrida</u>, (1919).
        SOURCE: KW-55
        COMMENT: Bilingual ed. English title: The
            Bullfight.
433. Blasco Ibanez, Vicente. <u>Novelas</u> <u>de</u> <u>la</u> <u>Costa</u> <u>Azul</u>,
        (1924).
        SOURCE: KW-55
434. Blasco Ibanez, Vicente. <u>Sangre</u> <u>Y</u> <u>Arena</u>, (1908).
        SOURCE: KW-40
        COMMENT: See Blood and Sand.
435. Bleu, F. <u>Antes</u> <u>Y</u> <u>Despues</u> <u>del</u> <u>Guerra</u> <u>(medio</u> <u>siglo</u> <u>de</u>
        <u>toreo),</u> <u>(1914)</u>.
        SOURCE: KW-40
436. Blixen-Finecke, Bror von. <u>African</u> <u>Hunter</u>, 1938.
        SOURCE: SCRBNR; KW-40
        COMMENT: Trans. from Swedish by F. H. Lyon.
437. Bloomfield, Paul. <u>The</u> <u>Travelers</u> <u>Companion</u>, (1931).
        SOURCE: KW-55
        COMMENT: Trav. info.
438. Blunden, Edmund. <u>Undertones</u> <u>of</u> <u>War</u>, (1928).
        SOURCE: KW-55
439. Blunt, Commander David Enderby. <u>Elephant</u>, (1933).
        SOURCE: KW-40
440. Boas and Smith. <u>Enjoyment</u> <u>of</u> <u>Literature</u>, (1934).
        SOURCE: KW-55
        COMMENT: Three copies.
441. Boccaccio. <u>The</u> <u>Decameron</u>.
        SOURCE: <u>KW-55</u>
442. Bodenheim, Maxwell. <u>Sixty</u> <u>Seconds</u>, (1929).
        SOURCE: KW-40

443. Boethius. The Consolation of Philosophy, (524).
          SOURCE: KW-55
444. Boileau, Ethel. Clansmen, 1936,June.
          SOURCE: SCRBNR
445. Bolderwood, Rolf. Robbery Under Arms (Vols.I&II),
          (1888).
          SOURCE: KW-55
446. Boleslavski, Richard. Way of the Lancer, (1932).
          SOURCE: KW-55
447. Bone, Charles **. Immigrants **.
          SOURCE: KW-40
448. Boner, Charles. Chamois Hunting, 1934,Mar.
          SOURCE: KL:Brentanos; KW-40
          COMMENT: Pub.1860. Bavaria and Tyrol.
449. Borel, Pierre. Le Destin Tragique de Guy de
          Maupassant, (1927).
          SOURCE: KW-40
450. Borrow, George Henry. The Bible in Spain, 1926,June.
          SOURCE: EH-Isidor Schneider; KW-40; KW-55
          COMMENT: EH: has the mind of a YMCA gym
              instructor. Probably read earlier.
451. Borrow, George Henry. Lavengro, 1926.
          SOURCE: EH-Guy Hickok; KW-40; KW-55
          COMMENT: EH: he has a YMCA mind.
452. Bosis, Lauro de. Icaro, 1934,Mar.
          SOURCE: SB; KW-40
          COMMENT: Trans. from Italian by Ruth Draper and a
              preface by Gilbert Murray.
453. Boswell, James. The Life of Samuel Johnson, (1791).
          SOURCE: KW-40
454. Botsford, G.W. and L.S. The Story of Rome, 1915.
          SOURCE: OPHS
          COMMENT: Assigned reading, HS.
455. Boucard, Robert. Les Dessous de L'Espionnage Anglais,
          (1926).
          SOURCE: KW-55
456. Boulestin, X. Marcel. Having Crossed the Channel,
          (1934).
          SOURCE: KW-40
457. Bourman, Anatole. The Tragedy of Nijinsky, 1936,Mar.
          SOURCE: SCRBNR; KW-55
          COMMENT: Russian dancers.
458. Bowers, Claude Gernade. The Tragic Era, (1929).
          SOURCE: KW-40; KW-55
          COMMENT: Reconstruction.
459. Bowers, Dorothy. Shadows Before, Book III, (1939).
          SOURCE: KW-40
          COMMENT: A Crime Club pub. EH and PH may have had
              a membership.
460. Boyd, James. Bitter Creek, 1939, March.
          SOURCE: EH-MP
          COMMENT: EH sent to children.

461.   Boyd, James.   <u>Drums</u>, 1934, May.
           SOURCE: EH-MP;   SCRBNR
           COMMENT: Ordered by EH.
462.   Boyd, James.   <u>Long Hunt</u>, 1930,May.
           SOURCE: EH-MP;   KW-40
           COMMENT: EH ordered and read.
463.   Boyd, James.   <u>Marching On</u>, 1934,Mar.
           SOURCE: EH-MP; SCRBNR
           COMMENT: EH ordered and received.
464.   Boyd, Thomas.   <u>Mad Anthony Wayne</u>, (1929).
           SOURCE: KW-40
465.   Boyd, Thomas.   <u>Samuel Drummond</u>, 1925,Dec.
           SOURCE: EH-FSF
           COMMENT: EH: compares unfavorably with The Growth
               of the Soil.
466.   Boyd, Thomas.   <u>Through the Wheat</u>, 1926,Apr.
           SOURCE: EH-MP
           COMMENT: EH: compared to Thomason's book, Boyd's
               awfully good.
467.   Boyes, John.   <u>The Company of Adventures</u>, (1928).
           SOURCE: KW-40
468.   Boyle, Kay.   <u>Gentlemen, I Address You Privately</u>,
               (1933).
           SOURCE: KW-55
469.   Boyle, Kay.   <u>Short Stories</u>, (1929).
           SOURCE: KW-40
           COMMENT: Black Sun Press. 185 numbered copies.
470.   Boyle, Kay.   <u>Year Before Last</u>, 1932,July.
           SOURCE: EH-MP; KW-55
           COMMENT: EH ordered.
471.   Boyton, Neil.   <u>Whoopee! the Story of a Catholic Summer
               Camp</u>, (1923).
           SOURCE: KW-55
472.   Brackett, Charles.   <u>Entirely Surrounded</u>, 1934, Oct.
           SOURCE: EH-MP
           COMMENT: Ordered by EH.
473.   Bradford, Roark.   " Child of God," 1928,Feb.
           SOURCE: EH-MP
           COMMENT: EH: compared with "Owl Creek Bridge", a
               weak story.
474.   Bradley, R. F. and R. B. Michell.   <u>French Literature
               of the Nineteenth Century</u>, (1935).
           SOURCE: KW-55
475.   Brandes, Georg M.C.   <u>William Shakespeare: a Critical
               Study</u>, 1916.
           SOURCE: KL
           COMMENT: Assigned reading, HS.
476.   Breasted, James Henry.   <u>The Conquest of Civilization</u>,
               (1926).
           SOURCE: KW-55
477.   Breder, Charles Marcus.   <u>Field Book of Marine Fishes
               of the Atlantic Coast</u>, (1929).
           SOURCE: KW-40; KW-55

478. Brent, Newell. Jungle Giants , 1936,June.
     SOURCE: SCRBNR; KW-40
     COMMENT: Tanganyika.
479. Breuer, Bessie. The Daughter, (1938).
     SOURCE: KW-40
     COMMENT: Bound galleys.
480. Bridge, Ann. Enchanter's Nightshade, (1937).
     SOURCE: KW-55
     COMMENT: Pseud. of Mary D. O'Malley.
481. Briggs, Clare A. Oh Man, (1919).
     SOURCE: KW-55
     COMMENT: Humor.
482. Briggs, Clare A. Oh Skin-nay!, (1913).
     SOURCE: KW-55
     COMMENT: Humor.
483. Brinley, Gordon. Away to the Gaspe, 1935, Aug.
     SOURCE: EH-MP
     COMMENT: Gaspe district, Quebec.
484. Bromfield, Louis. Early Autumn, a Story of a Lady,
     (1926).
     SOURCE: KW-40
485. Bromfield, Louis. The Rains Came, (1937).
     SOURCE: KW-55
486. Bronte, Charlotte. Jane Eyre, (1848).
     SOURCE: KW-40
     COMMENT: Probably read in HS.
487. Bronte, Emily. Wuthering Heights, (1847).
     SOURCE: KW-55
488. Brooks, George S. Spread Eagle, 1927,Nov.
     SOURCE: EH-MP
     COMMENT: EH requests copy.
489. Brooks, Van Wyck. The Flowering of New England, 1936,
     June.
     SOURCE: SCRBNR; KW-55
490. Brousson, Jean Jacques, ed. Anatole France en
     Patoufles, (1924).
     SOURCE: KW-55
491. Brown, Bruce. Arkansas Tales, (1937).
     SOURCE: KW-55
492. Brown, Horatio F. Dalmatia, (1925).
     SOURCE: KW-55
493. Brown, Rollo Walter, ed. The Writer's Art by Those
     Who Have Practiced It, (1921).
     SOURCE: KW-40
     COMMENT: Literary style.
494. Browne, Jefferson B. Key West, the Old and the New,
     (1912).
     SOURCE: KW-55
495. Browning, Robert. The Collected Works of Robert
     Browning, (1914).
     SOURCE: KW-55
     COMMENT: Six vols.

496.   Browning, Robert. <u>The Poems and Plays of Robert Browning</u>, 1918.
     SOURCE: KW-55; Baker
     COMMENT: 6 vol. set left in Key West. Read Browning in Kansas City in 1918.

497.   Browning, Robert.   "The Year's at the Spring," 1914, Apr.
     SOURCE: OPHS
     COMMENT: Memorized for HS.

498.   Brownlee, Raymond B.   <u>First Principles of Chemistry</u>, 1915.
     SOURCE: OPHS
     COMMENT: HS text.

499.   Bruce, Ethel and Bert O.   <u>Tennis, Fundamentals and Timing</u>, (1938).
     SOURCE: KW-55

500.   Bruette, William Arthur.   <u>American Duck Goose and Brant Shooting</u>, (1929).
     SOURCE: KW-40

501.   Bryant, William C.   " Thanatopsis," 1915, Apr.
     SOURCE: OPHS
     COMMENT: Memorized for HS.

502.   Bryant, William C.   " To a Water Fowl," 1915, Mar.
     SOURCE: OPHS
     COMMENT: Memorized for HS.

503.   Buchell **.   <u>The Complete Shot</u> **.
     SOURCE: KW-40

504.   Buck, Pearl S.   <u>The First Wife and Other Stories</u>, (1933).
     SOURCE: KW-55

505.   Budge, John D.   <u>Budge on Tennis</u>, (1939).
     SOURCE: KW-55

506.   Bugnet, Charles.   <u>En Ecoutant le Marechal Foch</u>, (1929).
     SOURCE: KW-55

507.   Bulliet, Clarence J.   <u>The Significant Moderns and Their Pictures</u>, 1936, May.
     SOURCE: SCRBNR

508.   Bunyan, John.   <u>Pilgrim's Progress</u>, 1914.
     SOURCE: OPHS
     COMMENT: HS reading.

509.   Burch, John P.   <u>Charles W. Quantrell</u>, (1923).
     SOURCE: KW-40

510.   Burke, Edmund.   " Speech Against Force," 1916, Mar.
     SOURCE: OPHS
     COMMENT: From Conciliation. EH memorized paragraphs 32-36.

511.   Burke, Edmund.   " Speech on Conciliation," 1915.
     SOURCE: OPHS

512.   Burman, Ben Lucien.   <u>Big River to Cross: Mississippi Life Today</u>, 1940.
     SOURCE: EH-MP
     COMMENT: Ordered by EH.

513. Burnett, Robert. The Life of Paul Gauguin, (1936).
      SOURCE: KW-55
514. Burnett, William Riley. Good-bye to the Past, (1934).
      SOURCE: KW-55
515. Burnham, David. This Our Exile, 1931,Apr.
      SOURCE: EH-MP; KW-40
      COMMENT: EH ordered.
516. Burns, Robert. " Afton Waters," 1915,Nov.
      SOURCE: OPHS
      COMMENT: EH memorized for HS.
517. Burrard, Gerald. The Modern Shotgun, 1931,Apr.
      SOURCE: MP-EH; EH-MP; KW-40
518. Burton, Richard Francis. First Footsteps in East
      Africa, (1856).
      SOURCE: KW-55
519. Burton, Richard Francis, trans. The Arabian Nights,
      (1885).
      SOURCE: KW-55
520. Busch, Ernst, ed. Canciones de las Brigadas
      Internacionales, (1938).
      SOURCE: KW-40
      COMMENT: EH mentioned in book.
521. Butler, Ellis P. Dollarature: The Drug-store Book,
      (1930).
      SOURCE: KW-40
      COMMENT: Publishing and bookselling.
522. Butler, Frank Hedges. Wine and Wine Lands of the
      World, (1926).
      SOURCE: KW-40
      COMMENT: Wine and wine-making - history.
523. Butler, N.M. The Path to Peace, 1929,Dec.
      SOURCE: Donovan-EH
      COMMENT: Vincent C. Donovan sent EH a copy.
524. Butler, Samuel. Hudibras.
      SOURCE: KW-55
      COMMENT: Two copies.
525. Butler, Samuel. The Way of All Flesh, (1903).
      SOURCE: KW-40
526. Butts, Mary. Armed With Madness, (1928).
      SOURCE: KW-55
527. Buxton, Sydney Charles, 1st Earl. Fishing and
      Shooting, (1903).
      SOURCE: KW-40
528. Buzzacott, Francis. The Complete American and
      Canadian Sportsman's Encyclopedia, (1905).
      SOURCE: KW-55
529. Byne, Arthur and Mildred Stapley. Spanish Interiors
      and Furniture (Vols. I&II), (1921).
      SOURCE: KW-55
530. Byron, George Gordon, Lord. Childe Harold, (1816).
      SOURCE: KW-55

531. Byron, George Gordon, Lord. "The Destruction of
      Sennacherib," 1914,Feb.
         SOURCE: OPHS
         COMMENT: EH memorized.
532. Byron, George Gordon, Lord. The Letters of Lord
      Byron, (1936).
         SOURCE: KW-40
         COMMENT: Ed. Robert Guy Howarth.
533. Byron, George Gordon, Lord. Poetical Works of Byron.
         SOURCE: KW-55
534. Cabell, James Branch. Jurgen, (1919).
         SOURCE: KW-40; Fenton
         COMMENT: Probably read by 1923.
535. Cabell, James Branch. Special Delivery, (1933).
         SOURCE: KW-55
536. Cadby, Will and C. Switzerland in Winter, (1914).
         SOURCE: KW-55
537. Caesar, Julius. Caesar's Gallic War.
         SOURCE: OPHS; KL
         COMMENT: Eds. Role and Roberts. HS text.
538. Caine, Louis S. Gamefish of the South and How to
      Catch Them, (1935).
         SOURCE: KW-40
539. Calder-Marshall, Arthur. At Sea, 1934, Oct.
         SOURCE: MP-EH; KW-55
540. Caldwell, Erskine. American Earth, 1931, April.
         SOURCE: EH-MP; KW-40
         COMMENT: EH:just read; seems very honest.
541. Caldwell, Erskine. Tobacco Road, (1932).
         SOURCE: KW-40
542. Callaghan, Morley. " Backwater," 1928, Jan.
         SOURCE: EH-MP
         COMMENT: EH: read book two or three years ago,
         remembers it vividly.
543. Callaghan, Morley. A Native Argosy, 1928,Mar.
         SOURCE: MP-EH; EH-MP; KW-55
         COMMENT: "American Made" is Sec.I.
544. Callaghan, Morley. Strange Fugitive, 1928,Aug.
         SOURCE: EH-MP
         COMMENT: EH orders copy.
545. Callwell, Sir E.C. Sir Henry Wilson: His Life and
      Diaries (2 vol.), (1927).
         SOURCE: KW-40
546. Calmer, Edgar. Beyond the Street, (1934).
         SOURCE: KW-40
547. Camoens, Luiz de. La Lusiada, (1804).
         SOURCE: KW-55
548. Camoens, Luiz de. Obras Completas, (1834).
         SOURCE: KW-55
         COMMENT: Two copies.
549. Camoens, Luiz de. Poesias Castellanas, (1927).
         SOURCE: KW-55

550. Campbell, Gordon. Mes Naviers Mysterieux, (1928).
       SOURCE: KW-55
       COMMENT: Naval history.
551. Campbell, Roy. Taurine Provence, (1932).
       SOURCE: KW-40
       COMMENT: Two copies?
552. Campbell, T. " Ye Mariners of England," 1916,June.
       SOURCE: OPHS
       COMMENT: EH memorized.
553. Cantwell, Robert. The Land of Plenty, (1934).
       SOURCE: KW-40; EH-MP
       COMMENT: EH: one of the new writers of note.
554. Carco, Francis. De Montmartre au Quartier Latin,
       (1927).
       SOURCE: KW-55
555. Carco, Francis. Perversity, (1928).
       SOURCE: KW-40
       COMMENT: Trans. by F.M.Ford.
556. Carco, Francis. Tenebres, (1935).
       SOURCE: KW-55
557. Cardozo, Harold G. The March of a Nation, (1937).
       SOURCE: KW-40
558. Carlyle, Thomas. Essay on Burns, 1914.
       SOURCE: OPHS
559. Carlyle, Thomas. The French Revolution, (1837).
       SOURCE: KW-55
       COMMENT: Vols. I & II.
560. Carlyle, Thomas. Heroes and Hero-Worship, (1838-41).
       SOURCE: KW-55
561. Carmer, Carl Lamson. Listen for a Lonesome Drum,
       1936, July.
       SOURCE: SCRBNR
       COMMENT: N.Y.state: Spiritualism and folk-lore.
562. Carnahan, David H. Alternate French Review Grammar,
       (1924).
       SOURCE: KW-55
563. Carnahan, David H. Short French Grammar Review,
       (1920).
       SOURCE: KW-55
564. Carr, John Dickson. The Crooked Hinge, (1938).
       SOURCE: KW-55
565. Carroll, Lewis. Alice in Wonderland and Through the
       Looking Glass.
       SOURCE: KW-55
       COMMENT: Pseud. of Charles Dodgson.
566. Carroll, Lewis. Through the Looking Glass.
       SOURCE: KW-55
       COMMENT: Pseud. of Charles Dodgson.
567. Carswell, Catherine Mc. The Savage Pilgrimage,
       (1932).
       SOURCE: KW-40
       COMMENT: "a narrative of D.H.Lawrence."

568. Carter, J. and G.Pollard. An Enquiry into the Nature
     of Certain 19th century Pamphlets, (1934).
     SOURCE: KW-40
     COMMENT: Literary forgeries.
569. Casson, Stanley. Progress and Catastrophe: an Anatomy
     of Human Adventure, 1937, June.
     SOURCE: SCRBNR; KW-55
570. Caswell, John. Sporting Rifles and Rifle Shooting,
     (1920).
     SOURCE: KW-40
571. Cather, Willa Sibert. A Lost Lady, 1937,Apr.
     SOURCE: SCRBNR
     COMMENT: Sent to Mrs. Hemingway.
572. Cather, Willa Sibert. One of Ours, 1923,Nov.
     SOURCE: EH-Edmund Wilson; EH-GS
     COMMENT: EH: battle scenes came from Birth of a
        Nation. Can't understand people taking it
        seriously. Gets good about p.425. (459pp).
573. Cather, Willa Sibert. Shadows on the Rock, (1931).
     SOURCE: KW-55
574. Cato. Guilty Men, 1940, Oct.
     SOURCE: EH-MP
     COMMENT: Ordered by EH. Pseud. Owen, Frank with
        Michael Foote and Peter Howard.
575. Caulaincourt, Armand, Marquis de. With Napoleon in
     Russia, 1936,Feb.
     SOURCE: EH-MP; SCRBNR
     COMMENT: EH ordered. Napoleon: Invasion of Russia,
        1812.
576. Caulfield, Vivian. How to Ski and How Not to, (1913).
     SOURCE: KW-40
577. Caumery. Becassine fait du Scoutisme, (1931).
     SOURCE: KW-55
     COMMENT: Pseud. of Maurice Languereau.
578. Celine, Louis Ferdinand. Mort a Credit, (1936).
     SOURCE: KW-55
     COMMENT: Pseud. of L.F.Destouches.
579. Celine, Louis Ferdinand. Voyage au Bout de la Nuit,
     (1932).
     SOURCE: KW-40
     COMMENT: Pseud. of Louis Ferdinand Destouches.
580. Cellini, Benvenuto. Memoirs.
     SOURCE: KW-55
581. Cendrars, Blaise. Moravagine, (1926).
     SOURCE: KW-40
     COMMENT: Trans. from Fr. by Alan Brown.
582. Cervantes, Miguel de. Don Quixote.
     SOURCE: KW-55
     COMMENT: Two copies.
583. Cervantes, Miguel de. Tragedia en Tres Journadas
     Numancia, (1937).
     SOURCE: KW-40
     COMMENT: Adaptation by Rafael Alberti.

584. Chadourne, Marc. Chine, (1931).
     SOURCE: KW-55
585. Chadourne, Marc. Vasco, (1927).
     SOURCE: KW-55
     COMMENT: Le roseau d'or; oeuvres et chroniques.
586. Champsaur, Felicien. Nora, La Guenon Devenue Femme,
     (1900).
     SOURCE: KW-55
587. Chamson, Andre. The Road, 1929,Feb.
     SOURCE: MP-EH
     COMMENT: MP: sending new C.novel. May be this or
        Roux the Bandit.
588. Chandler, Raymond. Farewell My Lovely, 1940,Nov.
     SOURCE: EH-MP
589. Channing, Edward. A Student's History of the U.S.,
     1915.
     SOURCE: OPHS; KL
     COMMENT: HS text.
590. Chapman, Abel. Savage Sudan, 1934,Mar.
     SOURCE: KL:Brentanos; KW-40
     COMMENT: Pub.1921.
591. Chapman, Frank Michler. Handbook of Birds of Eastern
     North America, (1895).
     SOURCE: KW-40
592. Chapman, Guy. Beckford, 1937.
     SOURCE: SCRBNR
     COMMENT: William Beckford 1760-1844.
593. Chase, R. H. The Works of Horace, (1870).
     SOURCE: KW-55
594. Chatterton, E. Keble. Les Bateaux-Pieges, (1922).
     SOURCE: KW-55
     COMMENT: "Q-Ships and their story".
595. Chaucer, Geoffrey. Canterbury Tales (Gen.Prol.),
     1914.
     SOURCE: OPHS
     COMMENT: EH read Gen. Prol. in 1914. Memorized
        first 18 lines in Sept.1916.
596. Chaucer, Geoffrey. "The Knight's Tale," 1916.
     SOURCE: OPHS
     COMMENT: Assigned reading in HS.
597. Chekhov, Anton. "The Horse Thieves," 1929,Feb.
     SOURCE: EH-MP
     COMMENT: In an unidentified collection of Russian
        short stories sent by MP.
598. Chekhov, Anton. The Schoolmaster, (1921).
     SOURCE: KW-40
     COMMENT: Stories trans. by Constance Garnett.
599. Chekhov, Anton. The Wife, (1918).
     SOURCE: KW-40
     COMMENT: Trans. by Constance Garnett.
600. Chester, Samuel Beach. Round the Green Cloth,
     1929,June.
     SOURCE: SB
     COMMENT: Gambling.

601. Chesterton, Gilbert Keith. The Ballad of the White
     Horse, (1911).
     SOURCE: KW-55
     COMMENT: Alfred the Great, 891-901. Poetry.
602. Chesterton, Gilbert Keith. The Incredulity of Father
     Brown, (1926).
     SOURCE: KW-55
603. Chesterton, G.K. The New Jerusalem, 1925,Dec.
     SOURCE: KL
     COMMENT: Palestine, Jewish question and Zionism.
604. Cheyney, Edward P. A Short History of England,
     (1904).
     SOURCE: KW-55
605. Childers, Erskine. The Riddle of the Sands, 1935.
     SOURCE: KL:EH Collection
606. Childs, Herbert. El Jimmy, Outlaw of Patagonia,
     1936,June.
     SOURCE: SCRBNR; KW-40
     COMMENT: Subj. James Radburne.
607. Chitambar, Jashwant R. Mahatma Gandhi, (1933).
     SOURCE: KW-55
608. Christie, Dame Agatha Miller. ABC Murders, (1936).
     SOURCE: KW-40
609. Churchill, Winston. The Crossing, (1904).
     SOURCE: KW-40
610. Churchill, Winston. Richard Carvel, (1899).
     SOURCE: KW-40
     COMMENT: Fiction: revolution, U.S. & Maryland.
611. Churchill, Winston L.S. The Aftermath 1918-1928,
     (1929).
     SOURCE: KW-40
612. Churchill, Winston L.S. A Roving Commission,
     1931,Dec.
     SOURCE: EH-MP; KW-55
     COMMENT: EH read.
613. Churchill, Winston L.S. The Unknown War: the Eastern
     Front, (1931).
     SOURCE: KW-40
614. Cicero. Orations, 1916.
     SOURCE: OPHS
     COMMENT: HS reading.
615. Cicero. Select Orations of Cicero.
     SOURCE: KW-55
616. Ciria y Nassare, H. Los Toros de Bonaparte, (1903).
     SOURCE: KW-40
617. Claretie, Jules. Histoire de la Revolution de
     1870-71, (1872).
     SOURCE: KW-40
618. Clark, Walter Van Tilburg. The Ox-Bow Incident, 1940,
     Nov.
     SOURCE: EH-MP; KW-55
     COMMENT: EH ordered.

619. Clausewitz, Karl Philipp G. von. On War (3 vols.),
      (1873).
      SOURCE: KW-40
      COMMENT: Trans. 1873, revised 1908.
620. Cleaton, Irene and Allen. Books and Battles: American
      Literature 1920-1930, 1937.
      SOURCE: SCRBNR
621. Clendening, Logan. The Care and Feeding of Adults,
      with doubts about children, (1931).
      SOURCE: KW-40
622. Clum, Woodworth. Apache Agent: The Story of John P.
      Clum, 1936, March.
      SOURCE: SCRBNR
623. Coates, Henry. A Short History of the American
      Trotting and Pacing Horse, (1901).
      SOURCE: KW-55
624. Coburn, Alvin Langdon. Men of Mark, 1925,Feb.
      SOURCE: EH-Ernest Walsh
625. Coburn, Alvin Langdon. More Men of Mark, 1925,Feb.
      SOURCE: EH-Ernest Walsh
626. Cocteau, Jean. Les Enfants Terribles, (1929).
      SOURCE: KW-40
627. Cocteau, Jean. Le Potomak, (1919).
      SOURCE: KW-55
628. Cocteau, Jean. Thomas L'Imposteur, (1923).
      SOURCE: KW-40; KL:EH Collection
      COMMENT: Owned Gertrude Stein's copy signed by
          Cocteau.
629. Codman, Charles. Contact, 1937, July.
      SOURCE: SCRBNR
630. Coffey, Brian. Three Poems, 1934,Mar.
      SOURCE: SB
631. Cohan, George M. The Tavern, 1920.
      SOURCE: EH-Bill Smith
      COMMENT: EH: best show he has ever seen.
632. Cohn, Louis Henry. A Bibliography of the Works of
      Ernest Hemingway, 1931.
      SOURCE: EH-MP; KW-40
      COMMENT: EH:crazy to say EH had not read Anderson
          when he wrote "My Old Man."
633. Cole, George D.H. The Brothers Sackville, 1937.
      SOURCE: SCRBNR; KW-55
634. Cole, George D.H. Practical Economics, (1938).
      SOURCE: KW-55
635. Coleridge, S. T. "The Rime of the Ancient Mariner,"
      1913.
      SOURCE: OPHS
636. Colette, Sidonie Gabrielle. Quatre Saisons, (1928).
      SOURCE: KW-40
637. Collins, Joseph. The Doctor Looks at Literature,
      1926,Jan.
      SOURCE: SB
      COMMENT: Joyce, Dostoevsky, D. Richardson, Proust,
          K. Mansfield, R. West, V. Woolf, D.H.Lawrence.

638. Collins, Wilkie. Jezebel's Daughter, (1880).
        SOURCE: KW-55
639. Colony, Horatio. Free Forester: a Novel of Pioneer
        Kentucky, (1935).
        SOURCE: KW-40
640. Colum, Mary Maguire. From These Roots: the Ideas that
        Have Made Modern Literature, 1938, Feb.
        SOURCE: EH-MP
641. Confucius. The Wisdom of Confucius.
        SOURCE: KW-55
        COMMENT: Chinese: philosophy & ethics.
642. Connington, J. J. A Minor Operation, 1937, June.
        SOURCE: SCRBNR
        COMMENT: Pseud. of Alfred W. Stewart.
643. Connolly, James Brendan. Gloustermen, Stories of the
        Fishing Fleet, 1930, April.
        SOURCE: EH-MP
        COMMENT: Ordered and received by EH.
644. Conrad, Jessie. Joseph Conrad and His Circle, (1935).
        SOURCE: KW-55
645. Conrad, Joseph. The Complete Short Stories of Joseph
        Conrad, (1933).
        SOURCE: KW-55
646. Conrad, Joseph. Lord Jim, (1900).
        SOURCE: KW-55
        COMMENT: EH: unable to finish.
647. Conrad, Joseph. An Outcast of the Islands, 1926, Apr.
        SOURCE: SB
648. Conrad, Joseph. A Personal Record, (1912).
        SOURCE: KW-55
649. Conrad, Joseph. The Rover, 1923.
        SOURCE: Baker
650. Conrad, Joseph. Typhoon, (1902).
        SOURCE: KW-40
651. Conrad, Joseph. Victory, 1920,Apr.
        SOURCE: Ted Brumback-EH
        COMMENT: Brumback: As you recommended I have
            started Victory. Am in accord with you that J.C.
            is the king.
652. Conrad, Joseph. Within the Tides, 1925.
        SOURCE: Baker
653. Constans, M. L. Conjuracion de Catilina, (1861).
        SOURCE: KW-55
654. Constantin-Weyer, Maurice. Un Homme se Penche sur son
        Passe, (1933).
        SOURCE: KW-55
655. Cook, Capt. James. Voyages of Discovery, (1906).
        SOURCE: KW-40
656. Cooper, A.E., ed. Sea Fishing, (1934).
        SOURCE: KW-40
        COMMENT: Sportsman's Library, Vol.III.
657. Cooper, Courtney Ryley. Here's to Crime, (1937).
        SOURCE: KW-55

658. Cooper, James Fenimore. The Last of the Mohicans, (1826).
     SOURCE: KW-55
659. Copeland, Charles. The Copeland Reader, (1926).
     SOURCE: KW-55
660. Coquiot, Gustave. Vincent Van Gogh, (1923).
     SOURCE: KW-55
661. Corcoran, William. This Man, Joe Murray, (1937).
     SOURCE: KW-55
662. Corey, Lewis. The House of Morgan: A Social Biography
     of the Masters of Money, 1930, Dec.
     SOURCE: MP-EH
663. Cormack, Bartlett. The Racket, (1928).
     SOURCE: KW-55
664. Corman, Mathieu. Salud Comarada, (1937).
     SOURCE: KW-40
665. Corneille, Pierre. The Cid, 1916.
     SOURCE: Fenton
666. Coulon, Marcel. Au Coeur de Verlaine et de Rimbaud, (1925).
     SOURCE: KW-55
667. Coulton, George Gordon. Life in the Middle Ages, 1929.
     SOURCE: SB
     COMMENT: Vol.II: Chronicles, Science & Art;
        vol.III: Men and Manners.
668. Covarrubias, Miguel. Island of Bali, (1937).
     SOURCE: KW-55
669. Cowan, John Franklin. The Jo-Boat Boys, (1891).
     SOURCE: KW-40
670. Coward, Noel. To Step Aside, (1939).
     SOURCE: KW-55
671. Cowley, Malcolm, ed. After the Genteel Tradition, 1937.
     SOURCE: SCRBNR; KW-55
     COMMENT: "American writers since 1910."
672. Cox, William D., ed. Boxing in Art and Literature, (1935).
     SOURCE: KW-40
673. Craige, John H. Black Bagdad, (1933).
     SOURCE: KW-55
     COMMENT: Haiti.
674. Crane, Hart. The Bridge, 1930, April.
     SOURCE: EH-MP; KW-55
     COMMENT: EH ordered and received.
675. Crane, Hart. The Collected Poems of Hart Crane, 1933,Apr.
     SOURCE: SCRBNR
676. Crane, Hart. White Buildings, 1927,May.
     SOURCE: EH-Isidor Schneider
     COMMENT: EH ordered.

677. Crane, Stephen. <u>Maggie</u>, <u>a Girl of the Streets</u>,
       (1896).
       SOURCE: KW-40
       COMMENT: Mod. Library ed. came out in 1933.
678. Crane, Stephen. <u>Pictures of War</u>, (1898).
       SOURCE: KW-40
679. Crane, Stephen. <u>The Red Badge of Courage</u>, 1926,May.
       SOURCE: EH-MP
       COMMENT: Probably read earlier but not before
          1924. EH: a tour de force.
680. Craven, Thomas. <u>Men of Art</u>, (1931).
       SOURCE: KW-40
681. Craven, Thomas. <u>Modern Art</u>: <u>the Men</u>, <u>the Movements</u>,
       the Meaning, 1934, May.
       SOURCE: EH-MP; SCRBNR; KW-40
       COMMENT: EH ordered.
682. Crockett, David. <u>Autobiography of David Crockett</u>,
       1933, Jan.
       SOURCE: EH-MP; KW-40
       COMMENT: Intro. by Hamlin Garland.
683. Crofts, Freeman Wills. <u>The Ponson Case</u>, (1921).
       SOURCE: KW-55
684. Cronin, A. J. <u>Hatter's Castle</u>, (1931).
       SOURCE: KW-55
685. Crosby, Caresse. <u>Poems for Harry Crosby</u>, (1931).
       SOURCE: KW-40
       COMMENT: Prvt. printed, limited to 44 lettered
          copies.
686. Crossman, Edward Cathcart. <u>The Book of the</u>
       <u>Springfield</u>, (1932).
       SOURCE: KW-40
       COMMENT: Textbook on rifles, military and
          sporting.
687. Crossman, Edward Cathcart. <u>Military Sporting Rifle</u>,
       (1932).
       SOURCE: KW-40
688. Crossman, Edward Cathcart. <u>Small-Bore Rifle Shooting</u>,
       (1927).
       SOURCE: KW-40
       COMMENT: Pub. Marshallton, Del.: Small Arms
          Technical Pub. Co.
689. Cummings, Edward Estlin. <u>Eimi</u> , 1934.
       SOURCE: EP-EH; KW-40
690. Cummings, Edward Estlin. <u>The Enormous Room</u>, 1922.
       SOURCE: EH-Edmund Wilson; <u>EH-Bill Smith</u>; EH-MP
       COMMENT: EH: loaned to Gertrude Stein. Best book
          published last year. One of the best written by
          an American.
691. Cummings, Edward Estlin. <u>Is 5</u>, (1926).
       SOURCE: KW-40
692. Cunningham, Eugene. <u>Triggernometry</u>: <u>a Gallery of Gun</u>
       <u>Fighters</u>, (1934).
       SOURCE: KW-40

693. Curry, Manfred. Yacht Racing, 1927.
     SOURCE: KL:EH Collection
     COMMENT: EH made notes on back of book jacket.
694. Curtis, Caldwell & Sherman, eds. Everyday Biology,
     (1940).
     SOURCE: KW-55
695. Curtis, Charles P. Hunting in Africa East and West,
     1935,Sept.
     SOURCE: EH-MP
     COMMENT: Probably read in 1934.
696. Curtis, Paul Allan. American Game Shooting, (1927).
     SOURCE: KW-40
697. Curtis, Paul Allan. Sporting Firearms of Today in
     Use, (1922).
     SOURCE: KW-40
698. Custer, Mrs. Elizabeth Bacon. Tenting on the Plains:
     or, Gen'l Custer in Kansas and Texas, (1887).
     SOURCE: KW-40
699. Dahlberg, Edward. From Flushing to Calvary, (1932).
     SOURCE: KW-55
700. Dalgliesh, Alice. America Begins, 1938, March.
     SOURCE: SCRBNR
     COMMENT: Juvenile lit; sent to Mrs. EH.
701. Dalgliesh, Alice. Happily Ever After, (1939).
     SOURCE: KW-40
     COMMENT: Likely. EH lists author as Arnold
        Gingrich. A joke? Dalgliesh pub. by Scribners.
702. Dall, Ian. Here Are Stones, An Account of a Journey
     to the Aran Islands, (1931).
     SOURCE: KW-40
703. Daly, Marcus. Big Game Hunting and Adventure, (1937).
     SOURCE: KW-40
704. Dana, Richard Henry. Two Years Before the Mast.
     SOURCE: KW-40
705. Dane, Richard M. Sport in Asia and Africa, 1934,Mar.
     SOURCE: KL:Brentanos; KW-40
706. D'Annunzio, Gabriele. The Flame, 1920.
     SOURCE: Baker
707. Dante. The Divine Comedy, (1867).
     SOURCE: KW-40
     COMMENT: 3 vol. trans. by Longfellow.
708. Dante. The Divine Comedy.
     SOURCE: KW-55
709. Dard, Emile. Napoleon and Talleyrand, (1937).
     SOURCE: KW-55
710. Darrah, Henry Zouch. Sport in the Highlands of
     Kashmir, 1934,Mar.
     SOURCE: KL:Brentanos; KW-40
     COMMENT: Pub.1898.
711. Darrow, Clarence. The Story of My Life, (1932).
     SOURCE: KW-55
712. Darwin, Bernard R. M. John Gully and His Times,
     (1935).
     SOURCE: KW-40

713. Daudet, Alphonse. Numa Roumestan, (1881).
         SOURCE: KW-55
714. Daudet, Alphonse. Sapho, (1884).
         SOURCE: KW-55
715. Daudet, Leon. La Police Politique.
         SOURCE: KW-55
716. Davenport, Marcia. Mozart, (1932).
         SOURCE: KW-55
717. Davis, Clyde Brion. The Great American Novel,
         1938,May.
         SOURCE: SCRBNR; KW-55
         COMMENT: EH sent copy to V. Pfeiffer.
718. Davis, Owen. The Great Gatsby, 1927,Nov.
         SOURCE: EH-MP
         COMMENT: Play adapted from FSF novel. EH admired
         the play.
719. Davis, Richard Harding. Miss Civilization, 1914,May.
         SOURCE: OPHS
720. de Kruif, Paul. Hunger Fighters, (1928).
         SOURCE: KW-55
         COMMENT: Wheat, agriculture, veterinarians,
         scientists, food, food supply.
721. de Kruif, Paul. Men Against Death, (1932).
         SOURCE: KW-55
722. Defoe, Daniel. Captain Singleton, (1720).
         SOURCE: KW-40; KW-55
723. Defoe, Daniel. Memoirs of a Cavelier.
         SOURCE: KW-40
         COMMENT: Everyman edition pub. 1933.
724. Defoe, Daniel. Roxana: the Fortunate Mistress,
         (1724).
         SOURCE: KW-40
725. Delafield, E. M. The Provincial Lady in America,
         (1934).
         SOURCE: KW-55
         COMMENT: Pseud. of De La Pasture, Edmee Elizabeth.
726. Delgado, Jose. Paginas Tauromacas, (1929).
         SOURCE: KW-40
727. Dell, Robert. My Second Country, (1920).
         SOURCE: KW-40
728. Dempsey, Jack. Round by Round, an Autobiography,
         1940,Oct.
         SOURCE: EH-MP
         COMMENT: EH ordered.
729. Denison, J. H. Emotional Currents in American
         History, (1932).
         SOURCE: KW-55
730. Desnos, Robert. Corps et Biens, (1930).
         SOURCE: KW-55
731. Desnos, Robert. Les Sans Cou, 1934.
         SOURCE: KL:EH Collection
         COMMENT: Inscribed by author. Pages uncut.
732. DeVoto, Bernard A. Mark Twain's America, (1932).
         SOURCE: KW-40

733. DeVoto, Bernard A.   We Accept with Pleasure, (1934).
     SOURCE: KW-40
734. Dickens, Charles.   A Christmas Carol, (1843).
     SOURCE: KW-40
735. Dickens, Charles.   Christmas Stories for Children,
     1909.
     SOURCE: Baker
736. Dickens, Charles.   David Copperfield, 1914.
     SOURCE: OPHS; KW-55
737. Dickens, Charles.   Great Expectations, (1860).
     SOURCE: KW-55
738. Dickens, Charles.   Pictures From Italy, (1843).
     SOURCE: KW-40
739. Dickens, Charles.   A Tale of Two Cities, 1920.
     SOURCE: EH-Grace Quinlan
     COMMENT: Probably read in HS. See comment: Andrea
        Chenier.
740. Dickinson, Edward.   Music in the History of the
     Western Church, (1902).
     SOURCE: KW-55
741. Dickson, Carter.   Bowstring Murder, (1933).
     SOURCE: KW-40
     COMMENT: Pseud. for John Dickson Carr.
742. Dimock, Anthony Weston.   The Book of the Tarpon,
     (1911).
     SOURCE: KW-40
743. Dinesen, Isak.   Out of Africa, 1938, Mar.
     SOURCE: SCRBNR
     COMMENT: Pseud. of Karen Blixen.
744. Dinesen, Isak.   Seven Gothic Tales, (1934).
     SOURCE: KW-55
     COMMENT: Pseud. of Karen Blixen.
745. Don Parando.   Resumen Pitonudo de 1929, (1930).
     SOURCE: KW-40
     COMMENT: Pseud. of Jose Rivera. Critical and
        statistical summary of year's bullfighting.
746. Don Ventura.   Efemerides Taurinas, (1928).
     SOURCE: KW-55
     COMMENT: Pseud. for Ventura Bagues.
747. D'Ooge, Benjamin L.   Latin for Beginners, 1913.
     SOURCE: OPHS
     COMMENT: HS text.
748. Doolittle, Hilda.   Collected Poems of H.D., (1925).
     SOURCE: KW-40
749. Dorrance, Ward Allison.   Where Rivers Meet, 1939,Dec.
     SOURCE: EH-MP
     COMMENT: EH ordered. EH: has truly fine things in
        it.
750. Dos Passos, John.   In All Countries, (1934).
     SOURCE: KW-40

751. Dos Passos, John. Manhattan Transfer, 1926,Apr.
       SOURCE: EH-MP; KL
       COMMENT: EH:started it twice. Style tiring. Gets
          more interesting. (Wrote a review which praised
          it.)
752. Dos Passos, John. One Man's Initiation, 1925.
       SOURCE: EH-FSF
       COMMENT: EH:first book was lousy.
753. Dos Passos, John. Rosinante to the Road Again,
       (1922).
       SOURCE: KW-55
754. Dos Passos, John. Streets of Night, 1925,Dec.
       SOURCE: EH-FSF
       COMMENT: EH: subject matter made it a lousy book.
755. Dos Passos, John. Three Plays, (1934).
       SOURCE: KW-55
756. Dos Passos, John. Three Soldiers, 1923,Aug.
       SOURCE: EH-William Bird; EH-FSF; KW-40; KW-55
       COMMENT: EH owns copy in 1923. Recommends it to
          FSF in 1925.
757. Dos Passos, John. U.S.A., (1937).
       SOURCE: KW-55
       COMMENT: EH read trilogy as it was pub. See other
          Dos Passos entries.
758. Dos Passos, John. 1919, 1932,June.
       SOURCE: EH-Samuel Putnam
       COMMENT: EH: one of the three best books pub. in
          1932.
759. Dos Passos, John. The 42nd Parallel, 1929.
       SOURCE: KW-55; Baker
760. Dosch-Fleurot, Arno W. Through War to Revolution,
       1931.
       SOURCE: Guy Hickok-EH
       COMMENT: EH probably read it. Strongly recommended
          to him by Guy Hickok.
761. Dostoevskaia, Anna G. The Diary of Dostoevsky's Wife,
       1929,May.
       SOURCE: SB
       COMMENT: Borrowed in May, returned July 2.
762. Dostoevsky, Fyodor. The Brothers Karamazov, (1912).
       SOURCE: KW-40
       COMMENT: Trans. from Russian by Constance Garnett.
763. Dostoevsky, Fyodor. The Gambler and Other Stories,
       1927,Dec.
       SOURCE: SB
       COMMENT: Rtrnd. Feb.13,1928.
764. Dostoevsky, Fyodor. The Idiot, 1929,Sept.
       SOURCE: SB
       COMMENT: Rtrnd. Jan.23,1930.
765. Dostoevsky, Fyodor. The Insulted and Injured,
       1927,Dec.
       SOURCE: SB
       COMMENT: Trans. Constance Garnett. Borrowed Dec.7,
          1927, rtrnd Feb.13,1928.

766. Doughty, Charles M. <u>Passages</u> <u>from</u> <u>Arabia</u> <u>Deserta</u>,
     (1931).
     SOURCE: KW-55
767. Doughty, Charles M. <u>Travels</u> <u>in</u> <u>Arabia</u> <u>Deserta</u>, 1925,
     April.
     SOURCE: EH-MP
     COMMENT: EH: wants to do book on bull ring like
        Arabia Deserta.
768. Douglas, Alfred. <u>Autobiography</u> <u>of</u> <u>Lord</u> <u>Alfred</u>
     <u>Douglas</u>, 1929, April.
     SOURCE: SB
769. Douglas, Norman. <u>Looking</u> <u>Back:</u> <u>an</u> <u>Autobiographical</u>
     <u>Excursion</u>, 1933, May.
     SOURCE: SCRBNR
770. Dowsett, J. Morewood. <u>The</u> <u>Spanish</u> <u>Bull</u> <u>Ring</u>,
     1926,Jan.
     SOURCE: SB; KW-40
     COMMENT: Borrowed and returned Jan.30. Purchased
        later.
771. Doyle, Sir Arthur Conan. <u>Sherlock</u> <u>Holmes</u>, (1892).
     SOURCE: KW-40
     COMMENT: Eds. pub. in 1932 and 1936.
772. Drake, Lawrence. <u>Don't</u> <u>Call</u> <u>Me</u> <u>Clever</u>, 1929,Nov.
     SOURCE: EH-Lawrence Drake; KW-40
     COMMENT: Drake sent EH complimentary copy.
773. Drieu La Rochelle, Pierre. <u>La</u> <u>Comedie</u> <u>de</u> <u>Charleroi</u>,
     (1934).
     SOURCE: KW-40
774. Drieu La Rochelle, Pierre. <u>Le</u> <u>Jeune</u> <u>Europeen</u>, (1927).
     SOURCE: KW-55
775. Drinkwater, John. <u>Outline</u> <u>of</u> <u>Literature</u>, 1934,Mar.
     SOURCE: SB
776. Du Bos, Charles. <u>Extraits</u> <u>d'un</u> <u>Journal</u>, <u>1908-1928</u>,
     (1929).
     SOURCE: KW-40
777. Dudley, Dorothy. <u>Forgotten</u> <u>Frontiers</u>, (1932).
     SOURCE: KW-55
     COMMENT: About T. Dreiser:"A novel of facts."
778. Duguid, Julian. <u>Green</u> <u>Hell</u>, 1931, April.
     SOURCE: EH-MP
     COMMENT: Ordered by EH. About jungles.
779. Duguid, Julian. <u>Tiger-Man</u>, <u>an</u> <u>Odyssey</u> <u>of</u> <u>Freedom</u>,
     (1932).
     SOURCE: KW-40
780. Dumas, Alexandre. <u>Black</u> <u>Tulip</u>, (1877).
     SOURCE: KW-40
781. Dumas, Alexandre. <u>Le</u> <u>Chevalier</u> <u>de</u> <u>Maison-Rouge</u>,
     (1846).
     SOURCE: KW-55
     COMMENT: French Revolution. Fiction. Vols.I&II of
        6 vol. work.
782. Dumas, Alexandre. <u>Les</u> <u>Compagnons</u> <u>de</u> <u>Jehu</u>, (1859).
     SOURCE: KW-40

783. Dumas, Alexandre. La Reine Margot.
       SOURCE: KW-55
       COMMENT: 2 copies of 2 vol. ed. 2 copies of a 1
           vol. ed.
784. Dumas, Alexandre. The Three Musketeers, 1914.
       SOURCE: Baker; KW-55
785. Dumas, Alexandre. Twenty Years After, (1845).
       SOURCE: KW-55
786. Dumas, Alexandre and Auguste Marquet. Les Quarante-
       Cinq (Vols. I,II&III of 10 vols.), (1847).
       SOURCE: KW-55
       COMMENT: Fiction: Henry III,1574-1589.
787. DuMaurier, George L. Peter Ibbetson, (1891).
       SOURCE: KW-40
788. DuMaurier, George L. Trilby, (1893).
       SOURCE: KW-40
       COMMENT: Reprnt. in Everyman's Library in 1931.
789. Dunne, Finley Peter. Mr. Dooley in Peace and War,
       (1898).
       SOURCE: KW-40
790. Dunsany, Edward J.M. Fifty One Tales, 1920,Aug.
       SOURCE: EH-Grace Quinlan
       COMMENT: EH:he's great.
791. Durtain, Luc. Captain O.K., (1935).
       SOURCE: KW-55
792. Duval, Marie Jean B.P.G. Les Lecons de la Guerre
       d'Espagne, (1938).
       SOURCE: KW-40
793. Dyer, George Bell. The People Ask Death, 1940,Apr.
       SOURCE: EH-MP
       COMMENT: EH: fresh of its kind. Enjoyed it.
794. Eastman, Max. The End of Socialism in Russia, (1937).
       SOURCE: KW-55
795. Eastman, Max. Kinds of Love, (1931).
       SOURCE: KW-55
796. Eastman, Max. The Literary Mind:It's Place in an Age
       of Science, 1931,Dec.
       SOURCE: EH-MP
       COMMENT: EH: pretentious rubbish.
797. Edmunds, Murrell. Earthenware, (1930).
       SOURCE: KW-40
798. Ehrenburg, Ilya. Vus Par un Ecrivain d'U.S.S.R.,
       (1934).
       SOURCE: KW-40
       COMMENT: 20th.C.Fr.Lit.: Duhamel, Gide, Malraux,
           Moriac, Morand, Romains, Unamuno.
799. Eisenschiml, Otto. Why Was Lincoln Murdered,
       1937,July.
       SOURCE: SCRBNR
800. Eliot, George. Adam Bede, 1916.
       SOURCE: Fenton
       COMMENT: HS reading.
801. Eliot, George. Silas Marner, 1914.
       SOURCE: OPHS

802. Eliot, T.S. After Strange Gods: A Primer of Modern
     Heresy, (1934).
     SOURCE: KW-40
803. Eliot, T.S. The Collected Poems of T.S.Eliot,
     1936,June.
     SOURCE: SCRBNR; KW-55
     COMMENT: Two copies.
804. Eliot, T.S. Dante, 1934,Mar.
     SOURCE: SB; KW-40
805. Eliot, T.S. For Lancelot Andrews, 1934,Mar.
     SOURCE: SB
     COMMENT: Purchased copy.
806. Eliot, T.S. John Dryden, 1934,Mar.
     SOURCE: SB
     COMMENT: Purchased copy.
807. Eliot, T.S. Journey of the Magi, 1934,Mar.
     SOURCE: SB
     COMMENT: Ariel poem.
808. Eliot, T.S. Murder in the Cathedral, (1935).
     SOURCE: KW-55
809. Eliot, T.S. Poems 1909-1925, 1934,Mar.
     SOURCE: SB; KW-40
     COMMENT: Two copies.
810. Eliot, T.S. The Sacred Wood, 1934,Mar.
     SOURCE: SB
811. Eliot, T.S. Selected Essays, 1934,Mar.
     SOURCE: SB; KW-55
812. Eliot, T.S. The Use of Poetry and the Use of
     Criticism, 1934,Mar.
     SOURCE: SB; KW-40
813. Eliot, T.S. The Waste Land, 1922.
     SOURCE: Baker
814. Ellis, Ernest T., ed. Black's Gardening Dictionary,
     (1921).
     SOURCE: KW-55
815. Ellis, Havelock. The Dance of Life, 1921.
     SOURCE: Baker
816. Ellis, Havelock. Erotic Symbolism, 1920,Mar.
     SOURCE: Bill Smith-EH
     COMMENT: Smith returned EH's copy to him.
817. Ellis, Havelock. My Life, 1939, Oct.
     SOURCE: EH-MP; KW-55
     COMMENT: Ordered by EH.
818. Ellis, Havelock. Studies in The Psychology of Sex (4
     vols.), 1936,Mar.
     SOURCE: SCRBNR; KW-55
819. Elson, Henry William. History of the United States,
     1916.
     SOURCE: OPHS; KL
     COMMENT: HS text.
820. Emerson, Ralph Waldo. " Concord Hymn," 1915,June.
     SOURCE: OPHS
     COMMENT: EH memorized for HS.

821. Emerson, Ralph Waldo. " Fable," 1915,Mar.
         SOURCE: OPHS
         COMMENT: EH memorized for HS.
822. Emmerson, Peter Henry. Caoba the Guerilla Chief: a
         real romance of the Cuban rebellion, (1897).
         SOURCE: KW-40
823. Empey, Guy. Over the Top, 1926,Apr.
         SOURCE: EH-MP
         COMMENT: Probably read in 1918. EH: a little Empey
         is poisonous.
824. Endore, Guy. Babouk, 1934, Oct.
         SOURCE: EH-MP
         COMMENT: EH ordered copy.
825. Endore, Guy. The Werewolf of Paris, 1933,Apr.
         SOURCE: SCRBNR
         COMMENT: Occult.
826. Erckmann, Emile and Alexandre Chatrian. History of
         Conscript 1813 and Waterloo, (1909).
         SOURCE: KW-40
         COMMENT: Trans. R.D.Gillman.
827. Erckmann, Emile and Alexandre Chatrian. Tales,
         (1933).
         SOURCE: KW-55
828. Ernst, Clayton H., ed. Deep River Jim's Wilderness
         Trail Book, (1935).
         SOURCE: KW-40
829. Ernst, Morris Leopold and William Seagle. To the
         Pure: a Study of Obscenity and the Censor, (1928).
         SOURCE: KW-40
830. Ervine, St.John. Parnell, 1927,June.
         SOURCE: SB
         COMMENT: Ireland.
831. Esher, Reginald B.B. The Captains and Kings Depart,
         1938,Dec.
         SOURCE: EH-MP
         COMMENT: EH:utter tripe, an idiot in military
         affairs, disgusting reading.
832. Esquire, Inc. The Third New Year, (1935).
         SOURCE: KW-40
         COMMENT: Essays and fiction from Esquire.
833. Euripides. Alcestis.
         SOURCE: KW-40
834. Evans, Walker. American Photographs, 1938,Dec.
         SOURCE: MP-EH; EH-MP
         COMMENT: Intro. by Lincoln Kirstein. EH:
         photographs superb.
835. Farlow & Co., Charles. Catalogue of High-Class
         Fishing Tackle.
         SOURCE: KW-40
         COMMENT: No date. Annual catalog.
836. Farrar, Guy B. The Feathered Folk of an Estuary,
         1939, June.
         SOURCE: EH-MP

837. Farrell, James T. Calico Shoes, (1934).
          SOURCE: KW-55
838. Farrell, James T. Father and Son, (1940).
          SOURCE: KW-55
839. Farrell, James T. A Note on Literary Criticism,
          (1936).
          SOURCE: KW-55
840. Farrell, James T. Studs Lonigan, 1936,May.
          SOURCE: SCRBNR; EH-MP; KW-40
          COMMENT: EH: marvelous parts in it. Gives a fine
              picture of the utter horror of the South Side.
841. Farrell, James T. A World I Never Made, (1936).
          SOURCE: KW-55
842. Farrington, Kip. Atlantic Game Fishing, 1937.
          SOURCE: AH; KW-40
          COMMENT: Intro. by EH.
843. Farson, Negley. The Way of the Transgressor,
          1936,Mar.
          SOURCE: SCRBNR; KW-40
844. Fauconnier, H. Malaisie, (1931).
          SOURCE: KW-40
845. Faulkner, William. Absalom, Absalom|, (1936).
          SOURCE: KW-55
846. Faulkner, William. As I Lay Dying, 1930.
          SOURCE: KW-40; Baker
          COMMENT: See Death in the Afternoon.
847. Faulkner, William. Light in August, 1932, Oct.
          SOURCE: EH-MP; KW-55
848. Faulkner, William. Sanctuary, 1930.
          SOURCE: Baker
          COMMENT: See DIA.
849. Faulkner, William. Soldiers' Pay, 1926,May.
          SOURCE: EH-Isidor Schneider; KW-40
          COMMENT: EH: could not finish it.
850. Fearing, Kenneth. Poems, (1935).
          SOURCE: KW-55
851. Ferguson, Robert. Harpooner, 1936,May.
          SOURCE: SCRBNR
          COMMENT: Four year voyage of barque Kathleen.
              Penn. U. Press.
852. Fernandez Coello de Portugal, A. Belmonte, (1919).
          SOURCE: KW-40
853. Fernandez Martinez, Fidel. Sierra Nevada, (1931).
          SOURCE: KW-55
854. Feuchtwanger, Lion. Jud Gub**, (1925).
          SOURCE: KW-40
          COMMENT: Probably Jud Suss.
855. Feuchtwanger, Lion. The Ugly Duchess, (1927).
          SOURCE: KW-40
856. Field, R.L. American Folk and Fairy Tales, 1929, Nov.
          SOURCE: MP-EH
          COMMENT: EH sent copy to son.

857. Fielding, Henry. The Adventures of Joseph Andrews,
          1925,Dec.
          SOURCE: EH-Horace Liveright; KW-40
858. Fielding, Henry. Tom Jones, 1925.
          SOURCE: EH-Isidor Schneider; SB; KW-40; KW-55
          COMMENT: One copy to Cuba. Two copies left in Key
          West.
859. Figgis, Darrell. Recollections of the Irish War,
          1928, Feb.
          SOURCE: SB
860. Figuier, Louis. The World Before the Deluge, (1865).
          SOURCE: KW-40
          COMMENT: Geology.
861. Fisher, Herbert A.L. A History of Europe, (1935).
          SOURCE: KW-55
862. Fitch, Clyde. Beau Brummel, 1917,Feb.
          SOURCE: OPHS
          COMMENT: EH played role in Sr. class play.
863. Fitzgerald, F. Scott. All the Sad Young Men, 1926.
          SOURCE: EH-MP; FSF-EH
          COMMENT: EH says he read when published.
864. Fitzgerald, F. Scott. Taps at Reveille, 1935,Apr.
          SOURCE: MP-FSF
          COMMENT: MP sent EH a copy.
865. Fitzgerald, F.Scott. The Crack Up, 1936,Jan.
          SOURCE: EH-Dos Passos:UVa
          COMMENT: EH sickened by FSF's public confessional.
866. Fitzgerald, F.Scott. The Great Gatsby, 1925,June.
          SOURCE: EH-MP
          COMMENT: EH: just read. An absolutely first rate
          book.
867. Fitzgerald, F.Scott. Tender is the Night, 1934,Apr.
          SOURCE: EH-MP; EH-FSF
          COMMENT: In 1934 EH critiqued it severely. Re-read
          in 1939. EH: much so good it was frightening.
868. Fitzgerald, Zelda S. Save Me the Waltz, 1932,Nov.
          SOURCE: EH-MP
          COMMENT: EH: completely and absolutely unreadable.
869. Flaherty, Robert Joseph. The Captain's Chair, 1938.
          SOURCE: PH-MP
          COMMENT: Pauline: We both liked The Captain's
          Chair.
870. Flandrau, Charles M. Viva Mexico, 1925,Feb.
          SOURCE: EH-GS; KW-40
          COMMENT: EH: splendid. Wish I could write like he
          can.
871. Flaubert, Gustave. L' Education Sentimental, 1932.
          SOURCE: EH-Paul Romaine
          COMMENT: Probably read prior to 1929. EH: a great
          writer with one great book - Bovary - and half a
          great book - L'Education.

872. Flaubert, Gustave. Madame Bovary, 1922.
     SOURCE: EH-William Bird; EH-Paul Romaine; KL;
     KW-55
     COMMENT: EH: his one great novel.Owns copy by
     1923.
873. Flaubert, Gustave. Sentimental Education, 1925,Oct.
     SOURCE: SB; EH-Paul Romaine
     COMMENT: Oct.12-27. EH: a great writer with one
     great book - Bovary - and half a great book -
     L'Education.
874. Flaubert, Gustave. Trois Contes, (1877).
     SOURCE: KW-40
     COMMENT: Cont: "Un Coeur Simple," "La Legende de
     Saint Julien l'Hospitalier," "Herodias.".
875. Flechtheim Galerie. Ausstellungen,1929, (1929).
     SOURCE: KW-40
     COMMENT: Art exhibition catalog: Braque, Gris,
     Grosz, Klee, Matisse, Picasso.
876. Fleischer, Nat S. Young Griffo, (1928).
     SOURCE: KW-40
     COMMENT: Boxing.
877. Fleischmann, Hector. Pauline Boneparte et ses Amants,
     (1910).
     SOURCE: KW-55
878. Fleming, Peter. Brazilian Adventure, 1933.
     SOURCE: KL:Cape
879. Fleming, Peter. News from Tartary, 1936.
     SOURCE: KL:Cape; KW-55
     COMMENT: China.
880. Fleming, Peter. One's Company: a Journey to China,
     (1934).
     SOURCE: KW-40
881. Fletcher, Frank Irving. Lucid Interval, (1938).
     SOURCE: KW-55
882. Flory, Jean **. Sons la Foi du Sermont **.
     SOURCE: KW-40
     COMMENT: May be Sans la Foi du Serment, but still
     unfound.
883. Flotow, Friedrich von. Martha, 1916,Mar.
     SOURCE: OPHS
     COMMENT: OPHS produced the opera.
884. Fodor, Marcel William. South of Hitler, (1938).
     SOURCE: KW-55
885. Ford, Ford Madox. The Good Soldier, (1915).
     SOURCE: KW-40
     COMMENT: Probably read in 1924.
886. Ford, Ford Madox. It Was the Nightingale, (1933).
     SOURCE: KW-40
887. Ford, Ford Madox. A Mirror to France, 1926, Aug.
     SOURCE: SB
888. Ford, Ford Madox. No More Parades, 1925.
     SOURCE: KL:EH Collection
     COMMENT: EH owned typescript. May have read it in
     1924.

889.   Ford, Ford Madox. Portraits From Life, 1937,Apr.
            SOURCE: SCRBNR
            COMMENT: Memories and criticism of James, Conrad,
                Hardy, Wells, Crane, Lawrence, Turgenev, Hudson,
                etc.
890.   Ford, Ford Madox. Return to Yesterday, 1932, Jan.
            SOURCE: EH-MP; KW-40
            COMMENT: EH ordered.
891.   Ford, Ford Madox. Thus to Revisit, (1921).
            SOURCE: KW-40
            COMMENT: Reminiscences on Conrad, Crane, Flint,
                James and Pound.
892.   Ford, Leslie. False to Any Man, 1940,Mar.
            SOURCE: EH-MP
            COMMENT: EH: hell of a good mystery writer. Pseud.
                of Zenith (Jones) Brown.
893.   Ford, Leslie. Old Lover's Ghost, (1940).
            SOURCE: KW-40
            COMMENT: Pseud. of Zenith Jones Brown.
894.   Ford, Richard. Gatherings from Spain, (1849).
            SOURCE: KW-40
895.   Forester, Cecil Scott. The African Queen, 1936,
            March.
            SOURCE: EH to "Mr. Reed"; SCRBNR; KW-55; KL
            COMMENT: EH:enjoyed immensely; missing a fine
                story if not read.
896.   Forester, Cecil Scott. Beat to Quarters, (1937).
            SOURCE: KW-55
897.   Forester, Cecil Scott. Captain Horatio Hornblower,
            (1939).
            SOURCE: KW-40; KW-55
898.   Forester, Cecil Scott. Flying Colours, (1938).
            SOURCE: KW-55
            COMMENT: Two copies.
899.   Forester, Cecil Scott. The General, 1936, March.
            SOURCE: SCRBNR; KW-40
900.   Forester, Cecil Scott. The Gun, (1933).
            SOURCE: KW-40
901.   Forester, Cecil Scott. Ship of the Line, 1938,Mar.
            SOURCE: SCRBNR
902.   Forester, Frank. The Complete Manual for Young Sport,
            (1857).
            SOURCE: KW-40
            COMMENT: Pseud. of Henry William Herbert.
903.   Forester, Frank. Frank Forester's Fish and Fishing,
            (1849).
            SOURCE: KW-40
            COMMENT: Pseud. of Henry William Herbert.
904.   Foresti, Antonio. Del Mappamondo Istorico **.
            SOURCE: KW-40
            COMMENT: Took 13 vols. No title. This may be title
                but no 13 vol. edition.

905. Forman, Harrison. Through Forbidden Tibet, 1936,Mar.
     SOURCE: SCRBNR; KW-55
     COMMENT: Lamaism.
906. Forsyth, William. History of the Captivity of
     Napoleon at St. Helena, (1853).
     SOURCE: KW-40
     COMMENT: Probably Vol.I. Vols.II&III in KW.
907. Forsyth, William. The History of the Captivity of
     Napoleon at St. Helena (Vols. II&III), (1853).
     SOURCE: KW-55
908. Forsythe, Robert. Redder Than the Rose, (1935).
     SOURCE: KW-40
     COMMENT: Pseud. of Kyle Samuel Crichton.
         Satirical.
909. Foss, William and Cecil Gerhty. Spanish Arena,
         (1938).
     SOURCE: KW-40
910. Fox, Paul Hervey. Sailor Town, (1935).
     SOURCE: KW-55
911. France, Anatole. Balthasar, (1898).
     SOURCE: KW-55
     COMMENT: Written in English.
912. France, Anatole. Le Crime de Sylvestre Bonnard,
         (1891).
     SOURCE: KW-55
913. France, Anatole. Thais , (1891).
     SOURCE: KW-55
914. Francis. Book on Angling**.
     SOURCE: KW-40
915. Frank, Waldo D. The Rediscovery of America, 1929,Feb.
     SOURCE: EH-MP; KW-40
916. Frank, Waldo D. Virgin Spain, 1926,Mar.
     SOURCE: EH-Isidor Schneider; KW-55
     COMMENT: EH mixed reaction.
917. Frank, Waldo D., ed. Tales from the Argentine,
         (1930).
     SOURCE: KW-40
     COMMENT: Trans. by Anita Brenner.
918. Frank, Waldo D. et al., eds. America and Alfred
         Stieglitz, (1934).
     SOURCE: KW-40
     COMMENT: Photography.
919. Frankfurter, Felix. The Case of Sacco and Vanzetti,
         (1927).
     SOURCE: KW-55
920. Franklin, Benjamin. The Autobiography of Benjamin
         Franklin, 1913.
     SOURCE: OPHS; KW-40
921. Frave **. Letters of Napoleon 1810-1814 **.
     SOURCE: KW-40
     COMMENT: May be Letters of Napoleon to Marie-
         Louise, 1810-1814 (1935).

922. Fredenburgh, Theodore. Soldiers March|, (1930).
          SOURCE: KW-40
          COMMENT: Fiction:WWI.
923. Freeman, Douglas S. Robert E. Lee, 1934,Oct.
          SOURCE: MP-EH; KW-40
          COMMENT: 4 vols.
924. Freeston, Charles L. The Cream of Europe for the
          Motorist, (1928).
          SOURCE: KW-55
925. Freund, Philip. The Snow, (1935).
          SOURCE: KW-55
926. Fuller, John Frederick C. Decisive Battles, 1939,Dec.
          SOURCE: EH-MP
          COMMENT: EH:extremely interesting. Has more sound
             imagination than most British.
927. Fuller, John Frederick C. Grant and Lee: A Study in
          Personality and Generalship, 1935, August.
          SOURCE: EH-MP
928. Funchal, Domingos Antonio. La Guerre de la Peninsule,
          1807-1814, (1816).
          SOURCE: KW-40
929. Fyleman, Rose. Book of Saints, (1939).
          SOURCE: KW-40
930. Galsworthy, John. On Forsyte Change, 1931,Nov.
          SOURCE: EH-MP; KW-55
          COMMENT: EH disliked.
931. Galsworthy, John. The White Monkey, (1924).
          SOURCE: KW-40; KW-55
932. Gano, Darwin C. Commercial Law, 1916.
          SOURCE: OPHS
          COMMENT: HS text.
933. Garcia Carraffa, Alberto. Frases Celebres del Ingenio
          espanol de Toreros, (1918).
          SOURCE: KW-40
          COMMENT: Ser.1-3,5.
934. Garcia Lorca, Federico. Lament for the Death of a
          Bullfighter and other poems, (1937).
          SOURCE: KW-55
935. Garcia Lorca, Federico. Romancero Gitano, (1935).
          SOURCE: KW-55
          COMMENT: "Poema del cante jonda."
936. Garland, Hamlin. The Long Trail, (1907).
          SOURCE: KW-55
          COMMENT: Rev. 1935.
937. Garnett, David. Beany-Eye, (1935).
          SOURCE: KW-40
938. Garnett, David. Go She Must, 1927.
          SOURCE: SB
          COMMENT: Borrowed and returned same day.
939. Garnett, David. The Grasshoppers Come, (1931).
          SOURCE: KW-40; KW-55
940. Garnett, David. No Love, (1929).
          SOURCE: KW-55

941. Garnett, David. Pocahontas, (1933).
          SOURCE: KW-40
          COMMENT: Historical fiction.
942. Garnett, David. The Sailor's Return, 1926,Nov.
          SOURCE: SB
          COMMENT: No record of return.
943. Garnett, Edward, ed. Capajon, (1933).
          SOURCE: KW-40
          COMMENT: Fifty-four short stories published
             1921-1933.
944. Gattorno, A. Gattorno, 1935.
          SOURCE: KW-40
          COMMENT: EH wrote intro.
945. Gautier, Theophile. Mademoiselle de Maupin, (1834).
          SOURCE: KW-55
946. Gayley, Charles Mills. The Classic Myths in English
          Literature, 1913.
          SOURCE: OPHS; KL
          COMMENT: HS text book heavily read.
947. Gellhorn, Martha. Detresse Americaine, (1938).
          SOURCE: KW-40
948. Gellhorn, Martha. A Stricken Field, 1940.
          SOURCE: AH
          COMMENT: EH wrote epigraph.
949. Gellhorn, Martha. The Trouble I've Seen, (1936).
          SOURCE: KW-55
          COMMENT: Pref. by H. G. Wells.
950. George, Henry, Jr. Life of Henry George, 1839-1897,
             (1900).
          SOURCE: KW-40
951. George, Walter Lionel. The Second Blooming, 1924.
          SOURCE: KL
952. Geraldy, Paul. Aimer, (1921).
          SOURCE: KW-55
953. Gerbault, Alain. Seul, a travers l'Atlantique,
             (1924).
          SOURCE: KW-55
954. Gide, Andre. L' Affaire Redureau, (1930).
          SOURCE: KW-40
955. Gide, Andre. Les Caves du Vatican, (1914).
          SOURCE: KW-55
956. Gide, Andre. Corydon, (1924).
          SOURCE: KW-55
957. Gide, Andre. Divers, (1931).
          SOURCE: KW-40
958. Gide, Andre. L' Ecole des Femmes, (1929).
          SOURCE: KW-40
959. Gide, Andre. Les Faux-Monnayeurs, (1925).
          SOURCE: KW-55
960. Gide, Andre. Nouvelles Pages de Journal, (1936).
          SOURCE: KW-40
961. Gide, Andre. Si le Grain ne Meurt, (1925).
          SOURCE: KW-55
          COMMENT: Vols.I,II & III.

962. Gide, Andre. Strait is the Gate, 1926,Apr.
    SOURCE: SB
    COMMENT: April 11-25.
963. Gide, Andre. La Symphonie Pastorale, (1919).
    SOURCE: KW-55
964. Gill, Eric. Clothes, (1931).
    SOURCE: KW-40
    COMMENT: Nature and significance of clothes.
965. Gilligan, Edmund. One Lives to Tell the Tale, (1931).
    SOURCE: KW-40
966. Gilpatric, Guy. The Compleat Goggler, 1938,May.
    SOURCE: SCRBNR; KW-40
967. Ginisty, Paul. The Old Boulevards, (1925).
    SOURCE: KW-55
    COMMENT: Trans. from French. Paris streets.
968. Giordano, Umberto. Andrea Chenier, 1920, Nov.
    SOURCE: EH-Grace Quinlan
    COMMENT: EH: same plot as Tale of Two Cities.
969. Glazier, Willard. Down the Great River, (1888).
    SOURCE: KW-40
970. Goering, Dimitroff. Incendie du Reichstag, (1934).
    SOURCE: KW-40
971. Gogarty, Oliver St. John. As I Was Going Down
    Sackville Street, 1937.
    SOURCE: SCRBNR; KW-55
972. Gold, Michael. 120 Million, (1929).
    SOURCE: KW-55
    COMMENT: Proletarian
      sketches,chants,&recollections.
973. Golding, Harry, ed. The Wonder Book of the Wild,
    1928,Mar.
    SOURCE: SB
    COMMENT: 200 illus.
974. Goldsmith, Oliver. "The Deserted Village," 1917.
    SOURCE: OPHS
    COMMENT: EH memorized first 35 lines for HS.
975. Goldsmith, Oliver. She Stoops to Conquer.
    SOURCE: KW-55
976. Goll, Iwan. Sodome et Berlin, (1929).
    SOURCE: KW-55
977. Gomez Carrillo, E. Le Mystere de la Vie et de la Mort
    de Mata Hari, (1924).
    SOURCE: KW-55
978. Goode, George B. and Theodore N. Gill. American
    Fishes, (1888).
    SOURCE: KW-40
    COMMENT: Rprtd. 1926.
979. Goodman, Henry, ed. Creating the Short Story, (1929).
    SOURCE: KW-40
980. Gordon, Caroline. Alek Maury, Sportsman, 1934, Nov.
    SOURCE: EH-MP; KW-40
981. Gordon, Caroline. The Garden of Adonis, (1937).
    SOURCE: KW-55

982. Gordon, Gen. J.M.   The Chronicles of a Gay Gordon,
          (1921).
          SOURCE: KW-40
983. Gorer, Geoffrey. Africa Dances: a Book about West
          African Negroes, (1935).
          SOURCE: KW-40
984. Gorki, Maxim. Bystander , 1930,May.
          SOURCE: EH-MP; KW-55
          COMMENT: EH ordered and received.
985. Gorman, Herbert S. The Incredible Marquis, Alexandre
          Dumas, (1929).
          SOURCE: KW-40
986. Gorman, Herbert S. James Joyce, (1924).
          SOURCE: KW-55
987. Goya y Lucientes, Francisco Jose de. Tauromaquia,
          (1923).
          SOURCE: KW-40
          COMMENT: 2 vols. 43 drawings by Goya. Probably
              acquired summer, 1924.
988. Gozlan, Leon. Balzac in Slippers, 1929, Oct.
          SOURCE: SB
          COMMENT: Trans. Babette and Glenn Hughes.
989. Graham, Joseph Alexander. The Sporting Dog, (1904).
          SOURCE: KW-40
          COMMENT: The American Sportsman's Library ed. by
              C. Whitney.
990. Graham, Robert Bontine Cunninghame. Thirty Tales and
          Sketches, (1929).
          SOURCE: KW-40
          COMMENT: Ed. by Edward Garnett.
991. Graham, Stephen. A Private in the Guards, (1919).
          SOURCE: KW-55
992. Grant, Ulysses Simpson. Personal Memoirs of
          U.S.Grant, (1885).
          SOURCE: KW-40
          COMMENT: Two vols.
993. Graves, Robert. Goodbye to All That: An
          Autobiography, (1929).
          SOURCE: KW-55
994. Graves, Robert. Lawrence and the Arabs, 1928.
          SOURCE: SB
995. Gray, Prentiss Nathaniel. Records of North American
          Big Game, (1932).
          SOURCE: KW-40
          COMMENT: Publ. under auspices of the Nat'l
              collection of heads & horns, N.Y. Zoo. Soc.
996. Gray, Thomas. " Elegy Written in a Country
          Churchyard," 1916,Feb.
          SOURCE: OPHS
          COMMENT: EH memorized for HS.
997. Grayson, Charles. Flight South, (1935).
          SOURCE: KW-40
998. Green, Julien. Christine, (1930).
          SOURCE: KW-55

999.   Green, Julien. Le Voyageur sur la Terre, (1927).
          SOURCE: KW-40
1000.   Greene, Graham. Journey Without Maps, 1937,June.
          SOURCE: SCRBNR; KW-40
1001.   Greene, Graham. The Man Within, (1929).
          SOURCE: KW-55
1002.   Greener, William Wellington. The Gun and Its
          Development, 1934,Mar.
          SOURCE: KL:Brentanos; KW-40
          COMMENT: Pub.1881.
1003.   Greenwood, James. Wild Sports of the World: a Book
          of Natural History and Adventure, (1870).
          SOURCE: KW-40
1004.   Gregg, William H. Where, When, and How to Catch Fish
          on the East Coast of Florida, (1902).
          SOURCE: KW-40
1005.   Greville, Charles Cavendish Fulke. The Greville
          Memoirs, (1896).
          SOURCE: KW-40
          COMMENT: 8 vols.
1006.   Greville, Charles Cavendish Fulke. The Greville
          Memoirs, (1874).
          SOURCE: KW-55
          COMMENT: Vols. I & II of III vols.
1007.   Grey, Edward, Viscount. The Charm of Birds, (1927).
          SOURCE: KW-55
1008.   Grey, Romer C. Adventures of a Deep-Sea Angler,
          1935,April.
          SOURCE: EH-MP; SCRBNR
          COMMENT: Ordered by EH.
1009.   Grey, Zane. An American Angler in Australia, (1937).
          SOURCE: KW-40
1010.   Grey, Zane. Tales of Swordfish and Tuna, 1928,June.
          SOURCE: EH-Waldo Peirce
1011.   Grey, Zane. Tales of Tahitian Waters, (1931).
          SOURCE: KW-40
1012.   Grey, Zane. Tales of the Angler's Eldorado, New
          Zealand, (1926).
          SOURCE: KW-40
          COMMENT: Famous Fishing Books edition.
1013.   Gribble, Harry Wagstaff. March Hares, (1923).
          SOURCE: KW-55
1014.   Griffith, D.W.(director). Birth of a Nation, 1915.
          SOURCE: KL:EH Scrap Books
          COMMENT: EH's father took him to see movie.
1015.   Grimm, Jacob. Grimm's Fairy Tales, 1929, Nov.
          SOURCE: SB
          COMMENT: Purchased by EH.
1016.   Grogan, E. S. From the Cape to Cairo, (1900).
          SOURCE: KW-40
1017.   Guedalla, Philip. The Hundred Years, (1936).
          SOURCE: KW-40

1018. Guedalla, Philip. The Second Empire, (1922).
       SOURCE: KW-40
       COMMENT: Napoleon III.
1019. Guilloux, Louis. Le Sang Noir, (1935).
       SOURCE: KW-55
1020. Guim, Juan B. Cornelii Nepotis Vitae Excellentium
       Imperatorum, (1888).
       SOURCE: KW-55
1021. Gulick, C.B. Life of the Ancient Greeks, 1915.
       SOURCE: OPHS
       COMMENT: Assigned reading, HS.
1022. Gumbel, Emil J. Les Crimes Politiques en Allemagne,
       (1925).
       SOURCE: KW-55
1023. Gunther, John. Inside Europe, 1936,Mar.
       SOURCE: EH-MP; SCRBNR; KW-40
       COMMENT: EH ordered and received.
1024. Gwynn, Stephen Lucius. The Happy Fisherman,
       1936,Nov.
       SOURCE: MP-EH; EH-MP; KW-40
1025. Hackett, Francis. Henry the Eighth, (1929).
       SOURCE: KW-40
1026. Hafiz. The Tongue of the Hidden.
       SOURCE: KW-55
       COMMENT: Persian poet 14th.C.
1027. Haines, Edith Key. Tried Temptations Old and New ,
       (1926).
       SOURCE: KW-55
       COMMENT: American cookery.
1028. H.A.L. Sport in Many Lands, 1934,Mar.
       SOURCE: KL:Brentanos; KW-40
       COMMENT: Pub. 1879 in 2 vols. Pseud. of Henry A.
           Leveson.
1029. Haliburton, T.C. The Clockmaker, (1863).
       SOURCE: KW-40
       COMMENT: The sayings and doings of Sam Slick of
           Slickville. Illustrated by Darley.
1030. Halliburton, Richard. Seven League Boots, (1935).
       SOURCE: KW-55
1031. Halsey, Margaret. With Malice Toward Some,
       1938,Sept.
       SOURCE: SB
1032. Hamilton, Bruce. To Be Hanged, (1930).
       SOURCE: KW-55
       COMMENT: Publ. for the Crime Club.
1033. Hamilton, Sir Ian Standish Monteith. A Staff
       Officer's Scrap-Book (2 vol.), (1905).
       SOURCE: KW-40
       COMMENT: Russo-Japanese War (1904-1905).
1034. Hammer, Simon Christian. Things Seen in Norway,
       (1926).
       SOURCE: KW-40

1035.   Hammett, Dashiell. The Glass Key, 1931, April.
           SOURCE: EH-MP
           COMMENT: Ordered by EH.
1036.   Hammett, Dashiell. The Thin Man, (1934).
           SOURCE: KW-55
1037.   Hamp, Pierre. Gens, (1917).
           SOURCE: KW-55
1038.   Hamsun, Knut. Children of the Age, 1925, Dec.
           SOURCE: SB
           COMMENT: Not returned until April,1926.
1039.   Hamsun, Knut. The Growth of the Soil, 1925,Dec.
           SOURCE: EH-FSF
           COMMENT: Trans.1920. EH read and liked better than
               Thomas Boyd.
1040.   Hanley, James. Boy, 1931.
           SOURCE: EH-MP; KW-40
           COMMENT: Ordered by EH.
1041.   Hanley, James. The Furys, 1935, July.
           SOURCE: EH-MP; KW-40
           COMMENT: Ordered by EH.
1042.   Harborough, Robert. The Life, Work and Evil Fate of
           Guy de Maupassant, 1926,Oct.
           SOURCE: SB
1043.   Harding, Tex. Verschollen, auf den spuren des
           obersten Fawcett, (1933).
           SOURCE: KW-40
           COMMENT: Fawcett, Percy Harrison, 1867-1925.
1044.   Hardy, Thomas. The Return of the Native, (1878).
           SOURCE: KW-55
           COMMENT: Two copies.
1045.   Hardy, Thomas. Yuletide in a Younger Year, 1934,Mar.
           SOURCE: SB
           COMMENT: Ariel poem.
1046.   Harispe, Pierre. Le Pays Basque, (1929).
           SOURCE: KL:EH Collection
1047.   Harris, Cyril. Trumpets at Dawn, (1938).
           SOURCE: KW-55
           COMMENT: Historical fiction: Amer. Revolution.
1048.   Harris, Frank. Bernard Shaw, (1931).
           SOURCE: KW-40
1049.   Harris, Frank. Confessional, 1930,Apr.
           SOURCE: EH-MP; KW-55
           COMMENT: EH ordered and received copy.
1050.   Harris, Frank. The Man Shakespeare, (1909).
           SOURCE: KW-55
1051.   Harris, Frank. My Life and Loves, 1927.
           SOURCE: AH
           COMMENT: EH satire in New Yorker.
1052.   Harris, Frank. Oscar Wilde: His Life and
           Confessions, (1916).
           SOURCE: KW-55

1053.   Harris, William C.   Wild Sports of Southern Africa,
        1934,Mar.
        SOURCE: KL:Brentanos; EH-MP; KW-40
        COMMENT: Pub. 1839.
1054.   Hart, Henry.   The Great One, a Novel of American
        Life, 1934, May.
        SOURCE: EH-MP; SCRBNR; KW-55
        COMMENT: Ordered by EH.
1055.   Hart, Henry Hersch, comp. & tr.   A Chinese Market:
        Lyrics from the Chinese in English verse, (1931).
        SOURCE: KW-40
        COMMENT: Chinese poetry trans. into English.
1056.   Hart, William L.   Plane Trigonometry, (1933).
        SOURCE: KW-55
1057.   Harte, Bret.   The Luck of Roaring Camp, (1869).
        SOURCE: KW-55
1058.   Harte, Bret.   Tales and Poems, (1892).
        SOURCE: KW-40
1059.   Harvey, Sir Paul, ed.   The Oxford Companion to
        English, (1932).
        SOURCE: KW-40
        COMMENT: Dictionary.
1060.   Hasek, Jaroslav.   The Good Soldier: Schweik, (1930).
        SOURCE: KW-40; KW-55
1061.   Hastings, Lansford Warren.   The Emigrants' Guide to
        Oregon and California, (1932).
        SOURCE: KW-40
        COMMENT: Reprinted by Princeton U. Press in 1932
        from 1845 original.
1062.   Hastings, Walter S., ed.   The Student's Balzac,
        (1937).
        SOURCE: KW-55
1063.   Hately, T. L. and Hugh Copley.   Angling in East
        Africa, (1933).
        SOURCE: KW-40
1064.   Hauman,G.   Happy Harbour, 1938,Mar.
        SOURCE: SCRBNR
1065.   Hauteclocque, Xavier de.   Pegre et Police
        Internationales, (1934).
        SOURCE: KW-40
1066.   Hawker, Peter.   Colonel Hawker's Shooting Diaries,
        (1931).
        SOURCE: KW-40
        COMMENT: Edited by Eric Parker from 19th C. Ms.
1067.   Hawker, Peter.   Instructions to Young Sportsmen,
        (1826).
        SOURCE: KW-55
1068.   Hawthorne, Hildegarde.   Rising Thunder, 1938,Mar.
        SOURCE: SCRBNR; KW-55
        COMMENT: Sent to Mrs. Hemingway. Rev.War
        historical fiction.
1069.   Hawthorne, Nathaniel.   The Scarlet Letter, (1850).
        SOURCE: KW-55

1070.   Hay, Ian. <u>Happy</u> Go <u>Lucky</u>, 1920,Nov.
      SOURCE: EH-GH; EH-Grace Quinlan
      COMMENT: EH saw. Pseud. of John Hay Beith.
1071.   Hay, Ian. <u>The King's Service</u>, 1938,Oct.
      SOURCE: Brentanos; KW-55
      COMMENT: Pseud. of John Hay Beith.
1072.   Hay, Ian. <u>The Willing Horse</u>, (1921).
      SOURCE: KW-40
      COMMENT: Pseud. of John Hay Beith.   Historical
         fiction.
1073.   Hay, John. <u>Castilian Days</u>, (1871).
      SOURCE: KW-55
1074.   Hayes and Moon. <u>Ancient and Medieval History</u>,
         (1929).
      SOURCE: KW-55
1075.   Hazard, Paul. <u>La Vie de Stendhal</u>, (1927).
      SOURCE: KW-55
1076.   Hazlitt, William. <u>The Fight</u>, (1929).
      SOURCE: KW-40
      COMMENT: Boxing. 19th C. Ms.
1077.   Hazlitt, William. <u>Table Talk</u>.
      SOURCE: KW-55
      COMMENT: 18th.C.
1078.   Hedin, Sven Anders. <u>My Life As an Explorer</u>, (1925).
      SOURCE: KW-40
      COMMENT: Asia. Illus. by the author.   Trans. by
         Alfhild Huebsch.
1079.   Heilner, Van Campen. <u>A Book on Duck Shooting</u>,
         (1939).
      SOURCE: KW-55
1080.   Hemingway, Alfred T. <u>How to Make Good, or Winning</u>
         <u>Your Largest Success</u>, 1917.
      SOURCE: KL:EH Collection
      COMMENT: EH's uncle gave him copy of his book,
         June,1917, Kansas City.
1081.   Henderson, Alexander. <u>Aldous Huxley</u>, (1936).
      SOURCE: KW-55
1082.   Henley, William Ernest.   " Unconquered," 1915,Oct.
      SOURCE: OPHS
      COMMENT: EH memorized for HS.
1083.   Henriot, Emile. <u>Voltaire and Frederic II</u>, (1927).
      SOURCE: KW-40
1084.   Henry, O. <u>Cabbages and Kings</u>, 1920.
      SOURCE: Baker
      COMMENT: Pseud. of William Sydney Porter.
1085.   Henty, George A. <u>True to the Old Flag</u>, 1909.
      SOURCE: Baker
      COMMENT: Amer. Revolution: fiction.
1086.   Herbst, Josephine. <u>Nothing Is Sacred</u>, 1928.
      SOURCE: AH-2
      COMMENT: EH:"a fine book by an honest writer.".
1087.   Heredia, Fernadez de. <u>Doctrinal Tauromaco de Hache</u>,
         1930.
      SOURCE: GP-EH; KW-40

1088. Hergesheimer, Joseph. Love in the United States and
        The Big Shot, (1932).
            SOURCE: KW-40
1089. Hergesheimer, Joseph. San Cristobal de la Habana,
        (1920).
            SOURCE: KW-40
1090. Hernandes-Girbal, F. Una Vida Popular: Frascuelo,
        (1933).
            SOURCE: KW-40
            COMMENT: Biog. of Salvador Sanchez "Frascuelo" -
            bullfighter.
1091. Herndon, William Henry. Abraham Lincoln, (1892).
            SOURCE: KW-55
            COMMENT: Two copies.
1092. Herrmann, John. Summer Is Ended, 1932,Oct.
            SOURCE: AH
            COMMENT: EH: "Herrmann writes of the tragedy of
            the human heart as well as any writer that ever
            lived."
1093. Heuser, Kurt. The Journey Inward, (1932).
            SOURCE: KW-55
1094. Hewitt, Edward R. Better Trout Streams, 1931, April.
            SOURCE: EH-MP; KW-40
1095. Hewitt, Edward R. Telling on the Trout, (1926).
            SOURCE: KW-40
1096. Hielscher, Kurt. Deutschland, (1925).
            SOURCE: KW-40
1097. Highton, Hugh P. Shooting Trips in Europe and
        Algeria, 1934,Mar.
            SOURCE: KL:Brentanos; KW-40
            COMMENT: Pub. in 1921.
1098. Hilton, James. Lost Horizon, (1933).
            SOURCE: KW-55
1099. Hindus, Maurice G. Humanity Uprooted, (1929).
            SOURCE: KW-55
1100. Hoel, Sigurd. One Day in October, (1932).
            SOURCE: KW-55
1101. Hoffenstein, Samuel. Poems in Praise of Practically
        Nothing, (1928).
            SOURCE: KW-40
1102. Holden, Raymond. Chance Has a Whip, 1935.
            SOURCE: EH-MP; KW-40
            COMMENT: EH: looking forward to reading it.
1103. Holder, Charles Frederick. The Big Game Fishes of
        the U.S., (1903).
            SOURCE: KW-40
1104. Holling, Holling C. The Book of Cowboys, (1936).
            SOURCE: KW-55
1105. Holt, Luther Emmett. The Care and Feeding of
        Children, (1894).
            SOURCE: KW-40

1106. Homburg, Robert. Legal Rights of Performing Artists,
          (1934).
          SOURCE: KW-40
          COMMENT: Trans. Maurice Joseph Speiser.
1107. Homer. The Iliad, 1929.
          SOURCE: EH-MP; KW-40
          COMMENT: Eds. Lang,Leaf and Meyers. Excerpts read
          in HS.
1108. Homer. The Odyssey.
          SOURCE: KW-55
1109. Hoover, Irwin Hood (Ike). Forty-two Years in the
          White House, (1934).
          SOURCE: KW-40
          COMMENT: Chief usher.
1110. Hopkins, Gerard Manley. Poems of Gerard Manley
          Hopkins, 1931, Apr.
          SOURCE: EH-MP; KW-40
          COMMENT: EH ordered. Ed., Robert Bridges.
1111. Horton, Philip. Hart Crane, (1937).
          SOURCE: KW-55
1112. Horvath, Odon von. The Age of Fish, 1939.
          SOURCE: EH-MP
1113. Hough, Frank. Renown, 1938,Mar.
          SOURCE: SCRBNR
          COMMENT: Benedict Arnold. Fiction.
1114. Housman, A.E. Introductory Lecture, (1933).
          SOURCE: KW-55
1115. Howard, Sidney Coe. Half Gods, (1930).
          SOURCE: KW-40
1116. Howe, Edgar Watson. "The Anthology of Another Town,"
          1919,Nov.
          SOURCE: Bill Smith-EH
          COMMENT: EH read in Sat. Eve. Post.
1117. Howe, Julia Ward. "The Battle Hymn of the Republic,"
          1914,Sept.
          SOURCE: OPHS
          COMMENT: EH memorized for HS.
1118. Hudson, William Henry. Adventures Among Birds,
          (1913).
          SOURCE: KW-40
1119. Hudson, William Henry. Afoot in England, (1909).
          SOURCE: KW-55
1120. Hudson, William Henry. Birds in London, (1898).
          SOURCE: KW-40
1121. Hudson, William Henry. Birds in Town and Village,
          (1920).
          SOURCE: KW-40
1122. Hudson, William Henry. The Book of a Naturalist,
          (1919).
          SOURCE: KW-55
1123. Hudson, William Henry. Dead Man's Plack, An Old
          Thorn and Poems, (1924).
          SOURCE: KW-55

1124. Hudson, William Henry. Far Away and Long Ago,
          1926,May.
          SOURCE: SB; EH-Isidor Schneider
          COMMENT: EH: Hudson writes the best of anyone
             (June,1926).
1125. Hudson, William Henry. Hampshire Days, (1903).
          SOURCE: KW-40
1126. Hudson, William Henry. A Hind in Richmond Park,
          (1922).
          SOURCE: KW-55
1127. Hudson, William Henry. The Land's End: a
          Naturalist's Impression in West Cornwall, (1908).
          SOURCE: KW-40
1128. Hudson, William Henry. The Naturalist in La Plata,
          (1892).
          SOURCE: KW-40
          COMMENT: Argentine Republic.
1129. Hudson, William Henry. Nature in Downland, (1906).
          SOURCE: KW-40
1130. Hudson, William Henry. South American Sketches,
          (1909).
          SOURCE: KW-55
1131. Hudson, William Henry. A Traveller in Little Things,
          1926,Dec.
          SOURCE: EP-EH; KW-55
          COMMENT: EP: read for style, "the simple
             statement."
1132. Hughes, Thomas. Tom Brown's School Days, (1858).
          SOURCE: KW-40
          COMMENT: Pub. pseud. as "An Old Boy".
1133. Hugo, Victor. Notre Dame de Paris, (1831).
          SOURCE: KW-55
1134. Hume, H. Harold. Gardening in the Lower South,
          (1929).
          SOURCE: KW-55
1135. Hume, Martin A. S. The Spanish People, (1901).
          SOURCE: KW-55
          COMMENT: Bibliog.
1136. Hun, John. Logarithmic & Trigonometric & other
          tables, (1929).
          SOURCE: KW-55
1137. Huneker, James G. Egoists: a Book of Supermen,
          1926,May.
          SOURCE: SB
          COMMENT: Stendhal, Baudelaire, Flaubert, A.
             France, Huysmans, Barres, Nietzche, Blake,
             Ibsen.
1138. Huneker, James G. Steeplejack, 1926,May.
          SOURCE: SB
          COMMENT: Vol.2 of Memoirs.
1139. Hunt, Frazier. One American and His Attempt at
          Education, (1938).
          SOURCE: KW-55

1140. Hunt, Lynn Bogue. An Artist's Game Bag, (1936).
       SOURCE: KW-40
1141. Hunt, Violet. The Flurried Years, 1926,Apr.
       SOURCE: SB
1142. Hunt, Violet. More Tales of the Uneasy, 1925, Nov.
       SOURCE: SB
1143. Hunt, Violet. The Wife of Rossetti: Her Life and
       Death, (1932).
       SOURCE: KW-40
       COMMENT: Mrs. Elizabeth Eleanor Siddal Rossetti.
1144. Hutchinson, Horatio Gordon, ed. Big Game Shooting, 2
       vols., 1934, March.
       SOURCE: KL:Brentanos; KW-40
       COMMENT: Pub. in 1905.
1145. Huxley, Aldous. After Many a Summer Dies the Swan,
       (1939).
       SOURCE: KW-55
1146. Huxley, Aldous. Along the Road, 1926,Apr.
       SOURCE: SB
1147. Huxley, Aldous. Beyond the Mexique Bay, (1934).
       SOURCE: KW-40
1148. Huxley, Aldous. Brief Candles, (1930).
       SOURCE: KW-55
1149. Huxley, Aldous. Eyeless in Gaza, (1936).
       SOURCE: KW-55
1150. Huxley, Aldous. Jesting Pilate: an Intellectual
       Holiday, (1926).
       SOURCE: KW-40
1151. Huxley, Aldous. Limbo, (1920).
       SOURCE: KW-55
1152. Huxley, Aldous. Mortal Coils, (1922).
       SOURCE: KW-55
1153. Huxley, Aldous. Music at Night and Other Essays,
       (1931).
       SOURCE: KW-40
1154. Huxley, Aldous. The Olive Tree and Other Essays,
       1937, July.
       SOURCE: SCRBNR; KW-55
1155. Huxley, Aldous. On the Margin, (1923).
       SOURCE: KW-55
1156. Huxley, Aldous. Point Counter Point, (1928).
       SOURCE: KW-40
1157. Huxley, Elspeth. Murder on Safari, 1938,May.
       SOURCE: SCRBNR
       COMMENT: Sent to Pauline.
1158. Huysmans, Joris Kari. Against the Grain, (1922).
       SOURCE: KW-40
       COMMENT: Trans. from French by John Howard.
1159. Ibsen, Henrik. A Doll's House, (1889).
       SOURCE: KW-40
1160. Idriess, Ion L. Lasseter's Last Ride, 1936.
       SOURCE: KL:Cape
       COMMENT: The central Australian gold discovery.

1161. Imbs, Bravig. <u>Confessions of Another Young Man</u>,
    1936,May.
    SOURCE: SCRBNR; KW-40
    COMMENT: Paris intellectual life:George Antheil,
     Gertrude Stein.
1162. Irving, Robert L.G. <u>The Romance of Mountaineering</u>,
    (1935).
    SOURCE: KW-55
1163. Irving, Washington. <u>The Sketch Book of Geoffrey
    Crayon</u>, (1848).
    SOURCE: KW-55
1164. Isherwood, Christopher. <u>Lions and Shadows</u>, 1938,Mar.
    SOURCE: SB
    COMMENT: Purhcased copy.
1165. Jacks, Leo V. <u>Xenophon, Soldier of Fortune</u>, (1930).
    SOURCE: KW-55
1166. Jackson, Holbrook. <u>The Anatomy of Bibliomania</u>,
    (1931).
    SOURCE: KW-55
1167. Jackson, Sir Frederick John. <u>Notes on the Game Birds
    of Kenya and Uganda</u>, (1926).
    SOURCE: KW-40
1168. Jacoby, Oswald. <u>On Poker</u>, 1940, Nov.
    SOURCE: EH-MP
    COMMENT: EH ordered.
1169. James, Henry. <u>The American</u>, (1877).
    SOURCE: KW-40
1170. James, Henry. <u>Art of the Novel</u>, 1934,Nov.
    SOURCE: EH-MP; KW-40
    COMMENT: MP sent copy.
1171. James, Henry. <u>The Awkward Age</u>, 1927,Dec.
    SOURCE: EP-EH
    COMMENT: EH: an enormous fake. EP: "I never
     suggested that you read The Awkward Age."
1172. James, Henry. <u>Novels and Stories of Henry James</u>.
    SOURCE: KW-55
1173. James, Henry. <u>A Portrait of a Lady</u>, (1881).
    SOURCE: KW-40
1174. James, Will. <u>Big Enough</u>, 1931, Dec.
    SOURCE: EH-MP
    COMMENT: EH ordered for son.
1175. James, Will. <u>Sun Up</u>, 1931,Dec.
    SOURCE: EH-MP
    COMMENT: EH ordered for son.
1176. James, William. <u>Psychology</u>, (1892).
    SOURCE: KW-40
1177. Jamison, Alcinous. <u>Intestinal Ills</u>, (1901).
    SOURCE: KW-55
    COMMENT: Intestines; proctology.
1178. Jarrett, Cora. <u>Strange Houses</u>, (1936).
    SOURCE: KW-55
1179. Jeanjean, Marcel. <u>Les Aventures de Fricasson</u>,
    (1925).
    SOURCE: KW-55

1180. Jellinek, F. <u>Civil War in Spain</u>, 1938,Oct.
        SOURCE: Brentanos
1181. Jenkinson, Sir Anthony. <u>Where Seldom a Gun Is Heard</u>,
        (1937).
        SOURCE: KW-55
1182. Jennings, John. <u>Next to Valour</u>, (1939).
        SOURCE: KW-55
1183. Jennison, George. <u>Natural History: Animals</u>, 1929,
        Nov.
        SOURCE: SB; KW-40
        COMMENT: EH purchased.
1184. Jimenez, Max. <u>Revenar</u>, (1936).
        SOURCE: KW-40
        COMMENT: Publ. in Santiago, Chile.
1185. Jirku, Gusti. <u>We Fight Death</u>, (1937).
        SOURCE: KW-40
        COMMENT: Pamphlet. Medical Service of
           International brigades in Spain.
1186. Johnson, Clifford. <u>Pirate Junk</u>, 1934,July.
        SOURCE: MP-EH; EH-MP
        COMMENT: "Five months captivity with Manchurian
           bandits." Sent and received.
1187. Johnson, Eldridge Reeves. <u>Tarpomania</u>, (1910).
        SOURCE: KW-40
        COMMENT: Tarpon fishing.
1188. Johnson, Eldrige Reeves. <u>Buck Fever</u>, (1911).
        SOURCE: KW-40
        COMMENT: Private printing.
1189. Johnson, Overton. <u>Route Across the Rocky Mountains</u>,
        (1932).
        SOURCE: KW-55
        COMMENT: Reprint from 1843/46.
1190. Johnston, Harold W. <u>The Private Lives of the Romans</u>,
        1915.
        SOURCE: OPHS
        COMMENT: Assigned reading, HS.
1191. Jones, Elias Henry. <u>The Road to En-Dor</u>, (1919).
        SOURCE: KW-40
        COMMENT: Escape of two POWs from Turkish prison.
1192. Jordan, Philip. <u>The Grey Pilgrim</u>, (1927).
        SOURCE: KW-40
1193. Jordanoff, Assen. <u>Your Wings</u>, 1937,June.
        SOURCE: SCRBNR
        COMMENT: Airplanes, piloting.
1194. Jordon, David Starr. <u>Fishes</u>, (1907).
        SOURCE: KW-40
1195. Jordon-Hubbs **. <u>On Ichthyology</u>, 3 vols. **.
        SOURCE: KW-40
        COMMENT: See David Starr Jordan and Carl L. Hubbs
           in NUC.
1196. Josephson, Matthew. <u>Jean Jacques Rousseau</u>, (1931).
        SOURCE: KW-55
1197. Josephson, Matthew. <u>Zola and His Time</u>, 1929,Apr.
        SOURCE: SB

1198.   Joyce, James. Anna Livia Plurabelle, 1935.
            SOURCE: KL:EH Collection
            COMMENT: Sheet music and text. Review copy.
            Limited edition of 350.
1199.   Joyce, James. Chamber Music, 1934,Mar.
            SOURCE: SB; KW-40
1200.   Joyce, James. Dubliners, 1929,Oct.
            SOURCE: EH-"Mr. Gud"; KW-40; KL
            COMMENT: EH: Dubliners and end of Ulysses are
               "immortal" literature. (Probably read by 1924.)
1201.   Joyce, James. Portrait of the Artist as a Young Man,
            1934,Mar.
            SOURCE: SB; KW-40
            COMMENT: Probably read in the 1920s.
1202.   Joyce, James. Two Tales of Shem and Shaun, 1934,Mar.
            SOURCE: SB; KW-40
            COMMENT: "Fragment from Work in Progress".
1203.   Joyce, James. Ulysses, 1922,Mar.
            SOURCE: EH-Sherwood Anderson; G.Clark-EH; KL:EH
            Collection
            COMMENT: Owned unbound press copy. EH: most
               wonderful book. See Baker.
1204.   Kang, Younghill. East Goes West, 1940,Jan.
            SOURCE: EH-MP
1205.   Kang, Younghill. The Grass Roof, 1931,Jan.
            SOURCE: MP-EH; KW-40
1206.   Kantor, MacKinlay. Long Remember, (1934).
            SOURCE: KW-55
            COMMENT: Fiction: Battle of Gettysburg.
1207.   Kaplan, Moise N. Big Game Angler's Paradise, (1936).
            SOURCE: KW-40
1208.   Kauffman, Ray. Hurricane's Wake, 1940, Oct.
            SOURCE: EH-MP
            COMMENT: Ordered by EH.
1209.   Kaulback, Ronald. Tibetan Trek, (1934).
            SOURCE: KW-55
1210.   Keats, John. The Poetical Works of John Keats.
            SOURCE: KW-55
1211.   Kemp, Harry. More Miles, (1926).
            SOURCE: KW-55
            COMMENT: Autobiog. novel.
1212.   Kemp, Harry. Tramping on Life, 1927,Feb.
            SOURCE: EH-Isidor Schneider
            COMMENT: EH: my god what a book.
1213.   Kempis, Thomas a. L' Imitation de Jesus Christ,
            (1831).
            SOURCE: KW-55
            COMMENT: Trans. F. de Lamennais.
1214.   Kennedy, Charles. The Servant in the House, 1915.
            SOURCE: KL
            COMMENT: EH wrote outline of play in HS.
1215.   Kephart, Horace. Camping and Woodcraft, (1916).
            SOURCE: KW-55

1216. Kessel, Joseph E. L' Equipage, (1923).
           SOURCE: KW-40
1217. Keyserling, Hermann A. The Travel Diary of a
           Philosopher, 1925,Nov.
           SOURCE: SB
           COMMENT: Nov.16-24. 2 vols. Trans. by J. Holroyd-
               Reece.
1218. Keyserling, Hermann A. The World in the Making,
           (1927).
           SOURCE: KW-40
           COMMENT: Trans. of Die Neuentstehende Welt, pub.
               1926.
1219. King, Marian. Mirror of Youth, (1928).
           SOURCE: KW-55
           COMMENT: Youth, nature, poetry.
1220. King, Raymond Sherwood. Between Murders, (1935).
           SOURCE: KW-40
1221. King, Rosa Eleanor. Tempest over Mexico: a Personal
           Chronicle, 1935,July.
           SOURCE: EH-MP
           COMMENT: EH ordered.
1222. Kingsmill, Hugh. Frank Harris, (1932).
           SOURCE: KW-55
           COMMENT: Pseud. of Hugh Kingsmill Lunn.
1223. Kinloch, Col. Alexander Angus. Large Game Shooting,
           1934,Mar.
           SOURCE: KL:Brentanos; KW-40
           COMMENT: Pub.1885. Tibet and India.
1224. Kipling, Rudyard. Animal Stories, (1932).
           SOURCE: KW-55
1225. Kipling, Rudyard. Debits and Credits, (1926).
           SOURCE: KW-55
1226. Kipling, Rudyard. The Humorous Tales of Rudyard
           Kipling, (1931).
           SOURCE: KW-55
1227. Kipling, Rudyard. The Jungle Book, 1916.
           SOURCE: EH-Emily Goetsmann; KW-55
           COMMENT: EH quotes two stanzas in ltr.
1228. Kipling, Rudyard. Just So Stories, (1902).
           SOURCE: KW-55
           COMMENT: Read by 1916.
1229. Kipling, Rudyard. Life's Handicap: Being Stories of
           Mine Own People, (1891).
           SOURCE: KW-40
1230. Kipling, Rudyard. Mine Own People, (1890).
           SOURCE: KW-40
1231. Kipling, Rudyard. Plain Tales from the Hills,
           (1888).
           SOURCE: KW-40; KW-55
1232. Kipling, Rudyard. "The Recessional," 1915,Jan.
           SOURCE: OPHS
           COMMENT: EH memorized for HS.
1233. Kipling, Rudyard. The Second Jungle Book, (1895).
           SOURCE: KW-55

1234. Kipling, Rudyard. <u>Something of Myself</u>, 1937,May.
SOURCE: SB; KW-55
COMMENT: Sent to Majestic Hotel, Barcelona.
1235. Kipling, Rudyard. <u>Stalkey and Co.</u>, 1916,Mar.
SOURCE: EH-Emily Goetsmann; KW-40
COMMENT: EH recommended it.
1236. Kipling, Rudyard. <u>The Story of the Gadsbys</u>, 1938,
May.
SOURCE: EH-MP
1237. Kipling, Rudyard. <u>Works of Kipling</u>, 9 vols. **.
SOURCE: KW-40; KW-55
COMMENT: 8 vols. left in Key West. No 9 or 17 vol.
eds. of Kipling.
1238. Klotz, Helmut. <u>Military Lessons</u>, (1937).
SOURCE: KW-40
COMMENT: Maybe in French or German. No record of
book being trans. into English.
1239. Klotz, Helmut. <u>La Nouvelle Guerre</u>, (1937).
SOURCE: KW-40
COMMENT: Les lecons militaires de la guerre civile
en Espagne.
1240. Knox, John C. <u>A Judge Comes of Age</u>, 1940,Sept.
SOURCE: MP-EH
1241. Kobler, John, ed. <u>Trial of Ruth Snyder and Judd
Gray</u>, 1938,May.
SOURCE: SCRBNR
COMMENT: Trial case of Albert Snyder
murder,1927-28.
1242. Kock, Charles Paul de. <u>La Femme, La Mari et L'Amant</u>,
(1829).
SOURCE: KW-55
1243. Kock, Charles Paul de. <u>Jean</u>, (1828).
SOURCE: KW-40
1244. Koestler, Arthur. <u>Spanish Testament</u>, (1937).
SOURCE: KL:EH Collection
COMMENT: Some pencil markings.
1245. Komroff, Manuel. <u>The Grace of Lambs</u>, 1926,Sept.
SOURCE: EH-MP
COMMENT: EH probably read.
1246. Komroff, Manuel, ed. <u>The Travels of Marco Polo</u>,
1926,Sept.
SOURCE: EH-MP; KW-40
COMMENT: Asia, Mongols.
1247. Kreymborg, Alfred et al, eds. <u>American Caravan</u>,
(1927).
SOURCE: KW-40
COMMENT: "a yearbook of Amer. lit."
1248. Kromer, Tom. <u>Waiting for Nothing</u>, (1935).
SOURCE: KW-40
COMMENT: Intro. by Theodore Dreiser.
1249. Kuck, Loraine E. and R.C.Tongg. <u>Tropical Garden: Its
Design, Horticulture and Plant Materials</u>,
1937,June.
SOURCE: SCRBNR; KW-55

1250.   Kuncz, Aladar. Black Monastery, 1934.
          SOURCE: EH-MP
          COMMENT: EH ordered. Trans. by Ralph Murray.
1251.   Kuprin, Aleksandr. The Bracelet of Garnets, (1917).
          SOURCE: KW-55
1252.   Kurz, Marcel. Alpinisme Hivernal, (1925).
          SOURCE: KW-55
1253.   Kyne, Peter Bernard. Comrades of the Storm, (1933).
          SOURCE: KW-40
1254.   La Farge, Christopher. Each Other, 1939,Nov.
          SOURCE: EH-MP
          COMMENT: A novel in verse. EH: like wearing boxing
               gloves on hands and feet in six day bike race.
1255.   La Sage. Aventuras de Gil Blas de Santillana.
          SOURCE: KW-40
1256.   Labiche, Eugene M. and Edouard Martin. Le Voyage de
          Monsieur Perrichon, (1879).
          SOURCE: KW-55
          COMMENT: Comedy in 4 acts.
1257.   Ladoux, Georges. Les Chasseurs d'Espions, (1932).
          SOURCE: KW-40
          COMMENT: "comment j'ai fait arreter Mata-Hari."
1258.   Lafarge, Oliver. Sparks Fly Upward, (1931).
          SOURCE: KW-40
1259.   Lagerlof, Selma. Charlotte Lowenskold, (1927).
          SOURCE: KW-40
          COMMENT: Orig. in Swedish.
1260.   Lake, Stuart N. Wyatt Earp, Frontier Marshal ,
          (1931).
          SOURCE: KW-40
1261.   Landreth, Helen. Dear Dark Head, (1936).
          SOURCE: KW-55
          COMMENT: Ireland.
1262.   Lang, Andrew. The Yellow Fairy Book, 1929,Nov.
          SOURCE: SB
          COMMENT: Purchased copy.
1263.   Langdon-Davies, John. Behind the Spanish Barricades,
          (1936).
          SOURCE: KW-40
1264.   Langworthey, Franklin. Scenery of the Plains,
          Mountains and Mines, (1932).
          SOURCE: KW-40
          COMMENT: Pub. in 1855. Reissued by Princeton
               U.Press.Paul C. Philips, ed.
1265.   Lanham, Edwin M. Another Ophelia, (1938).
          SOURCE: KW-55
1266.   Lanham, Edwin M. Sailors Don't Care, (1929).
          SOURCE: KW-40
1267.   Lanslots, Don Ildephonse. Illustrated Explanation of
          the Prayers and Ceremonies of the Mass, (1897).
          SOURCE: KW-55
1268.   Larbaud, Valery. Jaune, Bleu, Blanc, (1927).
          SOURCE: KW-55

1269.   Lardner, Ring. Round Up, 1929,Apr.
          SOURCE: MP-EH; EH-MP; KW-40; KW-55
1270.   Lardner, Ring. The Story of a Wonder Man, 1927,June.
          SOURCE: SB
          COMMENT: June 11-13.
1271.   Larvie and Fleury. La Deuxieme Annee de Grammaire,
          (1887).
          SOURCE: KW-55
          COMMENT: Grammar, composition, exercises.
1272.   Latimer, Jonathan. The Dead Don't Care, 1938,March.
          SOURCE: SCRBNR; SB
          COMMENT: Received copy from SCRBNR in March.
              Checked out copy from SB in Sept.
1273.   Laughlin, Clara Elizabeth. So You're Going to
          Spain!, 1931,April.
          SOURCE: EH-MP
          COMMENT: EH ordered.
1274.   Laver, James. Whistler, 1931,Apr.
          SOURCE: EH-MP
          COMMENT: EH ordered. EH: not one by Pennell or any
              other of Mr. Royal Bengal Cortezoz's buddies.
1275.   Lawrence, D.H. Assorted Articles, 1930, May.
          SOURCE: EH-MP; KW-55
          COMMENT: EH ordered and received copy.
1276.   Lawrence, D.H. Lady Chatterley's Lover, 1929.
          SOURCE: SB
          COMMENT: Purchased copy Mar.,1934.
1277.   Lawrence, D.H. The Ladybird, (1923).
          SOURCE: KW-55
1278.   Lawrence, D.H. The Letters of D.H.Lawrence, 1932,
          Oct.
          SOURCE: EH-MP; KW-40
          COMMENT: EH ordered. Ed. & w. intro. by Aldous
              Huxley.
1279.   Lawrence, D.H. The Plumed Serpent, (1926).
          SOURCE: KW-55
1280.   Lawrence, D.H. Sons and Lovers, 1924.
          SOURCE: KL
1281.   Lawrence, D.H. Triumph of the Machine, 1934,Mar.
          SOURCE: SB
          COMMENT: Ariel poem.
1282.   Lawrence, D.H. The Virgin and the Gipsy, 1931,Sept.
          SOURCE: SB
1283.   Lawrence, D.H. The White Peacock, 1923.
          SOURCE: KL
1284.   Lawrence, T.E. Letters of T. E. Lawrence, (1938).
          SOURCE: KW-40
          COMMENT: Ed. David Gannett.
1285.   Lawrence, T.E. The Revolt in the Desert, 1931,Sept.
          SOURCE: EH-E.W.Titus
1286.   Lawrence, T.E. Seven Pillars of Wisdom, 1935,July.
          SOURCE: EH-MP
          COMMENT: EH orders in advance of pub.

1287.   Lawson, Henry Archibald Hertzberg. While the Billy
        Boils (2 vols.), 1927.
        SOURCE: KL:Cape; KW-40
1288.   Lay, Beirne. I Wanted Wings, 1937,June.
        SOURCE: SCRBNR
1289.   Le Gallienne, Richard. The Romance of Perfume,
        (1928).
        SOURCE: KW-40
1290.   Le Gallienne, Richard. The Romantic '90s, (1925).
        SOURCE: KW-40
1291.   Lear, Edward. Nonsense Songs, 1934,Mar.
        SOURCE: SB
1292.   Lecky, William Edward. The American Revolution
        1763-1783, 1916.
        SOURCE: OPHS; KL
        COMMENT: HS text heavily read.
1293.   Lecky, William Edward. History of European Morals,
        from Augustus to Charlemagne, (1869).
        SOURCE: KW-40
        COMMENT: 2 vols.
1294.   Lee, George W. Beale Street, Where the Blues Began,
        1934, Nov.
        SOURCE: EH-MP; KW-55
        COMMENT: EH ordered and received.
1295.   Lehmann, John, ed. New Writing I&II, 1937,May.
        SOURCE: SB
        COMMENT: Sent to Majestic Hotel, Madrid.
1296.   Lehmann, Rosamond. Invitation to the Waltz, (1932).
        SOURCE: KW-40
1297.   Lehmann, Rosamond. A Note in Music, (1930).
        SOURCE: KW-40
1298.   Lehmann, Rosamond. The Weather in the Streets,
        1936,May.
        SOURCE: SCRBNR; KW-55
1299.   Lenotre, G. The Guillotine and Its Servants,
        1929,Apr.
        SOURCE: SB
        COMMENT: Pseud. of Louis L. Gosselin. Trans. from
            French by Mrs. Rodolph Stawell.
1300.   Leoncavallo, Ruggiero. Pagliacci, 1920,Apr.
        SOURCE: EH-CH
1301.   Leopold, Aldo. Game Management, (1933).
        SOURCE: KW-40
1302.   Leslie, Sir Shane. Studies in Sublime Failure,
        (1932).
        SOURCE: KW-40
        COMMENT: Re: Cardinal Newman, Charles Stewart
            Parnell, Coventry Patmore.
1303.   Levin, Meyer. Citizens:A Novel, 1940,Mar.
        SOURCE: AH-2
        COMMENT: EH:"a fine exciting American novel."
1304.   Levin, Meyer. Frankie and Johnnie, a Love Story,
        (1930).
        SOURCE: KW-55

1305. Levin, Meyer. The Old Bunch, 1937,June.
       SOURCE: SCRBNR
1306. Lewis, C. Day. Dick Willoughby, 1938,March.
       SOURCE: SCRBNR
       COMMENT: EH sent copy to PH.
1307. Lewis, Cecil A. Sagitarius Rising, 1937,June.
       SOURCE: SCRBNR
       COMMENT: WWI: aerial operations. China:
         description and travel.
1308. Lewis, Flannery. Suns Go Down , (1937).
       SOURCE: KW-55
       COMMENT: Two copies.
1309. Lewis, Grace (Hegger). Half a Loaf, (1931).
       SOURCE: KW-55
1310. Lewis, Herbert Clyde. Gentleman Overboard, 1937,
       June.
       SOURCE: SCRBNR
1311. Lewis, Sinclair. Babbit, 1925, Dec.
       SOURCE: EH-FSF
1312. Lewis, Sinclair. Main Street, 1925,Dec.
       SOURCE: EH-FSF; KW-55
       COMMENT: May have read earlier. EH: compared to
         Mann, Lewis is nothing to get excited about.
1313. Lewis, Wyndham. Paleface, 1929,Nov.
       SOURCE: W.Lewis-EH
       COMMENT: Lewis pleased EH liked book.
1314. Lewis, Wyndham. Tarr, (1918).
       SOURCE: KW-55
1315. Lewis, Wyndham. Time and Western Man, 1927,Oct.
       SOURCE: SB; EP-EH
       COMMENT: Kept one day. Modern lit. EH disliked.
1316. Lewishon, Ludwig. Expression in America, 1932,Apr.
       SOURCE: EH-MP; KW-40
       COMMENT: EH ordered and received.
1317. Liddell, Donald M. Chess Men, (1937).
       SOURCE: KW-55
1318. Liddell Hart, Basil Henry. Colonel Lawrence,
       1934,Apr.
       SOURCE: EH-MP; SCRBNR
       COMMENT: EH ordered and received.
1319. Liddell Hart, Basil Henry. Decisive Wars of History,
       (1929).
       SOURCE: KW-40
1320. Liddell Hart, Basil Henry. Europe in Arms, (1937).
       SOURCE: KW-40
1321. Liddell Hart, Basil Henry. A History of the World
       War, 1914-1918, (1934).
       SOURCE: KW-40
1322. Liddell Hart, Basil Henry. The Real War, 1914-1918,
       1930, Nov.
       SOURCE: EH-MP; KW-40
       COMMENT: EH ordered by wire from Billings, Mont.

1323. Liddell Hart, Basil Henry. Through the Fog of War,
          1938,Oct.
          SOURCE: Brentanos; KW-40
1324. Linati, Carlo. Issione il Polifoniarca, (1922).
          SOURCE: KW-40
          COMMENT: Only 611 copies printed.
1325. Lincoln, Abraham. " Gettysburg Address," 1914,Mar.
          SOURCE: OPHS
          COMMENT: EH memorized for HS.
1326. Lindbergh, Anne Morrow. Listen! the Wind, (1938).
          SOURCE: KW-40
1327. Lindbergh, Anne Morrow. North to the Orient, (1935).
          SOURCE: KW-55
1328. Linklater, Eric. Juan in China, (1937).
          SOURCE: KW-55
1329. Linklater, Eric. Mangus Merriman, (1934).
          SOURCE: KW-55
1330. Linklater, Eric. The Men of Ness, 1933.
          SOURCE: SB; KW-40
          COMMENT: The saga of Thorlief Coalbiter's sons.
1331. Locke, William J. The Montebank, (1921).
          SOURCE: KW-40
1332. Lockhart, Robert Hamilton Bruce. British Agent,
          (1933).
          SOURCE: KW-40
          COMMENT: Intro. by Hugh Walpole.
1333. Lockhart, Robert Hamilton Bruce. Retreat from Glory,
          (1934).
          SOURCE: KW-40
          COMMENT: History: 1918: Czechoslovak Republik and
             Balkan peninsula.
1334. Loeb, Harold A. The Professors Like Vodka, 1927,May.
          SOURCE: EH-Isidor Schneider
1335. London, Geo. Les Grands Proces de l'annee 1927,
          (1928).
          SOURCE: KW-40
1336. London, Jack. The Call of the Wild, 1913.
          SOURCE: OPBE
1337. Long, G.M.V., ed. Great Tales of Horror, 1933,Dec.
          SOURCE: Brentanos
1338. Long, William Joseph. English Literature, 1916.
          SOURCE: OPHS
          COMMENT: Heavily used HS text.
1339. Loos, A. Gentlemen Prefer Blondes, 1926,Apr.
          SOURCE: EH-FSF
          COMMENT: EH:second rate Lardner and very dull.
1340. Lopez-Valdemoro, J.G. El Espectaculo mas Nacional,
          (1899).
          SOURCE: KW-40
1341. Loti, Pierre. Pecheur D'Islande, (1886).
          SOURCE: KW-55
          COMMENT: Pseud. of Julien Viaud.

1342. Loti, Pierre. Ramuntcho, (1896).
    SOURCE: KW-55
    COMMENT: Pseud. of Julien Viaud. A play in five
        acts.
1343. Lowell, Amy. Tendencies in Modern American Poetry,
    (1917).
    SOURCE: KW-55
    COMMENT: Re: E.A.Robinson, Frost, Masters,
        Sandburg, H.D. and Fletcher.
1344. Lowie, Robert H. The Crow Indians, 1935.
    SOURCE: EH-MP
    COMMENT: EH ordered.
1345. Lowndes, Marie Adelaide Belloc. The Bread of Deceit,
    1925, Nov.
    SOURCE: SB
1346. Lowndes, Marie Adelaide Belloc. The Chianti Flask,
    1934,Nov.
    SOURCE: EH-MP; KW-40
    COMMENT: EH ordered.
1347. Lowndes, Marie Adelaide Belloc. The Chink in the
    Armour, 1937,Apr.
    SOURCE: SCRBNR; AH
    COMMENT: EH:"uncanny little masterpiece of dread
        and suspense."
1348. Lowndes, Marie Adelaide Belloc. Good Old Anna,
    (1915).
    SOURCE: KW-40
1349. Lowndes, Marie Adelaide Belloc. The House by the
    Sea, (1937).
    SOURCE: KW-55
1350. Lowndes, Marie Adelaide Belloc. Lilla, (1916).
    SOURCE: KW-55
1351. Lowndes, Marie Adelaide Belloc. One of Those Ways,
    (1929).
    SOURCE: KW-55
1352. Lowndes, Marie Adelaide Belloc. The Story of Ivy,
    1927,Nov.
    SOURCE: SB
1353. Lowry, Malcolm. Ultramarine, (1933).
    SOURCE: KW-40
1354. Loy, Mina. Lunar, Baedecker, 1923,Aug.
    SOURCE: SB
1355. Loyola, Attilio. The Captivity of the Italians in
    Austria, (1918).
    SOURCE: KL:EH Collection
    COMMENT: Owned two copies.
1356. Lubbock, Percy. Roman Pictures, (1923).
    SOURCE: KW-55
1357. Luckner, Felix. The Last Privateer, 1928,Mar.
    SOURCE: EH-MP
    COMMENT: Trans. of Seeteufel.
1358. Ludendorf, Erich. My War Memories, 1925,Dec.
    SOURCE: EH-FSF
    COMMENT: German general. Maps. Trans. from German.

1359. Ludwig, Emil. Genius and Character, 1928,Mar.
          SOURCE: SB
          COMMENT: Bismarck, Stanley, Wilson, Lenin, da
             Vinci, Byron, Balzac,etc.
1360. Ludwig, Emil. The Nile, (1936).
          SOURCE: KW-55
1361. Luhan, Mabel Dodge. Edge of the Taos Desert, (1937).
          SOURCE: KW-55
          COMMENT: Vol.4 of Intimate Memoirs.
1362. Luhan, Mabel Dodge. European Experiences, 1936,Dec.
          SOURCE: EH-MP; KW-55
          COMMENT: EH ordered copy. Vol. 2 of Intimate
             Memoirs.
1363. Luhan, Mabel Dodge. Movers and Shakers, (1936).
          SOURCE: KW-55
          COMMENT: Vol. 3 of Intimate Memoirs.
1364. Luhan, Mabel Dodge. Winter in Taos, 1936,Dec.
          SOURCE: MP-EH
1365. Luhan, Mable Dodge. Lorenzo in Taos, 1932,Mar.
          SOURCE: EH-MP; KW-55
          COMMENT: EH ordered by wire.
1366. Lunn, Arnold Henry Moore. The Complete Ski-Runner,
             (1930).
          SOURCE: KW-40
1367. Lunn, Arnold Henry Moore. A History of Skiing,
             (1927).
          SOURCE: KW-40
1368. Lydekker, Richard. The Game Animals of Africa,
             (1908).
          SOURCE: KW-40
1369. Lyell, Denis D. The Hunting and Spoor of Central
             African Game, (1929).
          SOURCE: KW-40
1370. Lyell, Denis D., ed. African Adventure: Letters from
             Famous Big-Game Hunters, 1936.
          SOURCE: SCRBNR; KW-40
1371. Lynch, John Gilbert Bohun. The Prize Ring, (1925).
          SOURCE: KW-40
          COMMENT: Illus. by reproductions of old prints,
             several oil paintings, and of the famous Byron
             screen.
1372. Lyons, Eugene. Assignment in Utopia, (1937).
          SOURCE: KW-55
1373. Macartney, Clarence E. Lincoln and His Cabinet,
             1931.
          SOURCE: EH-MP
          COMMENT: EH:Thanks for the Lincoln book.
1374. Macaulay, Thomas B. Essay on Addison, 1914.
          SOURCE: OPHS
1375. Macaulay, Thomas B. The Life of Johnson, (1895).
          SOURCE: KW-55

1376.   Macauley, Thurston.   The Festive Board: a Literary
        Feast, 1932,Feb.
            SOURCE: MP-EH; KW-55
            COMMENT: Verse and prose on cooking and dining.
1377.   Mack, W.   Tiger Rose, 1920.
            SOURCE: EH-GHH
            COMMENT: EH saw play.
1378.   Mackenzie, Compton.   Athenian Reminiscences (vol.3),
        1932.
            SOURCE: EH-MP
            COMMENT: EH ordered.
1379.   MacKenzie, Compton.   First Athenian Memories, (1931).
            SOURCE: KW-40
1380.   MacKenzie, Compton.   Gallipoli Memories, 1929.
            SOURCE: EH-FSF; KW-55
            COMMENT: EH: best book since Repington's on WWI.
1381.   MacKenzie, Compton.   Greek Memories, 1932,Dec.
            SOURCE: EH-MP; KW-40
            COMMENT: Vol.3 of series. EH: he writes lousy
                fiction but great reminiscences.
1382.   Mackenzie, Compton.   Sylvia and Michael, (1919).
            SOURCE: KW-55
1383.   MacKready, Kelvin.   A Beginner's Star Book, (1912).
            SOURCE: KW-55
            COMMENT: Pseud. E.G.Murphy.
1384.   MacLeish, Archibald.   Air Raid, (1938).
            SOURCE: KW-55
            COMMENT: A Verse Play for Radio.
1385.   MacLeish, Archibald.   America Was Promises, (1939).
            SOURCE: KW-55
1386.   MacLeish, Archibald.   Conquistador, 1930.
            SOURCE: EH-MP; EH-S.Putnam; KW-40; KW-55; KL:EH
            Collection
            COMMENT: EH read draft in 1930. EH:one of three
                best books of 1932. Owned typescript.
1387.   MacLeish, Archibald.   The Hamlet of A. MacLeish,
        (1928).
            SOURCE: KW-55
1388.   MacLeish, Archibald.   New Found Land, (1930).
            SOURCE: KW-55
1389.   MacLeish, Archibald.   Public Speech, 1935,Aug.
            SOURCE: MacLeish-EH; KW-55
            COMMENT: MacLeish: pleased EH thought the book was
                all right.
1390.   MacManus, Seumas.   Ireland's Case, (1917).
            SOURCE: KW-55
1391.   Macy, Pierre and Emile Malakis.   Petite Histoire de
        la Civilization Francaise, (1932).
            SOURCE: KW-55
            COMMENT: History and language reader.
1392.   Madan, Arthur C.   English Swahili Dictionary (2
        vols.), (1902).
            SOURCE: KW-40

1393. Madariaga, Salvador de. <u>Anarchy or Hierarchy</u>, 1937, June.
    SOURCE: SCRBNR
1394. Madariga, Salvador de. <u>Spain</u>, (1930).
    SOURCE: KW-40
1395. Maine, R. <u>La Bataille du Jutland</u>, (1939).
    SOURCE: <u>KW-40</u>
1396. Malet, Rawdon. <u>Unforgiving Minutes</u>, (1934).
    SOURCE: KW-40
1397. Malraux, Andre. <u>La Condition Humaine</u>, (1933).
    SOURCE: KW-40
1398. Malraux, Andre. <u>Days of Hope</u>, (1938).
    SOURCE: KW-55
    COMMENT: Fiction.
1399. Malraux, Andre. <u>Days of Wrath</u>, (1936).
    SOURCE: KW-40
    COMMENT: Fiction:Germany.
1400. Malraux, Andre. <u>Le Temps du Mepris</u>, 1935,July.
    SOURCE: EH-MP
    COMMENT: EH: send as soon as it is out.
1401. Mann, Thomas. <u>Buddenbrooks</u>, 1925, Dec.
    SOURCE: SB; <u>EH-FSF</u>
    COMMENT: 2 vol.ed. EH finished vol.I five days
      after check out. EH to Fitzgerald:a pretty damn
      good book.
1402. Mann, Thomas. <u>The Magic Mountain</u>, 1928,Feb.
    SOURCE: SB; <u>KW-40</u>
    COMMENT: Trans. H.T.Lowe-Porter.
1403. Mann, Thomas. <u>Stories of Three Decades</u>, 1936,June.
    SOURCE: SCRBNR; KW-55
    COMMENT: Includes "Felix Krull", "Death in
      Venice," and "Disorder and Early Sorrow."
1404. Mann, Thomas. <u>Tonio Kroger</u>, (1922).
    SOURCE: KW-55
1405. Manning, Frederic. <u>Her Privates, We</u>, 1929.
    SOURCE: Fenton; KW-55
    COMMENT: Pseud: Private 19022. Republished as The
      Middle Parts of Fortune.
1406. Mapes, V. and W. Collier. <u>The Hottentot</u>, 1921.
    SOURCE: EH-GH
    COMMENT: EH saw.
1407. Maran, Rene. <u>Batouala</u>, 1922, March.
    SOURCE: AH; Fenton
    COMMENT: Probably read in trans. by A.S.Seltzer.
      EH wrote review in TSW.
1408. Marbot, Jean Baptiste A., Baron de. <u>Au Service de</u>
    <u>Napoleon</u>, 1940,Feb.
    SOURCE: EH-MP
    COMMENT: Pub. in 1928. Extracts from 4 vol.
      edition of the memoirs. EH: happy to read it in
      French.
1409. Marbury, Mary Oryis. <u>Favorite Flies and Their</u>
    <u>Histories</u>, (1892).
    SOURCE: KW-40

1410. Marcosson, Isaac. Adventures in Interviewing,
          (1920).
          SOURCE: KW-55
1411. Margueritte, Victor. Aristide Briand, (1932).
          SOURCE: KW-55
1412. Marjoribanks, Edward. Carson, the Advocate, (1932).
          SOURCE: KW-40
          COMMENT: Edward H.Carson 1854-1935; vol.1.
1413. Marryat, Capt. Frederick. The Dog Fiend, 1926,Feb.
          SOURCE: EH-FSF
          COMMENT: EH: read as a boy.
1414. Marryat, Capt. Frederick. Jacob Faithful, (1834).
          SOURCE: KW-55
          COMMENT: Fiction: African setting.
1415. Marryat, Capt. Frederick. Masterman Ready, (1841).
          SOURCE: KW-55
          COMMENT: Shipwreck survival.
1416. Marryat, Capt. Frederick. Mr. Midshipman Easy,
          1926,Feb.
          SOURCE: EH-FSF; KW-40
          COMMENT: EH: read as a boy. Good war descriptions.
1417. Marryat, Capt. Frederick. The Naval Officer,
          1926,Feb.
          SOURCE: EH-FSF
          COMMENT: EH: good war descriptions. Read as a boy.
1418. Marryat, Capt. Frederick. Peter Simple, 1926,Feb.
          SOURCE: EH-FSF
          COMMENT: EH: re-reading for first time since a
             kid.
1419. Marsh, Ngaio. Overture to Death, (1939).
          SOURCE: KW-40
1420. Marshall, Frank. Chess in a Hour, (1937).
          SOURCE: KW-55
1421. Martet, Jean. Le Tigre, (1930).
          SOURCE: KW-40
          COMMENT: Biog. of Clemenceau, Georges Eugene
             Benjamin.
1422. Martet, Jean, ed. M. Clemenceau, Peint par Lui-meme,
          (1929).
          SOURCE: KW-40
1423. Martin, Kingsley. The Magic of Monarchy, (1937).
          SOURCE: KW-55
1424. Marvell, Andrew. " To His Coy Mistress," 1926.
          SOURCE: EH-E.Walsh
          COMMENT: EH:great poetry. Probably read earlier.
1425. Marx, Karl and Fredrick Engels. Manifesto of the
          Communist Party, (1888).
          SOURCE: KW-55
1426. Mascagni, Pietro. Cavalleria Rusticana, 1920,Apr.
          SOURCE: EH-CH
1427. Masefield, John. " Laugh and Be Merry," 1917,June.
          SOURCE: OPHS
          COMMENT: Memorized for HS.

1428. Masefield, John. <u>Salt Water Ballads</u>, 1916,Mar.
        SOURCE: EH-"Emily"
        COMMENT: EH:read all Emily recommended and got
            Salt Water Ballads as well.Enjoyed.
1429. Masefield, John. <u>The Story of a Round-House</u>,
        1916,Mar.
        SOURCE: EH-"Emily"
        COMMENT: Recommends.
1430. Masefield, John. <u>The Taking of the Gry</u>, 1934, Nov.
        SOURCE: EH-MP; KW-55
        COMMENT: EH ordered.
1431. Masefield, John. <u>Victorious Troy</u>, (1935).
        SOURCE: KW-55
1432. Mathews, Ferdinand. <u>Field Book of Wild Birds and</u>
        <u>their Music</u>, (1904).
        SOURCE: KW-55
1433. Mathews, Ferdinand. <u>Fieldbook of American Wild</u>
        <u>Flowers</u>, (1902).
        SOURCE: KW-40
1434. Matson, Norman H. <u>Flecker's Magic</u>, (1926).
        SOURCE: KW-55
1435. Matthews, Brander. <u>The Short Story</u>, (1907).
        SOURCE: KW-40
1436. Matthews, Herbert L. <u>Two Wars and More to Come</u>,
        1938.
        SOURCE: KW-40; AH
        COMMENT: Italo-Ethiopian War and Sp. Civil War.
1437. Maugham, William Somerset. <u>Ah King</u>, (1933).
        SOURCE: KW-40
1438. Maugham, William Somerset. <u>Andalusia, Sketches and</u>
        <u>Impressions</u>, (1920).
        SOURCE: KW-55
1439. Maugham, William Somerset. <u>Cakes and Ale</u>, 1930,Nov.
        SOURCE: EH-MP
        COMMENT: EH:damn good.
1440. Maugham, William Somerset. <u>Christmas Holiday</u>,
        (1939).
        SOURCE: KW-55
1441. Maugham, William Somerset. <u>Cosmopolitans</u>, 1936,
        March.
        SOURCE: SCRBNR; KW-55
1442. Maugham, William Somerset. <u>Don Fernando</u>, 1935,Aug.
        SOURCE: EH-MP
        COMMENT: EH ordered.
1443. Maugham, William Somerset. <u>The Gentleman in the</u>
        <u>Parlour</u>, 1930,May.
        SOURCE: EH-MP
        COMMENT: EH ordered and received.
1444. Maugham, William Somerset. <u>The Moon and Sixpence</u>,
        (1919).
        SOURCE: KW-40; KW-55

1445. Maugham, William Somerset. The Narrow Corner, 1932,
      Nov.
      SOURCE: EH-MP; KW-40; KW-55
      COMMENT: EH ordered and received.
1446. Maugham, William Somerset. Of Human Bondage,
      1925,Dec.
      SOURCE: KL; KW-40
1447. Maugham, William Somerset. Plays, (1931).
      SOURCE: KW-55
1448. Maugham, William Somerset. Six Comedies, (1937).
      SOURCE: KW-55
      COMMENT: Comedies.
1449. Maugham, William Somerset. Six Stories Written in
      the First Person Singular, (1931).
      SOURCE: KW-40
1450. Maugham, William Somerset. Theatre, a Novel, (1937).
      SOURCE: KW-55
1451. Maupassant, Guy de. Les Dimanches d'un Bourgeois de
      Paris.
      SOURCE: KW-55
1452. Maupassant, Guy de. Huit Contes Choisis, (1900).
      SOURCE: KW-55
      COMMENT: Two copies.
1453. Maupassant, Guy de. Mademoiselle Fifi.
      SOURCE: KW-55
1454. Maupassant, Guy de. "La Maison Tellier," 1933,July.
      SOURCE: EH-MP; KW-55
      COMMENT: May have read as early as HS. EH: "Light
         of the World" is a better and shorter story.
1455. Maupassant, Guy de. Misti, (1890).
      SOURCE: KW-40
1456. Maupassant, Guy de. Une Vie, (1883).
      SOURCE: KW-40
1457. Maurois, Andre. Ariel: ou, La Vie de Shelley,
      (1923).
      SOURCE: KW-55
1458. Maurois, Andre. Byron, 1930.
      SOURCE: EH-MP; KW-40
      COMMENT: Ordered by EH. Trans. from French by
         Hamish Miles.
1459. Maurois, Andre. Climats, (1928).
      SOURCE: KW-55
1460. Maurois, Andre. Les Discours du Docteur O'Grady,
      (1922).
      SOURCE: KW-55
1461. Maurois, Andre. Etudes Anglaises, (1927).
      SOURCE: KW-55
      COMMENT: Dickens, Walpole, Ruskin, Wilde.
1462. Maurois, Andre. The Miracle of England, (1937).
      SOURCE: KW-55
1463. Maurois, Andre. Tourgueniev, (1931).
      SOURCE: KW-55

1464. Maurois, Andre. Tragedy in France, 1940,Oct.
           SOURCE: EH-MP
           COMMENT: EH ordered.
1465. Maycock, Alan Lawson. The Inquisition From Its
           Establishment to the Great Schism, 1927,Apr.
           SOURCE: SB
1466. Maydon, Hubert Conway, ed. Big Game Shooting in
           Africa, (1932).
           SOURCE: KW-40
1467. Mayne, Ethel Colburn. Byron, (1912).
           SOURCE: KW-55
1468. Mayne, Ethel Colburn. The Life of Lady Byron,
           (1929).
           SOURCE: KW-55
1469. Mayo, Katherine. Mother India, 1927, Oct.
           SOURCE: SB
1470. McAlmon, Robert. North America, (1929).
           SOURCE: KW-55
1471. McAlmon, Robert. Post-Adolescence, (1923).
           SOURCE: KW-40
           COMMENT: Contact Editions.
1472. McAlmon, Robert. Village, 1925,Jan.
           SOURCE: EH-Robert McAlmon; EH-SB; EH-MP
           COMMENT: EH:absolutely first rate and damned good
               reading. A knock out.
1473. McBride, Herbert Wes. A Rifleman Went to War,
           1936,July.
           SOURCE: SCRBNR; KW-40
           COMMENT: Canadian army; emphasis on sniping.
1474. McCoy, Horace. They Shoot Horses Don't They, 1935.
           SOURCE: KL:Simon and Schuster
1475. McEntee, Girard Lindsley. Military History of the
           World War, (1937).
           SOURCE: KW-40
           COMMENT: Contains 456 maps and diagrams.
1476. McHugh, Vincent. Sing before Breakfast, (1933).
           SOURCE: KW-55
1477. Meade, Patrick A. Born to Trouble, (1939).
           SOURCE: KW-40
1478. Meader, Stephen W. Who Rides in the Dark?, 1938,Mar.
           SOURCE: SCRBNR; KW-55
           COMMENT: Sent to Mrs. Hemingway.
1479. Meier-Graefe, Julius. The Spanish Journey, 1926,Dec.
           SOURCE: SB; KW-40
           COMMENT: Dec.16-Mar.12,1927. Illus.
1480. Meier-Graefe, Julius. Vincent Van Gogh, (1922).
           SOURCE: KW-55
1481. Melville, Herman. Typee, (1846).
           SOURCE: KW-55
           COMMENT: Two copies.
1482. Mencken, H.L., ed. Americana,1925, 1926,Oct.
           SOURCE: SB
           COMMENT: Collected from American Mercury.

1483. Menke, Frank G. Encyclopedia of Sports, (1939).
      SOURCE: KW-55
1484. Meyerstein, Edward H. W. A Life of Thomas
      Chatterton, (1930).
      SOURCE: KW-40
1485. Michelin. Guide Michelin pour la France, (1929).
      SOURCE: KW-40
1486. Michelsen, Andreas. La Guerre Sous-Marine,
      1914-1918, (1925).
      SOURCE: KW-55
      COMMENT: Submarine warfare.
1487. Millan, Pascual. Los Novillos, 1930.
      SOURCE: GP-EH
      COMMENT: GP ordered copy for EH. May have
        received.
1488. Millan, Pascual. Los Toros en Madrid, 1930.
      SOURCE: GP-EH
      COMMENT: GP ordered copy for EH. May have
        received.
1489. Millan, Pascual. Trilogia Taurina, 1930.
      SOURCE: KW-40
      COMMENT: 2 copies.
1490. Millay, Edna St. Vincent. Poems by Edna St. Vincent
      Millay, (1923).
      SOURCE: KW-55
1491. Millay, Edna St.Vincent. Second April, (1921).
      SOURCE: KW-55
1492. Miller, Francis Trevelyan. Portrait Life of Lincoln,
      1916.
      SOURCE: KL:EH Collection
      COMMENT: Birthday gift from the Hemingway
        grandparents to EH, July 21,1916.
1493. Miller, Joaquin. " Columbus," 1913,Oct.
      SOURCE: OPHS
      COMMENT: EH memorized.
1494. Miller, Webb. I Found No Peace, (1936).
      SOURCE: KW-55
      COMMENT: Journalism.
1495. Millis, Walter. Road to War, America, 1914-1917,
      (1935).
      SOURCE: KW-40
1496. Milton, John. "L' Allegro," 1916, Dec.
      SOURCE: OPHS
      COMMENT: Memorized lines 25-40.
1497. Milton, John. Minor Poems by John Milton.
      SOURCE: KW-55
1498. Milton, John. " On His Blindness," 1917,Jan.
      SOURCE: OPHS
      COMMENT: EH memorized.
1499. Milton, John. Paradise Lost, Bks.I&II, 1916.
      SOURCE: OPHS
      COMMENT: HS reading.
1500. Minguet, Enrique. Desde La Grada, (1928).
      SOURCE: KW-40; KW-55

1501. Mirrielees, Edith R., ed. Significant Contemporary
          Stories, (1929).
          SOURCE: KW-40
          COMMENT: Includes EH, Virginia Woolf, Conrad, H.G.
          Wells, and others.
1502. Mirskii, Dmitrii P. Contemporary Russian Literature:
          1881-1925, 1929,June.
          SOURCE: SB
1503. Mitchell, John Ames. Drowsy, 1920,Nov.
          SOURCE: EH-Grace Quinlan
1504. Mitchell, Margaret. Gone with the Wind, (1936).
          SOURCE: KW-55
1505. Mitchell-Hedges, F. A. Battles with Giant Fish,
          (1923).
          SOURCE: KW-40
1506. Mitchell-Henry, L. Tunny Fishing at Home and Abroad,
          1935,Apr.
          SOURCE: EH-MP; SCRBNR; KW-40
          COMMENT: EH ordered and received.
1507. Mitchison, Naomi. Cloud Cuckoo Land, (1925).
          SOURCE: KW-55
1508. Mizner, Addison. The Many Mizners, (1932).
          SOURCE: KW-40
1509. Moliere, Jean Baptiste. The Affected Ladies, 1914.
          SOURCE: OPHS
          COMMENT: English translation.
1510. Moliere, Jean Baptiste. Le Bourgeois Gentilhomme.
          SOURCE: KW-55
1511. Moliere, Jean Baptiste. Theatre de Moliere, Vols. I-
          VIII.
          SOURCE: KW-55
          COMMENT: 17th.C.
1512. Molony, John C. The Riddle of the Irish, 1928,Feb.
          SOURCE: SB
1513. Monfreid, Henri de. La Croisiere de Hachich, (1937).
          SOURCE: KW-55
          COMMENT: Hashish.
1514. Monfreid, Henri de. Le Drame Ethiopien, (1935).
          SOURCE: KW-55
1515. Monfreid, Henri de. Le Lepreux, (1935).
          SOURCE: KW-55
1516. Monfreid, Henri de. Le Masque D'Or, (1936).
          SOURCE: KW-55
          COMMENT: Haile Selassie and Ethiopia.
1517. Monfreid, Henri de. La Poursuite de Kaipan, (1934).
          SOURCE: KW-55
          COMMENT: Adventures in Red Sea, Indian Ocean.
1518. Monfreid, Henri de. Vers les Terres Hostiles de
          l'Ethiopie, (1933).
          SOURCE: KW-40
1519. Monroe, Harriet. A Poet's Life, (1938).
          SOURCE: KW-55
1520. Montaigne, Michel E. de. Essays of Montaigne.
          SOURCE: KW-55

1521. Montaigne, Michel E. de. Lettre de Montaigne,
      (1802).
         SOURCE: KW-55
1522. Montes, Francisco. Tauromachia Completa, 1930.
         SOURCE: GP-EH
         COMMENT: GP ordered copy for EH.
1523. Montherlant, Henry de. Mors et Vita, (1932).
         SOURCE: KW-55
1524. Moore, Audrey. Serengeti, 1939,July.
         SOURCE: EH-MP
         COMMENT: EH: knows Moore. Home sick for Africa.
1525. Moore, George. Avowals, 1926,Nov.
         SOURCE: EH-Isidor Schneider; KW-40; KW-55
         COMMENT: EH ordered copy.
1526. Moore, George. Conversations in Ebury Street,
      (1924).
         SOURCE: KW-55
1527. Moore, George. Evelyn Innes, (1898).
         SOURCE: KW-55
1528. Moore, George. Hail and Farewell, 1927,Feb.
         SOURCE: EH-MP; KW-40
         COMMENT: 2 vols.
1529. Moore, George. Heloise and Abelard (2 vols.),
      1925,Nov.
         SOURCE: HH-I.Godolphin; KW-40
         COMMENT: Prv. printing.
1530. Moore, Marianne. " Marriage," (1923).
         SOURCE: KL:EH Collection
         COMMENT: In Mannikin, No.3.
1531. Morand, Paul. Bouddha Vivant, (1927).
         SOURCE: KW-55
1532. Morand, Paul. France la Doulce, (1934).
         SOURCE: KW-55
1533. Morand, Paul. Rien que la Terre, (1926).
         SOURCE: KW-55
         COMMENT: Far East.
1534. Morand, Paul. La Route des Indes, (1936).
         SOURCE: KW-55
1535. Morey, William C. Ancient Peoples, 1915.
         SOURCE: OPHS
         COMMENT: HS text.
1536. Morey, William C. Outlines of Greek History, 1915.
         SOURCE: OPHS
         COMMENT: HS text.
1537. Morey, William C. Outlines of Roman History, 1915.
         SOURCE: OPHS
         COMMENT: HS text.
1538. Morgan, Deck. Deck Morgan's Winter Carnival, (1935).
         SOURCE: KW-40
1539. Morin, Henri. A L'Ecoute Devant Verdun, (1938).
         SOURCE: KW-40
1540. Mortane, Jacques. Evasions d'Aviateurs 1914-1918,
      (1934).
         SOURCE: KW-40

1541.   Mosher, Thomas Bird.   An Outline of Distinguished
       Reading, (1925).
       SOURCE: KW-55
       COMMENT: Authors: bio-bibliography.

1542.   Mottram, Ralph Hale.   The Crime at Vanderlynden's,
       1926,April.
       SOURCE: SB

1543.   Mowrer, Edgar A.   This American World, (1928).
       SOURCE: KW-40

1544.   Muirhead, James T.   Air Attack on Cities, (1938).
       SOURCE: KW-55

1545.   Mukerji, Dhan Gopal.   The Chief of the Herd, (1929).
       SOURCE: KW-55
       COMMENT: Elephants: legends and stories.

1546.   Munoz, Rafael F.   El Feroz Cabecilla, (1936).
       SOURCE: KW-40
       COMMENT: "cuentos de la revolucion en el norte.".

1547.   Munroe, Donald Gordon.   Distillate, (1935).
       SOURCE: KW-40
       COMMENT: Music. 250 copies printed.

1548.   Munthe, Axel.   The Story of San Michele, (1929).
       SOURCE: KW-55

1549.   Murray, Hugh.   Historical and Descriptive Account of
       British India, (1832).
       SOURCE: KW-40

1550.   Murry, John M.   The Autobiography of John Middleton
       Murry, 1936.
       SOURCE: SCRBNR

1551.   Muzzey, David Saville.   An American History, 1916.
       SOURCE: OPHS; KW-55
       COMMENT: HS text heavily read.

1552.   Myers, Leopold H.   The Root and the Flower, (1934).
       SOURCE: KW-55

1553.   Nabokov, Vladimir.   Laughter in the Dark, (1938).
       SOURCE: KW-40

1554.   Naether, Carl.   The Book of the Pigeon, (1939).
       SOURCE: KW-55
       COMMENT: Pigeon literature.

1555.   Nansen, Fridtjof.   The First Crossing of Greenland,
       1925.
       SOURCE: EH-Robert McAlmon; KW-55

1556.   Nathan, Robert.   One More Spring, 1937, April.
       SOURCE: SCRBNR
       COMMENT: Publ. 1933.

1557.   Nesbitt, Lewis M.   Hell-Hole of Creation, 1935,Apr.
       SOURCE: EH-MP; SCRBNR
       COMMENT: EH ordered. Planning a trip to Abyssinia.

1558.   Neumann, Arthur H.   Elephant Hunting in East
       Equatorial Africa, 1934,Mar.
       SOURCE: KL:Brentanos
       COMMENT: Pub.1898.

1559. Nevinson, Henry Woodd. Goethe: Man and Poet, (1931).
        SOURCE: KW-40
        COMMENT: Written for the centenary of Goethe's
        death on Mar. 22, 1832.
1560. Newbigin, Alice. A Wayfarer in Spain, (1926).
        SOURCE: KW-55
1561. Newcomer, A.G. and H.E.Andrews, eds. Twelve
        Centuries of English Poetry and Prose, 1916.
        SOURCE: OPHS
        COMMENT: HS text.
1562. Newhouse, Edward. This is Your Day, (1937).
        SOURCE: KW-55
1563. Newhouse, Edward. You Can't Sleep Here, (1934).
        SOURCE: KW-55
1564. Newman, Frances. Frances Newman's Letters, 1930,Feb.
        SOURCE: EH-MP; KW-40
        COMMENT: EH ordered.
1565. Newman, John Henry. Apologia Pro Vita Sua, (1864).
        SOURCE: KW-55
1566. Nichols, Beverly. Twenty-Five, (1926).
        SOURCE: KW-55
1567. Nicolson, Harold George. Byron, The Last Journey,
        April 1823 - April 1824, (1924).
        SOURCE: KW-40
1568. Nicolson, Harold George. Helen's Tower, (1937).
        SOURCE: KW-55
        COMMENT: In search of the past, geneological
        tables.
1569. Nicolson, Harold George. Small Talk, (1937).
        SOURCE: KW-40; KW-55
1570. Nicolson, Harold George. Some People, (1927).
        SOURCE: KW-40
1571. Nicolson, Marjorie **. The Realm O'Dreams **,
        1914,May.
        SOURCE: OPHS
1572. Niedieck, Paul. With Rifle in Five Continents,
        1934,Mar.
        SOURCE: KL:Brentanos; KW-40
        COMMENT: Trans. from German. Pub. in 1909.
1573. Nietzsche, Frederick. Thus Spake Zarathustra,
        1926,May.
        SOURCE: SB
        COMMENT: May 5-Sept.13.
1574. Nimrod. Memoirs of the Life of the Late John Mytton,
        (1925).
        SOURCE: KW-40
        COMMENT: Pseud. of C.J.Apperley. First pub. in
        19th. C. Reissued in 1925.
1575. Nitti, Francesco F. Escape, 1930,Feb.
        SOURCE: EH-MP
        COMMENT: Facism, Italy.
1576. Nixon, Laurence A. Vagabond Voyaging: the Story of
        Freighter Travel, (1938).
        SOURCE: KW-55

1577. Noel-Baker, Philip John. The Private Manufacture of
Armaments, (1936).
SOURCE: KW-40
1578. Nomad, Max. Rebels and Renegades, (1932).
SOURCE: KW-40
COMMENT: Socialism and anarchism.
1579. Nordhoff, Charles B. and James N. Hall. The Bounty
Trilogy, (1936).
SOURCE: KW-55
COMMENT: Three vols.: Mutiny on the Bounty: Men
Against the Sea: Pitcairn's Island.
1580. Nordhoff, Walter. The Journey of the Flame,
1937, June.
SOURCE: SCRBNR; KW-55
COMMENT: Historical fiction, Mexico 19th. C.
1581. Norris, Kathleen. Storm House, (1929).
SOURCE: KW-55
1582. Norris, Thaddeus. The American Anglers Book, (1864).
SOURCE: KW-40
1583. North, Sterling. So Red the Nose, or Breath in the
Afternoon, (1935).
SOURCE: KW-40
COMMENT: Cocktail recipes.
1584. Noth, Ernst Erich. L' Homme Contre le Partisan,
(1938).
SOURCE: KW-55
COMMENT: Pseud. of Paul Krantz.
1585. Noyes, Alfred. "The Highwayman," 1913, Dec.
SOURCE: OPHS
COMMENT: EH memorized for HS.
1586. Nunez Cabeza De Vaca, Alvar. Naufragios y
Comentarios, (1922).
SOURCE: KW-40
COMMENT: Spanish exploration to 1565. Other
editions: 1932, 1936.
1587. Nyabongo, Prince Akiki K. The Story of an African
Chief, (1935).
SOURCE: KW-40
1588. O'Brien, Edward J., ed. Best Short Stories of 1925,
1926, March.
SOURCE: SB
COMMENT: Retrnd. May 10, 1926.
1589. O'Brien, Edward J., ed. Best Short Stories of 1926,
1927.
SOURCE: EH-MP
COMMENT: EH: pretty lousy collection.
1590. O'Brien, Edward J., ed. Best Short Stories of 1927,
1928, Feb.
SOURCE: EH-MP
COMMENT: EH: enjoyed Wister story which was really
part of a novel.
1591. O'Brien, Edward J., ed. Best Short Stories of 1932,
(1933).
SOURCE: KW-40; KW-55

1592. O'Brien, Edward J., ed. Best Short Stories of 1933,
       1934,Mar.
       SOURCE: SB; KW-55
       COMMENT: English stories.
1593. O'Brien, Edward J., ed. Best Short Stories of 1936,
       1937,June.
       SOURCE: SCRBNR
1594. O'Brien, Edward J., ed. Best Short Stories of 1937,
       (1938).
       SOURCE: KW-55
1595. O'Brien, John S. Alone Across the Top of the World,
       (1935).
       SOURCE: KW-55
1596. O'Brien, Philadelphia Jack. Boxing, 1929.
       SOURCE: EH-MP
1597. O'Casey, Sean. The Plough and the Stars, 1928, Feb.
       SOURCE: SB
1598. O'Connell, Daniel M., ed. Favorite Newman Sermons,
       (1932).
       SOURCE: KW-55
       COMMENT: Cardinal Newman.
1599. O'Connor, Frank. The Saint and Mary Kate, (1932).
       SOURCE: KW-40
1600. O'Crohan, Tomas. The Islandman, (1934).
       SOURCE: KW-55
1601. O'Faolain, Sean. Bird Alone, 1936.
       SOURCE: KL:Cape
1602. O'Faolain, Sean. Midsummer Night Madness, 1933.
       SOURCE: KL:Cape
1603. O'Flaherty, Liam. The Short Stories of Liam
       O'Flaherty, (1937).
       SOURCE: KW-55
1604. O'Flaherty, Liam. Two Years, 1930,Nov.
       SOURCE: EH-MP
       COMMENT: EH wires for a copy of this book.
1605. O'Flahrety, Liam. The Mountain Tavern, 1929,Aug.
       SOURCE: EH-SB
       COMMENT: EH ordered book from SB.
1606. O'Hara, John. Appointment in Samarra, 1934, Oct.
       SOURCE: Ned Calmer-EH; KL
       COMMENT: Calmer: "O'Hara . . . will be delighted
          you like his novel."
1607. O'Hara, John. Butterfield 8, (1934).
       SOURCE: KW-55
1608. O'Hara, John. The Doctor's Son and Other Stories,
       (1935).
       SOURCE: KW-40
1609. O'Hara, John. Files on Parade, (1939).
       SOURCE: KW-55
1610. O'Malley, Ernie. Army Without Banners, 1937, Feb.
       SOURCE: SCRBNR
       COMMENT: "adventures of an Irish volunteer"; Sinn
          Fein rebellion.

1611. O'Neill, Eugene. The Emperor Jones, 1928,Feb.
         SOURCE: SB
1612. Oppenheim, Edward P. The Oppenheim Omnibus: Clowns
         and Criminals, (1933).
         SOURCE: KW-40
1613. Oppenheim, Edward P. The Terrible Hobby of Sir
         Joseph Londe, 1925,Nov.
         SOURCE: SB
         COMMENT: Nov.28-Dec.1.
1614. Oppenheimer, Franz. The State: Its History and
         Development Viewed Sociologically, (1914).
         SOURCE: KW-40
         COMMENT: Trans. by John M. Gitterman.
1615. Ortega y Gasset, Jose. Invertebrate Spain,
         1937,July.
         SOURCE: SCRBNR
1616. Ortega y Gasset, Jose. La Rebelion de las Masas,
         (1929).
         SOURCE: KW-55
1617. Ortega y Gasset, Jose. The Revolt of the Masses,
         (1932).
         SOURCE: KW-40
         COMMENT: Trans. authorized by Sr. Ortega y Gasset.
1618. Orwell, George. Down and Out in Paris and London,
         (1933).
         SOURCE: KW-55
1619. Orwell, George. Homage to Catalonia, 1938, Sept.
         SOURCE: SB
         COMMENT: Borrowed, no record of return.
1620. Osler, Sir William. A Way of Life, (1914).
         SOURCE: KW-55
         COMMENT: Philosophy.
1621. Otopalik, Hugo. Modern Wrestling, 1930,Feb.
         SOURCE: MP-EH
         COMMENT: MP sent unrequested.
1622. Otten, George. Tuberous-Rooted Begonias and Their
         Culture, (1935).
         SOURCE: KW-55
1623. Outhwaite, Leonard. Atlantic Circle: Around the
         Ocean With the Winds and Tides, (1931).
         SOURCE: KW-40
1624. Palgrave, Francis T., ed. Palgrave's Golden
         Treasury, (1929).
         SOURCE: KW-55
1625. Palmer, Joe. Recollections of a Boxing Referee,
         (1927).
         SOURCE: KW-40
         COMMENT: Intro. by Bohun Lynch.
1626. Pardo Bazan, Emilia. Los Pazos de Ulloa, (1886).
         SOURCE: KW-55
1627. Pareto, Vilfredo. The Mind and Society, 1935,July.
         SOURCE: EH-MP
         COMMENT: EH ordered.

1628.   Parijanine, Maurice. The Krassin, (1929).
        SOURCE: KW-40
1629.   Parker, Eric. Elements of Shooting, (1924).
        SOURCE: KW-40
1630.   Parker, Eric. Shooting by Moor, Field and Shore,
        (1929).
        SOURCE: KW-40; KW-55
1631.   Parrott, Katherine Ursula. Next Time We Live,
        (1935).
        SOURCE: KW-40
1632.   Parton, James. Life of Andrew Jackson, Vols. I, II &
        III, (1860).
        SOURCE: KW-55
1633.   Parviel **. Notre Dame de Praslin **.
        SOURCE: KW-40
1634.   Pascal, Blaise. Les Provinciales, (1656).
        SOURCE: KW-55
1635.   Pater, Walter. Marius the Epicurean, (1885).
        SOURCE: KW-55
1636.   Paul, Elliot Harold. The Life and Death of a Spanish
        Town, 1938.
        SOURCE: SB
        COMMENT: No record of return.
1637.   Paul, Louis. Pumpkin Coach, (1935).
        SOURCE: KW-40
        COMMENT: Pseud. of Felix L.P. Heink.
1638.   Peabody, Josephine P. The Piper, 1915,Feb.
        SOURCE: OPHS
        COMMENT: EH saw performance.
1639.   Pearson, Drew and C. Brown. The American Diplomatic
        Game, (1935).
        SOURCE: KW-40
        COMMENT: U.S.foreign rel. 20th.C.
1640.   Pease, Alfred Edward. The Book of the Lion,
        1934,Mar.
        SOURCE: KL:Brentanos; KW-40
        COMMENT: Pub.1914.
1641.   Peattie, Donald C., ed. Audubon's America, 1940.
        SOURCE: EH-MP
        COMMENT: Ordered by EH.
1642.   Peattie, Donald C., ed. A Gathering of Birds,
        (1939).
        SOURCE: KW-55
1643.   Peers, Edgar Allison. Spain: a Companion to Spanish
        Studies, (1929).
        SOURCE: KW-55
1644.   Peers, Edgar Allison. The Spanish Tragedy, 1930-36,
        (1936).
        SOURCE: KL:EH Collection
1645.   Peisson, Edouard. Parti de Liverpool, (1932).
        SOURCE: KW-55
1646.   Pena Martin, Alfredo. Tratado de las Aves
        Insectivoras, (1904).
        SOURCE: KW-40

1647. Pena y Goni, Antonio. Guerrita, (1894).
          SOURCE: KW-40
          COMMENT: "Vol.II de la Biblioteca de Sol y
              Sombra".
1648. Pena y Goni, Antonio. Lagartijo y Frascuelo y su
          Tiempo, (1914).
          SOURCE: KW-40
1649. Percival, Arthur Blayney. A Game Ranger on Safari,
          (1928).
          SOURCE: KW-40
1650. Percival, Arthur Blayney. A Game Ranger's Note Book,
          (1924).
          SOURCE: KW-40
1651. Perez de Ayala, Ramon. Tinieblas en las Cumbres,
          (1907).
          SOURCE: KW-55
          COMMENT: Novel.
1652. Perez Galdos, Benito. El Equipaje del Rey Jose,
          (1875).
          SOURCE: KW-55
          COMMENT: Fiction: Napoleonic Conquest.
1653. Perez Lugin, Alejandro. Currito de la Cruz, 2 Vols.,
          1933,April.
          SOURCE: EH-MP; KW-40
          COMMENT: Pub. in 1921. May have read before '33.
              EH:very readable local color novel. Accurate
              description of holy week and bull fights.
1654. Perez Lugin, Alejandro. Shadows of the Sun,
          1934,Jan.
          SOURCE: EH-MP; KW-40
          COMMENT: Trans. by Sidney Franklin.
1655. Perrin, Alice. Government House, (1925).
          SOURCE: KW-55
1656. Peterson, Houston. The Melody of Chaos, (1931).
          SOURCE: KW-40
          COMMENT: Study of Conrad Aiken's poetry.
1657. Peterson, Roger Tory. Field Guide to the Birds,
          (1934).
          SOURCE: KW-55
1658. Peyre, Joseph. Sang et Lumieres, 1936,Apr.
          SOURCE: SCRBNR; KW-55
          COMMENT: Two copies.
1659. Philippe, Charles Louis. Lettres de Jeunesse,
          (1911).
          SOURCE: KW-55
1660. Phillipps-Wolley, Clive. Big Game Shooting, 2 vols.,
          1934, March.
          SOURCE: KL:Brentanos; KW-40
          COMMENT: Pub. in 1894 in Badminton Library of
              Sports.
1661. Phillips, Henry Albert. Germany Today and Tomorrow,
          (1935).
          SOURCE: KW-40

1662. Pidgeon, Harry. Around the World Single-Handed: the
       Cruise of the "Islander," (1932).
           SOURCE: KW-40
1663. Pierrefeu, Jean de. Plutarque a Menti, (1923).
           SOURCE: KW-55
1664. Pigot, Brig.-Gen. R. Twenty Five Years' Big Game
       Hunting, (1928).
           SOURCE: KW-40
1665. Pike, James. Scout and Ranger, (1932).
           SOURCE: KW-40
           COMMENT: Pub.1865. Reissued by Princeton U.Press.
           Texas Rangers in 1859-60.
1666. Pilat, Oliver R. The Mate Takes Her Home, (1939).
           SOURCE: KW-55
1667. Pinchot, Gifford. Just Fishing Talk, (1936).
           SOURCE: KW-40
1668. Pirandello, Luigi. La Ragione Degli Altri, (1925).
           SOURCE: KW-55
1669. Plomer, William. Ali the Lion, (1936).
           SOURCE: KW-55
1670. Plomer, William. The Child of Queen Victoria, 1933.
           SOURCE: KL:Cape; KW-55
1671. Pochhammer, Hans. Graf Spee's Letzte Fahrt, (1918).
           SOURCE: KW-40
1672. Pollard, Hugh B. C. Game Birds: Rearing,
       Preservation and Shooting, (1929).
           SOURCE: KW-40
1673. Pollard, Hugh B. C. The Gun Room Guide, (1930).
           SOURCE: KW-40
1674. Pollard, Hugh B.C. Wild Fowl and Waders, 1929.
           SOURCE: EH-MP
           COMMENT: EH liked book.
1675. Poore, Charles Graydon. Goya, 1938, Oct.
           SOURCE: EH-MP; KW-55
           COMMENT: Sent to Pauline. 50 plates.
1676. Pope, Alexander. The Rape of the Lock, 1916.
           SOURCE: OPHS
           COMMENT: HS reading.
1677. Pope, Clark and Albion. Brief Biographies in Modern
       History, (1930).
           SOURCE: KW-55
1678. Pope, Clifford H. Turtles in the U.S. and Canada,
       (1939).
           SOURCE: KW-55
1679. Poulaille, Henry. Le Pain Quotidien, (1931).
           SOURCE: KW-55
1680. Pound, Ezra. ABC of Economics, 1934,Mar.
           SOURCE: SB; EP-EH; KW-40
1681. Pound, Ezra. The Cantos of Ezra Pound, 1933.
           SOURCE: KL:EH Collection
           COMMENT: With testimonies by EH, F.M.Ford,
               T.S.Eliot, Hugh Walpole, MacLeish, Joyce, and
               others.

1682. Pound, Ezra. XVI Cantos, (1925).
          SOURCE: KL:EH Collection
          COMMENT: Three Mountains Press limited edition of
              90 copies.
1683. Pound, Ezra. A Draft of XXX Cantos, 1933.
          SOURCE: EP-EH; KW-40
1684. Pound, Ezra. Gaudier-Brzeska: A Memoir, 1922,Nov.
          SOURCE: EP-EH
          COMMENT: EP asks EH to return his copy.
1685. Pound, Ezra. Guide to Kulchur, (1938).
          SOURCE: KW-40
1686. Pound, Ezra. Lustra, (1916).
          SOURCE: KW-40
1687. Pound, Ezra. Make It New, (1934).
          SOURCE: KW-55
1688. Pound, Ezra. Pavannes and Divisions, (1918).
          SOURCE: KW-40
1689. Pound, Ezra. Personae, 1926,Oct.
          SOURCE: EH-Isidor Schneider; KW-40
          COMMENT: EH ordered and received.
1690. Pound, Ezra. Profile, (1932).
          SOURCE: KW-40
          COMMENT: Prvt. printing. 250 numbered copies.
1691. Pound, Ezra. Selected Poems, 1934,Mar.
          SOURCE: SB; KW-40
          COMMENT: Ed. with intro. by T.S.Eliot.
1692. Pound, Ezra. Umbra: the Early Poems of Ezra Pound,
              (1920).
          SOURCE: KW-40
1693. Pound, Ezra, ed. Active Anthology, (1933).
          SOURCE: KW-40
          COMMENT: Includes: Williams, W.C.; Zukofsky;
              Aragon; Cummings; EH; Moore, Marianne; Eliot,
              T.S.; Pound.
1694. Pound, Ezra, ed. Catholic Anthology, 1914-15,
              (1915).
          SOURCE: KW-40
1695. Pound, Ezra, ed. The Exile, 1927.
          SOURCE: EP-EH; EH-EP; KW-40
          COMMENT: Nos.1-4: Spring,1927-Autumn,1928.
1696. Pourtales, Guy de. Nietzsche en Italie, (1929).
          SOURCE: KW-40
1697. Powell, Dawn. Angels on Toast, 1940,Sept.
          SOURCE: EH-MP
          COMMENT: EH: a literary idol. Best woman writing.
1698. Powell, Dawn. The Happy Island, (1939).
          SOURCE: KW-55
1699. Powell, Fred Wilbur. Hall Jackson Kelly, Prophet of
              Oregon, (1917).
          SOURCE: KW-40
1700. Powell, Hickman. Ninety Times Guilty, (1939).
          SOURCE: KW-40
          COMMENT: N.Y.C.: prostitution.

1701.   Powys, John C. Dorothy M. Richardson, 1934,Mar.
        SOURCE: SB; KW-40
        COMMENT: Limited edition.
1702.   Powys, Llewelyn. Love and Death, (1939).
        SOURCE: KW-55
1703.   Powys, Llewelyn. Skin for Skin, (1925).
        SOURCE: KW-40
1704.   Powys, T. F. Mr. Weston's Good Wine, (1927).
        SOURCE: KW-55
1705.   Pratt, Theodore. Big Blow, 1937.
        SOURCE: SCRBNR
1706.   Praz, Mario. Unromantic Spain, (1929).
        SOURCE: KW-55
1707.   Prevost, Jean. Les Freres Bouquinquant, (1930).
        SOURCE: KW-40
1708.   Prin, Alice. Kiki's Memoirs, 1930.
        SOURCE: AH; KL:EH Collection
        COMMENT: Trans. by Samuel Putnam. Intro. by EH.
1709.   Pritchett, Victor Sawdon. This England (No. 1),
        (1937).
        SOURCE: KW-40
        COMMENT: 78pp.
1710.   Proust, Marcel. A L'Ombre des Jeunes Filles en
        Fleurs, (1919).
        SOURCE: KW-55
        COMMENT: Remembrance of Things Past.
1711.   Proust, Marcel. Cities of the Plain, Vols. I&II,
        (1927).
        SOURCE: KW-40; KW-55
        COMMENT: Trans. by C.K. Scott Moncrieff.
1712.   Proust, Marcel. Du Cote de Chez Swann, (1914).
        SOURCE: KW-55
        COMMENT: Two copies.
1713.   Proust, Marcel. The Guermantes Way, (1925).
        SOURCE: KW-55
        COMMENT: Trans. of Le Cote de Guermantes. Vol.4 of
        Remembrance of Things Past.
1714.   Proust, Marcel. Swann's Way, (1922).
        SOURCE: KW-55
        COMMENT: Remembrance of Things Past; trans. of Du
        Cote de Chez Swann.
1715.   Proust, Marcel. The Sweet Cheat Gone, (1930).
        SOURCE: KW-55
        COMMENT: Remembrance of Things Past; trans. of
        Albertine Disparue.
1716.   Pupin, Michael Idvorsky. Romance of the Machine,
        (1930).
        SOURCE: KW-40
1717.   Puxley, W. Lavallin. Deep Seas and Lonely Shores,
        1936,March.
        SOURCE: SCRBNR; KW-40
1718.   Pyle, Howard. Howard Pyle's Book of Pirates, 1932.
        SOURCE: EH-MP
        COMMENT: Ordered book for his son.

1719. Pyle, Howard, illus. Howard Pyle's Book of the
       American Spirit, (1923).
       SOURCE: KW-55
1720. Pyle, Katharine. Tales from Greek Mythology, (1928).
       SOURCE: KW-55
       COMMENT: Fiction: juv. lit.
1721. Quennell, Peter. Byron: The Years of Fame, (1935).
       SOURCE: KW-40
1722. Quevedo, F. de. Los Suenos, (1916).
       SOURCE: KW-55
       COMMENT: Pseud. of Quevedo y Villegas, Francisco
       Gomez de (1580-1645).
1723. Quevedo y Villegas, Francisco de. Castellanos **.
       SOURCE: KW-40
       COMMENT: No such title in NUC, but edition
       Clasicos Castellanos of his works.
1724. Quiller-Couch, Arthur, ed. Oxford Book of English
       Verse 1250-1918, 1940,Apr.
       SOURCE: EH-MP; KW-40; KW-55
       COMMENT: Two copies owned. EH: title source for
       FWBT. See p.171.
1725. Quinche, Eugene. Haarmann, le Boucher de Hanovre,
       (1925).
       SOURCE: KW-40
1726. Quintanilla, Luis. All the Brave, 1939.
       SOURCE: KW-40; KL:EH Collection
       COMMENT: Wrote intro.; owned 2 copies.
1727. Radcliffe, William. Fishing from the Earliest Times,
       (1921).
       SOURCE: KW-40
1728. Radiguet, Raymond. The Devil in the Flesh, (1932).
       SOURCE: KW-40
       COMMENT: Forward by Aldous Huxley. Trans. by Kay
       Boyle.
1729. Railey, Hilton Howell. Touch'd with Madness, (1938).
       SOURCE: KW-55
1730. Randell, Jack. I'm Alone, (1930).
       SOURCE: KW-40
       COMMENT: As told to Meigs O. Frost. Seafaring life
       and Boer War.
1731. Ransome, Arthur. " Racundra's" First Cruise, (1923).
       SOURCE: KW-40
       COMMENT: Sailing on the Eastern Baltic.
1732. Ransome, Arthur. Rod and Line, (1929).
       SOURCE: KW-40
1733. Rascoe, Burton. Before I Forget, 1937.
       SOURCE: SCRBNR
1734. Rascoe, Burton. A Bookman's Daybook, 1929, June.
       SOURCE: SB
       COMMENT: "significant literary currents from
       April,1922-Aug.,1924".
1735. Raswan, Carl R. Black Tents of Arabia, (1935).
       SOURCE: KW-55

1736.   Rauschning, Hermann. The Revolution of Nihilism,
        1939, Oct.
            SOURCE: EH-MP; KW-55
            COMMENT: EH ordered. Pro-Hitler. "A Warning to the
                West".
1737.   Rawlings, Marjorie K. When the Whippoorwill,
        1940,Apr.
            SOURCE: EH-MP
            COMMENT: Sent to Martha Gelhorn.
1738.   Rawlings, Marjorie K. The Yearling, 1938,Mar.
            SOURCE: EH-MP; KW-40
1739.   Ray, Oscar. Espions et Espionnage, (1936).
            SOURCE: KW-40
1740.   Raymond, Charles Harlow. A Book of English: For
        Understanding, Expressing and Appreciating Thought,
        (1932).
            SOURCE: KW-55
1741.   Raynal, Maurice. Anthologie de la Peinture en France
        de 1906 a nos Jours, (1927).
            SOURCE: KW-40
1742.   Reade, Charles. The Cloister and the Hearth, 1916.
            SOURCE: Fenton
            COMMENT: A tale of the middle ages.
1743.   Redondo, Ladislao. Guerrita. Su Tiempo y su
        Retirada, (1899).
            SOURCE: KW-40
1744.   Reed, Alonzo and Brainerd Kellogg. Higher Lessons in
        English, (1878).
            SOURCE: KW-55
            COMMENT: A work on Engl. gram. & comp., in which
                the science of lang. is made tributary to the
                art of expression.
1745.   Reed, Chester A. Bird Guide Part 2: Land Birds East
        of the Rockies, 1910.
            SOURCE: KL:EH Collection
            COMMENT: Inscribed:"Ernest Hemingway bought May
                17,1910 at Mclures."
1746.   Reed, Douglas. Insanity Fair, (1938).
            SOURCE: KW-55
1747.   Regler, Gustav. The Great Crusade, 1940.
            SOURCE: AH
            COMMENT: See EH introduction to book.
1748.   Regler, Gustav. La Passion de Jass Fritz, (1937).
            SOURCE: KL:EH Collection
            COMMENT: Trans. into French from German.
1749.   Regny **. Les Golfs de France **.
            SOURCE: KW-40
            COMMENT: May be Annuaire de Golfs de France.
1750.   Reid, Mayne. The Boy Hunters, (1852).
            SOURCE: KW-55
1751.   Reignac, Jean. La Chasse Pratique, (1928).
            SOURCE: KW-55

1752.   Reitz, Deneys. <u>Trekking On</u>, 1934,May.
          SOURCE: EH-MP; SCRBNR
          COMMENT: South Africa and East Africa in WWI.
1753.   Remarque, Erich M. <u>All Quiet on the Western Front</u>,
          1929,May.
          SOURCE: FSF-EH; EH-MP
1754.   Renan, Ernest. <u>Souvenirs d'Enfance et de Jeunesse</u>,
          (1883).
          SOURCE: KW-55
1755.   Renn, Ludwig. <u>War</u>, 1929,Sept.
          SOURCE: SB
          COMMENT: Pseud. of Vieth von Golssenau, A.F.
             Trans. from German by Willa and Edwin Muir.
1756.   Repington, Col. Charles a Court. <u>The First World</u>
          <u>War, 1914-1918</u>, (1920).
          SOURCE: KW-40
          COMMENT: 2 vols.
1757.   Resquemores, ed. <u>Anales Taurinos</u>, (1900).
          SOURCE: KW-40
1758.   Reyls, Carlos. <u>Castanets</u>, (1929).
          SOURCE: KW-40
          COMMENT: El Embrujo de Sevilla, trans. by Jacques
             Le Clercq.
1759.   Reynolds, Jeremiah N. <u>Mocha Dick</u>, (1932).
          SOURCE: KW-55
          COMMENT: "The White Whale of the Pacific." Two
             copies. Scribner's reprnt of 1839 orig. A source
             of Moby Dick.
1760.   Rhodes, C.E., ed. <u>Old Testament Narratives</u>, 1913.
          SOURCE: OPHS; Fenton
          COMMENT: HS text.
1761.   Rhys, Jean. <u>After Leaving Mr. Mackenzie</u>, (1931).
          SOURCE: KW-55
1762.   Richards, Frank. <u>Old Soldier Sahib</u>, 1936, May.
          SOURCE: SCRBNR
          COMMENT: Pre-war soldiering in India and Burma.
1763.   Richards, Vyvyan. <u>Portrait of T.E.Lawrence</u>, 1936.
          SOURCE: KL:Cape; KW-55
1764.   Richardson, Dorothy M. <u>Dawn's Left Hand</u>, 1934,Mar.
          SOURCE: SB; KW-40
1765.   Richardson, Henry B., ed. <u>L' Attaque du Moulin par</u>
          <u>Emile Zola</u>, (1925).
          SOURCE: KW-55
          COMMENT: With questionnaire and French vocabulary.
1766.   Richardson, Henry Handel. <u>The Fortunes of Richard</u>
          <u>Mahony</u>, (1917).
          SOURCE: KW-55
          COMMENT: Pseud. of Henrietta Richardson.
1767.   Richardson, Henry Handel. <u>The Way Home</u>, (1925).
          SOURCE: KW-55
          COMMENT: Pseud. of Henrietta Richardson.
1768.   Riddell, John. <u>In the Worst Possible Taste</u>, (1932).
          SOURCE: KW-40
          COMMENT: Parodies. Pseud. of Corey Ford.

1769.   Riddell, John. The John Riddell Murder Case,
        1930,Nov.
           SOURCE: EH-MP; KW-40
           COMMENT: Pseud. of Corey Ford. Parody of Philo
              Vance. EH: could not read.
1770.   Rieger, Max. Espionnage en Espagne, (1938).
           SOURCE: KW-40
           COMMENT: Trans. Jean Cassou.
1771.   Rimbaud, Arthur. Lettres de la Vie Litteraire,
        (1931).
           SOURCE: KW-55
1772.   Rinehart, Mary Roberts. The Door, 1930.
           SOURCE: EH-MP
           COMMENT: Ordered and received May 22.
1773.   Rinehart, Mary Roberts. My Story, (1931).
           SOURCE: KW-55
1774.   Rintelen, Franz Von. The Dark Invader, (1933).
           SOURCE: KW-55
1775.   Ripley, Thomas Alexander. They Died with Their Boots
        On, 1935,July.
           SOURCE: EH-MP
           COMMENT: Texas desperados. EH ordered.
1776.   Robb, D.D. and J.J.Garrison. Art in the Western
        World, (1935).
           SOURCE: KW-55
1777.   Roberts, Frederick Sleigh Roberts. Forty-one Years
        in India, (1898).
           SOURCE: KW-40
1778.   Roberts, Kenneth Lewis. Arundel, 1937, June.
           SOURCE: SCRBNR; KW-55
           COMMENT: May have been for children.
1779.   Roberts, Kenneth Lewis. Captain Caution, 1937, June.
           SOURCE: SCRBNR
           COMMENT: Hist. Fiction: War of 1812.
1780.   Roberts, Kenneth Lewis. For Authors Only, and Other
        Gloomy Essays, (1935).
           SOURCE: KW-40
1781.   Roberts, Kenneth Lewis. The Lively Lady, 1937, June.
           SOURCE: SCRBNR
           COMMENT: Fiction: War of 1812, Dartmoor Prison.
1782.   Roberts, Kenneth Lewis. Northwest Passage, 1937,
        June.
           SOURCE: SCRBNR; KW-40
           COMMENT: Fiction: Courtmartial of Major Robert
              Rogers and Lt. Samuel Stephens.
1783.   Roberts, Kenneth Lewis. Rabble in Arms, 1937, June.
           SOURCE: SCRBNR
           COMMENT: Historical fiction.
1784.   Roberts, Michael, ed. New Country, (1933).
           SOURCE: KW-40
           COMMENT: W.H.Auden, Stephen Spender, C.Day
              Lewis,..."and other believers in social
              revolution."

1785. Roberts, Walter A. Sir Henry Morgan: Buccaneer and
      Governor, (1933).
      SOURCE: KW-40
1786. Robinson, Edward. Lawrence, 1937, June.
      SOURCE: SCRBNR
1787. Robinson, Edwin Arlington. The Three Taverns,
      (1920).
      SOURCE: KW-55
1788. Robinson, Jacob S. A Journal of the Santa Fe
      Expedition, (1932).
      SOURCE: KW-40
      COMMENT: Princeton U.Press.
1789. Robinson, Thomas. Buttons, (1938).
      SOURCE: KW-55
      COMMENT: Legends and stories of cats.
1790. Robinson, W. A. 10,000 Leagues Over the Sea, (1932).
      SOURCE: KW-55
      COMMENT: Voyages around the world.
1791. Rockwell, Paul Ayres. American Fighters in the
      Foreign Legion, 1914-1918, (1930).
      SOURCE: KW-40
1792. Rodman, Selden. Mortal Triumph and Other Poems,
      (1932).
      SOURCE: KW-55
1793. Rogers, Samuel. Lucifer in Pine Lake, 1937,June.
      SOURCE: SCRBNR
1794. Rogers, William G. Life Goes On, (1929).
      SOURCE: KW-55
1795. Rogerson, Sidney. Propaganda in the Next War,
      1938,Oct.
      SOURCE: Brentanos; KW-40
      COMMENT: Series ed. by Capt. Liddell Hart.
1796. Roget, Peter Mark. Thesaurus of English Words and
      Phrases, (1852).
      SOURCE: KW-40
      COMMENT: First publ. 1852.
1797. Rohmer, Sax. The Si-Fan Mysteries, (1917).
      SOURCE: KW-40
      COMMENT: Pseud. of Arthur S. Ward.
1798. Rolfe, Edwin. The Lincoln Battalion, 1939.
      SOURCE: AH-2
      COMMENT: Americans in the International Brigades.
1799. Rollins, William. The Shadow Before, (1934).
      SOURCE: KW-40
1800. Romains, Jules. Donogoo Tonka, (1920).
      SOURCE: KW-40
      COMMENT: "ou, Les miracles de la science, conte
      cinematographique."
1801. Romains, Jules. Les Hommes de Bonne Volonte, (1932).
      SOURCE: KW-55
      COMMENT: Two vol. in one: Le 6 Octobre; Crime de
      Quinette.

1802.   Romains, Jules. <u>Men</u> <u>of</u> <u>Good</u> <u>Will</u>, 1934,Mar.
        SOURCE: SB; KW-40
        COMMENT: Trans. Gerard Hopkins.
1803.   Rombauer, Irma. <u>The</u> <u>Joy</u> <u>of</u> <u>Cooking</u>, (1931).
        SOURCE: KW-55
1804.   Roosevelt, Robert Barnwell. <u>Superior</u> <u>Fishing</u>,
        (1865).
        SOURCE: KW-40
1805.   Roosevelt, Theodore. <u>African</u> <u>Game</u> <u>Trails</u>, (1910).
        SOURCE: KW-40
1806.   Roosevelt, Theodore. <u>The</u> <u>Deer</u> <u>Family</u>, (1902).
        SOURCE: KW-40
1807.   Roosevelt, Theodore and Kermit (sons). <u>Trailing</u> <u>the</u>
        <u>Giant</u> <u>Panda</u>, (1929).
        SOURCE: KW-40
        COMMENT: Field Museum expedition.
1808.   Ross, Leonard. <u>The</u> <u>Education</u> <u>of</u> <u>Hyman</u> <u>Kaplan</u>,
        1938,Nov.
        SOURCE: SB
        COMMENT: Pseud. of Leo C. Rosten.
1809.   Ross, Martin. <u>Music</u> <u>and</u> <u>James</u> <u>Joyce</u>, (1936).
        SOURCE: KL:EH Collection
        COMMENT: "To accompany Anna Livia Plurabelle by
        Hazel Felman."
1810.   Rossetti, D.G. and C.G. <u>The</u> <u>Poetical</u> <u>Works</u> <u>of</u> <u>the</u>
        <u>Rossettis</u>.
        SOURCE: KW-40
1811.   Rostand, Edmond. <u>Cyrano</u> <u>de</u> <u>Bergerac</u>, (1898).
        SOURCE: KW-40
        COMMENT: Intro,notes and vocabulary by Oscar Kuhns
        and H.W.Church.
1812.   Rothenstein, William. <u>Men</u> <u>and</u> <u>Memories</u>, 1931, April.
        SOURCE: EH-MP; KW-40
        COMMENT: EH ordered.
1813.   Rothenstein, William. <u>William</u> <u>Rothenstein's</u> <u>Memoirs</u>,
        <u>II</u>, 1932,July.
        SOURCE: EH-MP
        COMMENT: EH ordered second vol.
1814.   Roule, Louis. <u>Fishes</u>, <u>Their</u> <u>Journeys</u> <u>and</u> <u>Migrations</u>,
        1934, April.
        SOURCE: EH-MP; SCRBNR
        COMMENT: Ordered by EH. Trans. from French by
        Conrad Elphinstone.
1815.   Rourke, Thomas. <u>Haven</u> <u>for</u> <u>the</u> <u>Gallant</u>, (1936).
        SOURCE: KW-40
        COMMENT: Pseud. of Daniel J. Clinton.
1816.   Rourke, Thomas. <u>Stallion</u> <u>from</u> <u>the</u> <u>North</u>, 1932,Oct.
        SOURCE: EH-MP
        COMMENT: Pseud. of Daniel J.Clinton. EH: made him
        and want to keep track of him.
1817.   Rowan, Richard Wilmer. <u>Spy</u> <u>and</u> <u>Counter-spy</u>, (1928).
        SOURCE: KW-40
        COMMENT: The development of modern espionage.

1818. Roya, Louis. Histoire de Mussolini, (1926).
           SOURCE: KW-55
           COMMENT: Pseud. of Louis Toesca.
1819. Ruebens, Horatio Seymour. Liberty, the Story of
           Cuba, 1932,Oct.
           SOURCE: EH-MP; KW-40
           COMMENT: EH ordered.
1820. Ruiz, Juan. The Book of Good Love of the Archpriest
           of Hita, (1933).
           SOURCE: KW-40
           COMMENT: Prvt. printing. Trans. by Elisha K. Kane.
1821. Ruiz Vilaplana, Antonio. Doy Fe, (1939).
           SOURCE: KW-40
           COMMENT: Took 8 copies to Cuba. English trans.
           Burgos Justice.
1822. Russell, Bertrand. Problems of Philosophy, 1926,May.
           SOURCE: SB
           COMMENT: Rtrnd Sept.1926. May be same title by
           G.W.Cuningham.
1823. Russell, William. Falconry, 1940,Feb.
           SOURCE: EH-MP; KW-55
           COMMENT: EH enjoyed. Sent one to son.
1824. Ruttledge, Hugh. Attack on Everest, (1935).
           SOURCE: KW-55
1825. Ryvez, Henri. La Peche a la Ligne au Bord de la Mer,
           (1932).
           SOURCE: KW-40
           COMMENT: Pseud. of Henri Vezes.
1826. Sabatini, Rafael. St.Martin's Summer, (1924).
           SOURCE: KW-55
1827. Sachs, Hans. The Hot Iron, 1926.
           SOURCE: AH-2
           COMMENT: EH wrote review.
1828. Sackville-West, Hon. Victoria Mary. Thirty Clocks
           Strike the Hour, and other Stories, (1932).
           SOURCE: KW-40
1829. Saint-Simon, Louis de R. Memoires.
           SOURCE: KW-55
1830. Salisbury, Barrows & Tower. A Text Book in General
           Zoology, 1914.
           SOURCE: OPHS
1831. Salvemini, Gaetano. Under the Axe of Facism,
           1936,May.
           SOURCE: SCRBNR; KW-40
           COMMENT: Italy: economic conditions 1918.
1832. Sanchez Canton, Francisco Jauier. L' Espagne,
           (1926).
           SOURCE: KW-40
1833. Sanchez de Neira, J. Gran Dicionario Tauromaco,
           1897, 1930.
           SOURCE: GP-EH; KW-40
1834. Sand, George. Le Meunier d'Angibault, (1845).
           SOURCE: KW-55
           COMMENT: Pseud. of Mme. Dudevant.

1835. Sandburg, Carl. Selected Poems, 1926,Apr.
        SOURCE: SB
        COMMENT: April 13-25.
1836. Sandburg, Carl, ed. The American Song Bag, (1927).
        SOURCE: KW-55
1837. Sanderson, Ivan T. Caribbean Treasure, 1939,Oct.
        SOURCE: EH-MP
        COMMENT: EH ordered.
1838. Sandoz, Mari. Old Jules, (1935).
        SOURCE: KW-55
        COMMENT: Frontier life: Nebraska.
1839. Sanford, John B. The Old Man's Place, (1935).
        SOURCE: KW-40
1840. Sanford, Leonard C. et al. The Waterfowl Family,
        (1903).
        SOURCE: KW-40; KW-55
1841. Sannazzaro. Poemata, (1751).
        SOURCE: KW-55
1842. Santayana, George. The Last Puritan, (1935).
        SOURCE: KW-55
        COMMENT: Memoir in form of a novel.
1843. Sarl, Arthur J. Horses, Jockeys and Crooks, 1936,
        Mar.
        SOURCE: SCRBNR; KW-40
1844. Saroyan, William. The Daring Young Man on the Flying
        Trapeze, 1934.
        SOURCE: KW-55; Baker
1845. Saroyan, William. Inhale and Exhale, (1936).
        SOURCE: KW-55
1846. Sauvage, Henri Emile. La Grande Peche, les Poissons,
        (1833).
        SOURCE: KW-40
1847. Savtchenko, Elie. Les Insurges de Kouban, (1929).
        SOURCE: KW-55
1848. Sayers, Dorothy, ed. Omnibus of Crime, 1930, Nov.
        SOURCE: EH-MP
        COMMENT: Detective stories. EH ordered by telegram
            from Billings, Mont.
1849. Sayers, Dorothy, ed. Second Omnibus of Crime,
        1932,Jan.
        SOURCE: EH-MP
        COMMENT: EH ordered.
1850. Schillings, Carl George. In Wildest Africa, (1907).
        SOURCE: KW-40
        COMMENT: Trans. Frederic Whyte.
1851. Schlosser, Julius. Francisco Goya, (1922).
        SOURCE: KL:EH Collection
        COMMENT: 10 pp. 20 plates.
1852. Schmitz, Ettore. La Coscienza di Zeno, (1923).
        SOURCE: KW-40
        COMMENT: Pseud. of Italo Svevo. Protege of James
            Joyce.
1853. Schneider, Isidor. Doctor Transit, 1926,Mar.
        SOURCE: EH-Isidor Schneider

1854.   Schreiber, Georges, ed. Portraits and Self-
        Portraits, (1936).
        SOURCE: KW-40
        COMMENT: 40 contemporary authors, including EH.
        Pictures and biogs.
1855.   Schulberg, Sonya. They Cried a Little, (1937).
        SOURCE: KW-55
1856.   Schutz, Heinrich. When Mammoths Roamed the Frozen
        Earth, (1929).
        SOURCE: KW-55
        COMMENT: Animals: legends & stories.
1857.   Schwezoff, Igor. Russian Somersault, 1936,Mar.
        SOURCE: SCRBNR
        COMMENT: Dancer.
1858.   Scott, Peter. Wild Chorus, 1939,Feb.
        SOURCE: EH-MP; KW-55
        COMMENT: EH: marvelous book.
1859.   Scott, Sir Walter. Ivanhoe, 1909.
        SOURCE: Baker; OPHS
        COMMENT: Read again in 1913.
1860.   Seabrook, William B. Witchcraft, Its Power in the
        World Today, 1940,Oct.
        SOURCE: EH-MP
        COMMENT: EH ordered.
1861.   Sedgwick, Henry Dwight. Spain: a Short History of
        Its Politics, Literature and Art, (1926).
        SOURCE: KW-40
1862.   Selous, Frederick C. A Hunter's Wanderings in
        Africa, 1934,Mar.
        SOURCE: KL:Brentanos; KW-40
        COMMENT: Pub.1881.
1863.   Sencourt, Robert E. The Life of the Empress Eugenie,
        (1931).
        SOURCE: KW-55
1864.   Sencourt, Robert E. The Spanish Crown, 1808-1931,
        (1932).
        SOURCE: KW-40
1865.   Seneca, Lucius Annaeus. Lettres a Lucilius, (1895).
        SOURCE: KW-55
        COMMENT: French trans.
1866.   Sesgo, Una al. Los Ases del Toreo.
        SOURCE: KW-40
        COMMENT: Pseud. of Orts Ramos, Tomas.
1867.   Seton, Ernest Thompson. The Library of Pioneering &
        Woodcraft, (1926).
        SOURCE: KW-55
1868.   Seton, Ernest Thompson. Life Histories of Northern
        Animals, Vols. I & II, (1909).
        SOURCE: KW-55
1869.   Seton, Ernest Thompson. Rolf in the Woods, (1911).
        SOURCE: KW-55
        COMMENT: Fiction:camping, Indians, scouts.

1870. Seton, Ernest Thompson. <u>Wild</u> <u>Animals</u> <u>at</u> <u>Home</u>,
      (1913).
      SOURCE: KW-55
      COMMENT: Animals: habits & legends.
1871. Seton, Ernest Thompson. <u>Woodcraft</u>, (1918).
      SOURCE: KW-55
      COMMENT: "Camps of instruction".
1872. Seton, Ernest Thompson. <u>The</u> <u>Woodcraft</u> <u>Manual</u> <u>for</u>
      <u>Boys</u>, (1917).
      SOURCE: KW-55
      COMMENT: Outdoors.
1873. Seton, Ernest Thompson. <u>Woodland</u> <u>Tales</u>, (1921).
      SOURCE: KW-55
1874. Shakespeare, William. <u>As</u> <u>You</u> <u>Like</u> <u>It</u>, 1914.
      SOURCE: OPHS
1875. Shakespeare, William. <u>Hamlet</u>, 1915.
      SOURCE: OPHS; KL; KW-55
      COMMENT: EH read 1915-1916. Memorized Pol. advice
          to Laertes, Apr.1916. Memorized 40 lines III,ii
          on acting, Nov.1916.
1876. Shakespeare, William. <u>Julius</u> <u>Caesar</u>.
      SOURCE: KW-55
      COMMENT: Probably read in HS.
1877. Shakespeare, William. <u>King</u> <u>Lear</u>, 1916.
      SOURCE: OPHS; KW-55
      COMMENT: HS reading.
1878. Shakespeare, William. <u>Macbeth</u>, 1915.
      SOURCE: OPHS; KL; KW-55
      COMMENT: HS reading.
1879. Shakespeare, William. <u>The</u> <u>Merchant</u> <u>of</u> <u>Venice</u>.
      SOURCE: KW-55
1880. Shakespeare, William. <u>A</u> <u>Midsummernight's</u> <u>Dream</u>,
      1916.
      SOURCE: OPHS; KW-55
      COMMENT: Sr. Class play in Feb.1916.
1881. Shakespeare, William. <u>Much</u> <u>Ado</u> <u>About</u> <u>Nothing</u>, 1917.
      SOURCE: OPHS
1882. Shakespeare, William. <u>The</u> <u>Tragedy</u> <u>of</u> <u>Othello</u>.
      SOURCE: KW-55
1883. Shakespeare, William. <u>Plays</u> <u>of</u> <u>William</u> <u>Shakespeare</u>.
      SOURCE: KW-40
      COMMENT: 3 vol. edition.
1884. Shakespeare, William. <u>Romeo</u> <u>and</u> <u>Juliet</u>, 1914.
      SOURCE: KL
1885. Shakespeare, William. "The Seven Ages of Man,"
      1914,Nov.
      SOURCE: OPHS
      COMMENT: Memorized for HS.
1886. Shakespeare, William. <u>The</u> <u>Comedy</u> <u>of</u> <u>the</u> <u>Tempest</u>.
      SOURCE: KW-55
1887. Shakespeare, William. <u>Twelfth</u> <u>Night</u>, 1914.
      SOURCE: OPHS; KW-55

1888. Shaw, George Bernard. The Black Girl in her Search
       for God, 1934,Mar.
       SOURCE: SB
1889. Shaw, George Bernard. How He Lied to Her Husband,
       1926.
       SOURCE: AH-2
       COMMENT: EH saw play and wrote review.
1890. Shaw, George Bernard. Saint Joan, (1924).
       SOURCE: KW-55
1891. Sheean, Vincent. A Day of Battle, (1938).
       SOURCE: KW-55
       COMMENT: Battle of Fontenoy (1745).
1892. Sheean, Vincent. Personal History, (1935).
       SOURCE: KW-40
1893. Sheean, Vincent. Sanfelice, 1936,June.
       SOURCE: SCRBNR; KW-55
       COMMENT: Naples, historical fiction.
1894. Sheldon, Charles. The Wilderness of Denali,
       1930,Apr.
       SOURCE: EH-MP; KW-55
       COMMENT: EH: sort of book liked very much.
1895. Shelley, Percy B. "A Cloud," 1915,Dec.
       SOURCE: OPHS
       COMMENT: EH memorized for HS.
1896. Shelley, Percy B. Poems.
       SOURCE: KW-55
1897. Shepard, E.W. Tanks in the Next War, 1938,Oct.
       SOURCE: Brentanos
1898. Sherman, Harold Morrow. Tahara in the Land of
       Yucatan, (1933).
       SOURCE: KW-40
       COMMENT: Children's book.
1899. Sherman, Stuart Pratt. My Dear Cornelia, 1925,Feb.
       SOURCE: EH-GS
       COMMENT: EH impressed by structure and ending.
1900. Sherwood, Robert. There Shall Be No Night, 1940,Oct.
       SOURCE: MP-EH
       COMMENT: MP sent copy. Interesting forward. Russo-
       Finnish War 1939-40.
1901. Shiel, Matthew P. Cold Steel, (1929).
       SOURCE: KW-55
       COMMENT: Historical fiction:Henry VIII.
1902. Shuster, George Nauman. The Catholic Church and
       Current Literature, 1930,Apr.
       SOURCE: EH-MP
1903. Sienkiewicz, Henryk. Quo Vadis, (1897).
       SOURCE: KW-55
1904. Silone, Ignazio. Bread and Wine, 1937.
       SOURCE: SCRBNR
1905. Simenon, Georges. L' Assassin, (1937).
       SOURCE: KW-55
1906. Simenon, Georges. Au Rendezvous Des Terre-neuvas,
       1936.
       SOURCE: SCRBNR

1907.   Simenon, Georges.   Le Blanc a Lunettes, 1938, March.
            SOURCE: SCRBNR
1908.   Simenon, Georges.   Le Charretier de "La Providence,"
            1936, Mar.
            SOURCE: SCRBNR
1909.   Simenon, Georges.   Chez les Flamands, 1936,Mar.
            SOURCE: SCRBNR
1910.   Simenon, Georges.   Le Chien Jaune, 1936,Mar.
            SOURCE: SCRBNR
1911.   Simenon, Georges.   Le Coup de Lune, 1936,March.
            SOURCE: SCRBNR;   KW-40
1912.   Simenon, Georges.   Les Demoiselles de Concarneau,
            (1936).
            SOURCE: KW-55
1913.   Simenon, Georges.   L' Ecluse No. 1, 1936, March.
            SOURCE: SCRBNR
1914.   Simenon, Georges.   L' Evade, 1936, April.
            SOURCE: SCRBNR
1915.   Simenon, Georges.   Faubourg, 1938, March.
            SOURCE: SCRBNR
1916.   Simenon, Georges.   Le Fou de Bergerac, 1936, March.
            SOURCE: SCRBNR
1917.   Simenon, Georges.   " Liberty Bar," 1936,Mar.
            SOURCE: SCRBNR
            COMMENT: In French.
1918.   Simenon, Georges.   Le Locataire, 1936, Mar.
            SOURCE: SCRBNR
1919.   Simenon, Georges.   Maigret, 1936,Mar.
            SOURCE: SCRBNR; KW-55
1920.   Simenon, Georges.   La Maison du Canal, (1933).
            SOURCE: KW-40
1921.   Simenon, Georges.   Les 13 Mysteres, 1936,Apr.
            SOURCE: SCRBNR
1922.   Simenon, Georges.   La Nuit de Carrefour, 1936, Mar.
            SOURCE: SCRBNR
1923.   Simenon, Georges.   L' Ombre Chinoise, 1936,Mar.
            SOURCE: SCRBNR; KW-55
1924.   Simenon, Georges.   Le Passager du "Polarlys," (1932).
            SOURCE: KW-40
1925.   Simenon, Georges.   Pietr-le-Letton, 1936,Mar.
            SOURCE: SCRBNR; KW-55
1926.   Simenon, Georges.   Les Pitard, 1936,Mar.
            SOURCE: SCRBNR
1927.   Simenon, Georges.   Quartier Negre, 1936, Apr.
            SOURCE: SCRBNR
1928.   Simenon, Georges.   Les Rescapes du Telemaque,
            1938,May.
            SOURCE: SCRBNR
            COMMENT: Sent to Mrs. Hemingway.
1929.   Simenon, Georges.   Les Sept Minutes, 1938,May.
            SOURCE: SCRBNR; KW-55
            COMMENT: Sent to Mrs. Hemingway.
1930.   Simenon, Georges.   Les Suicides, 1936,April.
            SOURCE: SCRBNR; KW-55

1931.   Simenon, Georges.   La Tete d'un Homme, 1936,Mar.
      SOURCE: SCRBNR

1932.   Simenon, Georges.   Les Trois Crimes de Mes Amis,
      1938,May.
      SOURCE: SCRBNR; KW-55
      COMMENT: Sent to Mrs. Hemingway.

1933.   Simenon,Georges.   Le Pendu de Saint Pholien, (1931).
      SOURCE: KW-55

1934.   Simpson, Charles Torrey.   Ornamental Gardening in
      Florida, (1916).
      SOURCE: KW-55
      COMMENT: Tropical plants.

1935.   Simpson, Helen DeGuerry.   The Spanish Marriage,
      (1933).
      SOURCE: KW-40
      COMMENT: Mary Tudor and Felipe II.

1936.   Sinclair, Gordon.   Khyber Caravan, 1936,June.
      SOURCE: SCRBNR

1937.   Sinclair, Upton.   I, Candidate for Governor, (1935).
      SOURCE: KW-40

1938.   Sinclair, Upton.   Mammonart, 1925,Oct.
      SOURCE: SB

1939.   Sindral, Jaques.   Tallyrand, (1926).
      SOURCE: KW-40
      COMMENT: Pseud. of Alfred Fabre-Luce.

1940.   Sintenis, Renee.   Renee Sintenis, (1930).
      SOURCE: KW-40
      COMMENT: Paris 4th ed. printed 1930.

1941.   Sitwell, Edith.   I Live Under a Black Sun, 1938,Mar.
      SOURCE: SCRBNR; KW-55

1942.   Sitwell, Osbert.   Before the Bombardment, 1927, Nov.
      SOURCE: SB

1943.   Sitwell, Osbert.   Discursions on Travel, Art and
      Life, 1933,Nov.
      SOURCE: SB

1944.   Sitwell, Osbert.   The Man Who Lost Himself, (1929).
      SOURCE: KW-40

1945.   Sitwell, Sacheverell.   Roumanian Journey, (1938).
      SOURCE: KW-55

1946.   Skolsky, Sidney.   Times Square Tintypes, (1930).
      SOURCE: KW-55
      COMMENT: Actors & actresses.

1947.   Slesinger, Tess.   Time: The Present, 1935.
      SOURCE: KL:Simon and Schuster

1948.   Slocombe, George.   Paris in Profile, (1929).
      SOURCE: KW-55

1949.   Slocum, Joshua.   Sailing Alone Around the World,
      1925,Oct.
      SOURCE: SB

1950.   Small, John K.   Shrubs of Florida, (1913).
      SOURCE: KW-55

1951.   Smith and Thompson.   First Year Latin.
      SOURCE: KW-55

1952.   Smith, Henry Worcester. A Sporting Family of the Old
        South, (1936).
        SOURCE: KW-55
        COMMENT: Skinner family.
1953.   Smith, Lawrence B. Modern Shotgun Shooting,
        1935,June.
        SOURCE: MP-EH
        COMMENT: MP sent unrequested.
1954.   Smith, Lawrence B. Shotgun Psychology, 1938,Dec.
        SOURCE: EH-MP
        COMMENT: EH: very good.
1955.   Smith, Pauline. The Beadle, (1926).
        SOURCE: KW-55
1956.   Smith, Sir William. A Smaller Classical Dictionary,
        (1910).
        SOURCE: KW-55
1957.   Smith, Thorne. Topper   , (1926).
        SOURCE: KW-40
1958.   Smith, Walton H. and F.C.Helwig. Liquor: The Servant
        of Man, 1939,Oct.
        SOURCE: EH-MP
        COMMENT: EH ordered it.
1959.   Smith, Walton Hall. Shadow River, 1927,Nov.
        SOURCE: SB
        COMMENT: Nov.23-Dec.7.
1960.   Smith-Dorrien, Gen. Horace L. Memories of 48 Years'
        Service, (1925).
        SOURCE: KW-40
1961.   Smollett, Tobias George. Humphry Clinker.
        SOURCE: KW-40
        COMMENT: Modern Library ed. 1929?.
1962.   Smythe, Francis Sydney. Climbs and Ski Runs, (1933).
        SOURCE: KW-40
1963.   Soglow, Otto. Everything's Rosy, (1932).
        SOURCE: KW-55
1964.   Sokolov, Nikolai A. Enquete Judiciaire sur
        L'Assassinat de la Famille Imperiale Russe, (1924).
        SOURCE: KW-55
        COMMENT: Nicholas II (1868-1918).
1965.   Solano, Solita. Statue in a Field, (1934).
        SOURCE: KW-55
1966.   Sonrel, Leon. Le Fond de la Mer, (1868).
        SOURCE: KW-40
1967.   Soulie, Maurice. Les Proces Celebres de L'Allemagne,
        (1931).
        SOURCE: KW-55
        COMMENT: History of German trials.
1968.   Southard, Charles Z. The Evolution of Trout and
        Trout Fishing in America, (1928).
        SOURCE: KW-55
1969.   Souvarine, Boris. Stalin, 1939,Oct.
        SOURCE: EH-MP; KW-55
        COMMENT: EH ordered.

1970. Souza, Ernest. Blue Rum, 1930,May.
          SOURCE: EH-MP; KW-55
          COMMENT: Pseud. of Evelyn Scott. EH ordered.
1971. Spaight, J.M. Air Power in the Next War, 1938,Oct.
          SOURCE: Brentanos
1972. Sparrow, Walter Shaw. Angling in British Art,
          (1923).
          SOURCE: KW-40
1973. Spaulding, Col. Oliver Lyman. The United States Army
          in War and Peace, 1937,June.
          SOURCE: SCRBNR; KW-40
1974. Spender, Stephen. The Burning Cactus, (1936).
          SOURCE: KW-55
1975. Spender, Stephen. Poems by Stephen Spender, (1933).
          SOURCE: KW-55
1976. Spender, Stephen. Trial of a Judge, 1938,Mar.
          SOURCE: SB
1977. Spengler, Oswald. The Decline of the West, (1932).
          SOURCE: KW-55
1978. Spenser, Edmund. The Fairy Queen, Books I&II, 1916.
          SOURCE: OPHS
          COMMENT: EH memorized stanza 41 in Oct.,1916. Read
              Books I&II.
1979. Spiess, Johannes. Six Ans de Croisieres en Sous-
          Marin, (1927).
          SOURCE: KW-55
1980. Spinelli, Marcos. From Jungle Roots, (1938).
          SOURCE: KW-55
1981. Spingarn, Joel Elias. Creative Criticism, (1931).
          SOURCE: KW-40
          COMMENT: May have been ed. of '17 or '25.
1982. Spink, Josetta Eugenia. Le Beau Pays de France,
          (1922).
          SOURCE: KW-55
          COMMENT: Fr. language:Chrestomathies.
1983. Spiridovich, Alexandre. Les Dernieres Annees de la
          Cour de Tzarskoie-Selo, (1928).
          SOURCE: KW-40; KW-55
          COMMENT: Trans. from Russ. to Fr. by M. Jeason.
1984. Stallings, Laurence, ed. The First World War: a
          Photographic History, (1933).
          SOURCE: KW-40
1985. Stanley, Edward, Bishop of Norwich. A Familiar
          History of Birds, (1840).
          SOURCE: KW-55
1986. Stanley, Sir Henry Morton. How I Found Livingstone,
          (1872).
          SOURCE: KW-40
1987. Stearns, Harold E. America, A Re-Appraisal, (1937).
          SOURCE: KW-55
1988. Steele, Wilbur D. The Man Who Saw Through Heaven,
          (1927).
          SOURCE: KW-40

1989. Steer, George L. The Tree of Gernika, 1938,July.
       SOURCE: EH-MP; SCRBNR
       COMMENT: EH wire: rush air express 3 copies needed
         for article writing.
1990. Stefansson, Vilhjalmur. The Friendly Arctic, the
       Story of Five Years in Polar Regions, 1925.
       SOURCE: EH-Robert McAlmon; KW-40
1991. Steffens, Joseph Lincoln. The Autobiography of
       Lincoln Steffens, 1931.
       SOURCE: EH-MP
       COMMENT: Ordered by EH.
1992. Steig, William. Man About Town, (1932).
       SOURCE: KW-55
1993. Stein, Gertrude. The Autobiography of Alice B.
       Toklas, 1933.
       SOURCE: KL
       COMMENT: Numerous comments in letters and unpub.
         Mss. See EH intro. to This Must Be the Place.
1994. Stein, Gertrude. Composition as Explanation,
       1926,Nov.
       SOURCE: SB
       COMMENT: EH borrowed Nov.,1926, returned
         Feb.28,1927.
1995. Stein, Gertrude. Descriptions of Literature,
       1926,Aug.
       SOURCE: EH-Miss Finch; KL:EH Collection
       COMMENT: EH owned #117 of 200 numbered copies.
1996. Stein, Gertrude. An Elucidation, 1927,Apr.
       SOURCE: KL:EH Collection
       COMMENT: From Transition magazine.
1997. Stein, Gertrude. Everybody's Autobiography, (1937).
       SOURCE: KW-55
1998. Stein, Gertrude. Geography and Plays, 1922,Mar.
       SOURCE: EH-Sherwood Anderson; EH-GS
       COMMENT: EH read in typescript with Anderson's
         introduction. Pub. in 1923.
1999. Stein, Gertrude. Lucy Church, Amiably, 1934,Mar.
       SOURCE: SB; KW-40
2000. Stein, Gertrude. The Making of Americans, 1922,May.
       SOURCE: EH-GS; EH-Sherwood Anderson
       COMMENT: See Baker's Life. EH: a wonderful book.
2001. Stein, Gertrude. Picasso, (1938).
       SOURCE: KW-55
       COMMENT: 63 reproductions; 8 in color.
2002. Stein, Gertrude. Portrait of Mabel Dodge at the
       Villa Curona, (1911).
       SOURCE: KL:EH Collection
       COMMENT: Inscribed:"To the two Hemingways with
         much affection, Gertrude Stein.".
2003. Stein, Gertrude. Portraits and Prayers, (1934).
       SOURCE: KW-40

2004. Stein, Gertrude. <u>Three Lives</u>, 1922.
   SOURCE: EH-Bill Smith; KL; Fenton; SB
   COMMENT: May have read as early as 1920. Read at
    SB's again June 5,1929.
2005. Steinbeck, John. <u>The Long Valley</u>, (1938).
   SOURCE: KW-55
2006. Steinbeck, John. <u>Of Mice and Men</u>, 1937,June.
   SOURCE: SCRBNR; EH-MP
   COMMENT: Received copy in 1937. In Oct.,1938,
    refers to reading it.
2007. Stendhal, Frederic. <u>The Abbess of Castro and Other</u>
   <u>Tales</u>, (1926).
   SOURCE: KW-40
   COMMENT: Trans. from French by C.K.Scott
    Moncrieff.
2008. Stendhal, Frederic. <u>The Charterhouse of Parma</u>,
   1925,Dec.
   SOURCE: SB; EH-FSF
   COMMENT: Pseud. of Marie Henri Beyle. Trans. by
    C.K. Scott Moncrieff.
2009. Stendhal, Frederic. <u>De L'Amour</u>, (1853).
   SOURCE: KW-55
2010. Stendhal, Frederic. <u>Le Rouge et le Noir</u>, 1927,Feb.
   SOURCE: EH-Isidor Schneider
2011. Stern, James. <u>The Heartless Land</u>, 1934,Mar.
   SOURCE: SB; KW-40
2012. Sterne, Laurence. <u>A Sentimental Journey</u>, 1927,Feb.
   SOURCE: EH-Isidor Schneider
2013. Sterne, Laurence. <u>Tristram Shandy</u>, (1769).
   SOURCE: KW-40
2014. Stevens, Wallace. <u>The Man With the Blue Guitar</u>,
   (1937).
   SOURCE: KW-55
2015. Stevenson, Robert. <u>The Works of Robert Louis</u>
   <u>Stevenson</u>, (1906).
   SOURCE: KW-40; ATH
   COMMENT: 10 vol. edition. May be the set from
    Hemingway home in Oak Park. EH reading HS or
    earlier.
2016. Stewart, Donald O. <u>Mr. and Mrs. Haddock Abroad</u>,
   1925,Feb.
   SOURCE: EH-Bill Smith
   COMMENT: EH: his copy loaned out.
2017. Stewart, Donald O. <u>A Parody Outline of History</u>,
   1925,Nov.
   SOURCE: SB
   COMMENT: Borrowed Nov.23. Retrnd Dec.10.
2018. Stewart, Donald O. <u>The Crazy Fool</u>, 1925,Apr.
   SOURCE: EH-Dos Passos
2019. Stewert, Re.Alex **. <u>In Darkest Spain</u> **.
   SOURCE: KW-40
2020. Stieglitz, Julius Oscar. <u>Chemistry in Medicine</u>,
   (1928).
   SOURCE: KW-40

2021. Stigand, Chauncey Hugh. Hunting the Elephant in Africa, 1934, Mar.
SOURCE: KW-40; KL:Brentanos
COMMENT: Intro. by Col. Theodore Roosevelt.

2022. Stigand, Chauncy Hugh. The Game of British East Africa, (1909).
SOURCE: KW-40

2023. Stoddard, Charles A. Spanish Cities, (1892).
SOURCE: KW-55

2024. Stoddard, Herbert L. The Bobwhite Quail, 1931.
SOURCE: EH-MP; KW-40
COMMENT: Ordered by EH.

2025. Stoker, Bram. Dracula, 1913.
SOURCE: Baker

2026. Stolberg and Vinton. The Economic Consequences of the New Deal, (1935).
SOURCE: KW-55

2027. Stone, I. Sailor on Horseback, 1938,Oct.
SOURCE: Brentanos
COMMENT: Biog. of Jack London.

2028. Stone, Irving. Lust for Life, 1934.
SOURCE: Baker; KW-55
COMMENT: Novel about Van Gogh.

2029. Stopes, Marie. Wise Parenthood, (1919).
SOURCE: KW-55
COMMENT: Birth control.

2030. Strachey, Giles Lytton. Landmarks in French Literature, 1934,Mar.
SOURCE: SB

2031. Strachey, Giles Lytton. Portraits in Miniature, and other essays, (1931).
SOURCE: KW-40

2032. Strange, Michael. Who Tells Me True, 1940,Apr.
SOURCE: MP-EH; KW-55
COMMENT: Sent to Mrs. Hemingway.

2033. Streeter, Daniel. An Arctic Rodeo, (1929).
SOURCE: KW-55

2034. Strickland, W.W. Vishnu, 1929.
SOURCE: EH-MP

2035. Strong, L.A.G. Shake Hands and Come Out Fighting, 1938,Oct.
SOURCE: Brentanos; KW-40

2036. Strutt, Joseph. The Sports and Pastimes of the People of England, (1801).
SOURCE: KW-40

2037. Stuart, Lee. " Que Pasa en Cuba".
SOURCE: KL:EH Collection
COMMENT: No date. Typescript. May be unpublished.

2038. Sturgis, Bertha. Field Book of Birds of the Panama Canal Zone, (1928).
SOURCE: KW-55

2039. Sturgis, W. B. Fly-Tying, 1940, June.
SOURCE: EH-MP

2040. Suarez, Georges. La Vie Orgeuilleuse de Clemenceau,
      (1930).
      SOURCE: KW-55
2041. Summers, Montague. The Werewolf, (1933).
      SOURCE: KW-55
2042. Surtees, Robert S. Plain or Ringlets? (1860).
      SOURCE: KW-55
2043. Sutten, Richard Lightburn. Tiger Trails in Southern
      Asia, (1926).
      SOURCE: KW-40
2044. Swainston, C.M. Reed's Seamanship , (1931).
      SOURCE: KW-40
      COMMENT: Nautical guide for candidates for
         certificates as mates and masters.
2045. Swinburne, Algernon Charles. Poems, (1866).
      SOURCE: KW-40
2046. Swinnerton, Frank Arthur. Swinnerton: an
      Autobiography, (1936).
      SOURCE: KW-55
2047. Tabouis, Genevieve R. Blackmail or War, (1938).
      SOURCE: KW-40
      COMMENT: Trans. from French by Paul Selver.
2048. Taggard, Genevieve. Words for the Chisel, 1926,May.
      SOURCE: Taggard-EH; KW-55
      COMMENT: Taggard sent EH a copy.
2049. Tambs, Erling. The Cruise of the Teddy, 1933.
      SOURCE: KL:Cape; KW-40
2050. Tannehill, Ivan Ray. Hurricanes, Their Nature and
      History, 1938,Mar.
      SOURCE: EH-MP
      COMMENT: EH:sound, interesting and useful.
2051. Tarkington, Booth. Seventeen, 1918.
      SOURCE: KL
2052. Tarkington, Booth. The Turmoil, (1915).
      SOURCE: KW-55
2053. Tarkington, Booth. Young Mrs. Greely, (1929).
      SOURCE: KW-55
2054. Tatchell, Frank. The Happy Traveller: a Book for
      Poor Men, (1923).
      SOURCE: KW-40
2055. Tate, Allen. The Fathers, (1938).
      SOURCE: KW-55
2056. Tate, Allen. Mr. Pope and Other Poems, (1928).
      SOURCE: KW-40
2057. Tate, Allen. Poems: 1928-1931, 1934,Mar.
      SOURCE: SB; KW-40
2058. Taverner, Eric. Trout Fishing from All Angles,
      (1929).
      SOURCE: KW-40
2059. Tavolato, Italo. Georg Grosz, (1924).
      SOURCE: KL:EH Collection
      COMMENT: 32 reproductions.

2060. Taylor, Carl N. Odyssey of the Islands, (1936).
       SOURCE: KW-55
       COMMENT: Philippine Islands.
2061. Tennant, Eleonora. Spanish Journey, (1936).
       SOURCE: KL:EH Collection
2062. Tennyson, Alfred. "The Charge of the Light Brigade,"
       1902.
       SOURCE: KL; EH Scrapbook
       COMMENT: GHH: EH knew a great deal of it by heart
       at age 4.
2063. Tennyson, Alfred. " Crossing the Bar," 1916,Jan.
       SOURCE: OPHS
       COMMENT: Memorized for HS.
2064. Tennyson, Alfred. Idylls of the King, 1913.
       SOURCE: OPHS
       COMMENT: HS text.
2065. Tennyson, Alfred. " Ulysses," 1917,May.
       SOURCE: OPHS
       COMMENT: Memorized for HS.
2066. Terhune, Albert P. To the Best of My Memory,
       1930,May.
       SOURCE: EH-MP; MP-EH
       COMMENT: EH orders and receives copy.
2067. Thackeray, William M. Vanity Fair, (1848).
       SOURCE: KW-55
2068. Tharaud, Jerome et Jean. Notre Cher Peguy, (1926).
       SOURCE: KW-55
2069. Thomas and Howe. Composition and Rhetoric, 1915.
       SOURCE: OPHS
       COMMENT: HS text.
2070. Thomas, George Clifford, Jr. and George C. Thomas,
       III. Game Fish of the Pacific: Southern
       Californian and Mexican, (1930).
       SOURCE: KW-40
2071. Thomason, John W. Fix Bayonets, 1926,Apr.
       SOURCE: EH-MP; EH-Isidor Schneider
       COMMENT: EH: disappointing. Too many bayonets.
2072. Thomason,, John W. Gone to Texas, (1937).
       SOURCE: KW-55
2073. Thomason, John W., ed. Adventures of General Marbot,
       1940,Feb.
       SOURCE: MP-EH
2074. Thompson, Cecil V.R. I Lost My English Accent,
       1939,Nov.
       SOURCE: EH-MP; KW-55
       COMMENT: EH ordered and received.
2075. Thorne, Anthony. Delay in the Sun, (1934).
       SOURCE: KW-40
2076. Thurber, James. My Life and Hard Times, 1933.
       SOURCE: Baker; AH
2077. Thurber, James. The Seal in the Bedroom, (1932).
       SOURCE: KW-55
       COMMENT: EH read and enjoyed Thurber.

2078. Thurston, Howard. 200 More Tricks You Can Do,
       (1927).
       SOURCE: KW-55
       COMMENT: Conjuring.
2079. Thurston, Howard. 200 Tricks You Can Do, (1926).
       SOURCE: KW-40
       COMMENT: Conjuring.
2080. Tinker, Frank Glasgow. Some Still Live, 1938,May.
       SOURCE: SCRBNR; Brentanos
       COMMENT: Bought three copies. "Fighting Plane
          Pilot in the Spanish War."
2081. Tolstoi, Leo. Anna Karenina, 1932.
       SOURCE: Carol Hemingway-EH; KW-55
       COMMENT: Two copies. Carol borrowed a copy in
          1932.
2082. Tolstoi, Leo. The Cossacks, 1933,Jan.
       SOURCE: EH-MP
2083. Tolstoi, Leo. The Journal of Leo Tolstoi, (1917).
       SOURCE: KW-40
       COMMENT: Trans. from Russian by Rose Strunsky.
2084. Tolstoi, Leo. War and Peace, 1925.
       SOURCE: Baker; EH-MP; KW-40
       COMMENT: EH: after reading it, decided there was
          no need to write a war book.
2085. Tomlinson, Henry Major. Gallions Reach, 1927,Dec.
       SOURCE: SB
       COMMENT: Rtrnd. Feb.6,1928.
2086. Tomlinson, Henry Major. London River, (1921).
       SOURCE: KW-40; KW-55
2087. Tomlinson, Henry Major. Old Junk, (1918).
       SOURCE: KW-40
       COMMENT: "Stories of travel and chance."
2088. Tomlinson, Henry Major. The Sea and the Jungle,
       1925,Oct.
       SOURCE: SB
       COMMENT: Brazil, Amazon river.
2089. Tomlinson, Henry Major, ed. Great Sea Stories of All
       Nations, (1930).
       SOURCE: KW-40
       COMMENT: Includes Conrad.
2090. Tosti, Amedeo. L' Italie dans la Guerre Mondiale
       (1915-1918), (1933).
       SOURCE: KW-40
2091. Train, Arthur C. The Adventures of Ephraim Tutt,
       1930, Nov.
       SOURCE: EH-MP
       COMMENT: EH wired MP for copy.
2092. Train, Arthur C. My Day in Court, (1939).
       SOURCE: KW-40
2093. Train, Arthur C. Puritan's Progress, (1931).
       SOURCE: KW-40
2094. Traven, B. The Death Ship, 1934,May.
       SOURCE: EH-MP; SCRBNR
       COMMENT: EH ordered and received.

2095. Travers, Pamela L. Mary Poppins, (1934).
       SOURCE: KW-55
2096. Trelawny, Edward John. The Adventures of a Younger
       Son, 1926.
       SOURCE: MP-EH; KW-40
       COMMENT: MP recommends book for material on
           Shelley and Byron.
2097. Trepte, Lois E. Pansies, 1934,Mar.
       SOURCE: SB
       COMMENT: Purchased copy.
2098. Trevelyan, George M. Garibaldi's Defense of the
       Roman Republic, (1907).
       SOURCE: KW-40
2099. Trollope, Anthony. An Autobiography, Vols. I&II,
       (1883).
       SOURCE: KW-55
2100. Trollope, Anthony. Barchester Towers, (1857).
       SOURCE: KW-55
2101. Trollope, Anthony. The Bertrams, (1859).
       SOURCE: KW-55
2102. Trollope, Anthony. The Last Chronicle of Barset,
       (1867).
       SOURCE: KW-55
       COMMENT: Two copies.
2103. Trollope, Anthony. North America, (1862).
       SOURCE: KW-40
2104. Trotsky, Leon. My Life, 1930,Apr.
       SOURCE: EH-MP
2105. Trotsky, Leon. The Revolution Betrayed, 1937, July.
       SOURCE: SCRBNR
       COMMENT: Trans. by Max Eastman.
2106. Tully **. Pour Diviner **.
       SOURCE: KW-40
2107. Tunney, Gene. A Man Must Fight, (1932).
       SOURCE: KW-55
2108. Turgenev, Ivan. A Desperate Character and Other
       Stories, 1929.
       SOURCE: SB
       COMMENT: Purchased copy.
2109. Turgenev, Ivan. The Diary of a Superfluous Man,
       1929.
       SOURCE: SB
       COMMENT: Purchased copy.
2110. Turgenev, Ivan. Dream Tales and Prose Poems, 1929.
       SOURCE: SB
       COMMENT: Purchased copy.
2111. Turgenev, Ivan. Fathers and Children, 1925,Dec.
       SOURCE: SB; EH-FSF; KW-55
       COMMENT: EH:not his best. More exciting when first
           written. Hell of a criticism for a book.
2112. Turgenev, Ivan. A House of Gentlefolk, 1925, Dec.
       SOURCE: SB
       COMMENT: Purchased copy in 1929.

2113. Turgenev, Ivan. The Jew and Other Stories, 1929.
       SOURCE: SB
       COMMENT: Purchased copy.
2114. Turgenev, Ivan. Knock,Knock,Knock and Other Stories,
       1926,May.
       SOURCE: SB
       COMMENT: Trans. Constance Garnett.Rtrnd.
          Nov.2,1926. Purchased copy 1929.
2115. Turgenev, Ivan. A Lear of the Steppes, 1925.
       SOURCE: SB
       COMMENT: Trans. Constance Garnett. Purchased copy
          1929.
2116. Turgenev, Ivan. Memoires d'un Seigneur Russe.
       SOURCE: KW-55
       COMMENT: Two copies.
2117. Turgenev, Ivan. On the Eve, 1926.
       SOURCE: SB; KW-55
       COMMENT: Borrowed May 10, 1926; returned Sept. 10,
          1926. Borrowed Sept. 27, 1929; no record of
          return.
2118. Turgenev, Ivan. The Plays of Ivan S. Turgenev, 1929.
       SOURCE: SB
       COMMENT: Purchased copy.
2119. Turgenev, Ivan. Rudin, 1929.
       SOURCE: SB
       COMMENT: Purchased copy.
2120. Turgenev, Ivan. Smoke, 1929.
       SOURCE: SB; KW-55
2121. Turgenev, Ivan. A Sportsman's Sketches, 1926,Sept.
       SOURCE: SB
2122. Turgenev, Ivan. A Sportsman's Sketches, 1925,Oct.
       SOURCE: SB
       COMMENT: Oct.22-Nov.16.
2123. Turgenev, Ivan. A Sportsman's Sketches, 1929,Sept.
       SOURCE: SB
       COMMENT: Purchased copy 1929.
2124. Turgenev, Ivan. The Torrents of Spring, 1928,Feb.
       SOURCE: SB
       COMMENT: Feb.8-Mar.3. Purchased copy 1929.
2125. Turgenev, Ivan. The Torrents of Spring, 1925,Oct.
       SOURCE: SB
       COMMENT: Oct.27-Nov.16. Trans. by Constance
          Garnett. Purchased copy 1929.
2126. Turgenev, Ivan. The Two Friends, 1926,May.
       SOURCE: SB
       COMMENT: May 10-Sept.10. Purchased copy 1929.
2127. Turgenev, Ivan. Virgin Soil, 1929.
       SOURCE: SB
       COMMENT: Purchased copy.
2128. Twain, Mark. The Adventures of Huckleberry Finn,
       1916.
       SOURCE: OPHS; KW-55
       COMMENT: EH: American Literature begins with Huck
          Finn.

2129. Twain, Mark. <u>The Adventures of Tom Sawyer</u>, (1876).
        SOURCE: KW-55
2130. Twain, Mark. <u>The Innocents Abroad</u>, (1869).
        SOURCE: KW-40
2131. Twain, Mark. <u>Tom Sawyer and Huckleberry Finn</u>.
        SOURCE: KW-55
2132. Tyndall, John. <u>The Glaciers of the Alps</u>, (1860).
        SOURCE: KW-40
2133. Ullivarri, Saturnino. <u>Piratas y Corsarios en Cuba</u>,
        (1931).
        SOURCE: KW-40
        COMMENT: Pub. in Cuba.
2134. Undset, Sigrid. <u>Kristin Lavransdatter</u>, (1929).
        SOURCE: KW-40
2135. Vale, Robert B. <u>Wings, Fur and Shot</u>, (1936).
        SOURCE: KW-40
2136. Valery, Paul. <u>Mer, Marines, Marins</u>, (1930).
        SOURCE: KW-40; KW-55
2137. Valery, Paul. <u>Monsieur Teste</u>, (1932).
        SOURCE: KW-55
2138. Valle-Inclan, Ramon del. <u>La Guerra Carlista</u>, (1908).
        SOURCE: KW-40
2139. Valle-Inclan, Ramon del. <u>La Pipa de Kif</u>, (1919).
        SOURCE: KW-40
2140. Van Cise, Philip S. <u>Fighting the Underworld</u>,
        1936,Mar.
        SOURCE: SCRBNR
        COMMENT: Crime and criminals.
2141. Van de Water, F.F. <u>Glory Hunter</u>, 1934, Nov.
        SOURCE: EH-MP
        COMMENT: Ordered by EH. Life of Custer.
2142. Van Doren, Carl Clinton, ed. <u>Modern American Prose</u>,
        (1934).
        SOURCE: KW-40
2143. Van Dyke, T.S. and Edwyn Sandys. <u>Upland Game Birds</u>,
        (1902).
        SOURCE: KW-40; KW-55
2144. Van Every, Edward. <u>Sins of New York as "Exposed" by
        the Police Gazette</u>, (1930).
        SOURCE: KW-55
2145. Van Loon, Hendrik Willem. <u>Van Loon's Geography</u>,
        (1932).
        SOURCE: KW-55
2146. Van Paassen, Pierre. <u>Days of Our Years</u>, (1939).
        SOURCE: KW-55
        COMMENT: 20th.C.
2147. Van Vechten, Carl. <u>Excavations</u>, (1926).
        SOURCE: KW-40
        COMMENT: EH inventory called it: Evacuations.
2148. Vanderbilt, Cornelius, Jr. <u>Farewell to Fifth Avenue</u>,
        (1935).
        SOURCE: KW-40

2149. Vanderbilt, Harold. Enterprise, 1931,Nov.
           SOURCE: MP-EH; EH-MP
           COMMENT: Sailing: Americas' Cup.
2150. Vandercook, John Womack. The Fools' Parade, 1930,
           May.
           SOURCE: EH-MP
           COMMENT: Ordered and received by EH.
2151. Vasari, Giorgio. Lives of the Painters, Sculptors
           and Architects (Vols.I-VI), (1885).
           SOURCE: KW-55
           COMMENT: The 6 vol. edition first pub. in 1885.
2152. Vasquez, Leopoldo et al. La Tauromachia de Rafael
           Guerra(Guerrita), 1930.
           SOURCE: GP-EH
           COMMENT: GP ordered copy for EH.
2153. Veblen, Thorstein. The Theory of the Leisure Class,
           (1899).
           SOURCE: KW-55
           COMMENT: Economics. Reissued in '24,'27, and '34.
2154. Velazques y Sanchez, D. Jose. Anales Del Toreo,
           (1919).
           SOURCE: KL:EH Collection
2155. Verga, Giovanni. Mastro-Don Gesualdo, 1926,Oct.
           SOURCE: SB
           COMMENT: Trans. by D.H.Lawrence.
2156. Verlaine, Paul. Poemes Saturniens, (1921).
           SOURCE: KW-40
2157. Verona, Guido da. "La Vita Comincia Domani," (1912).
           SOURCE: KW-55
2158. Verrill, A. Hyatt. Great Conquerors of South and
           Central America, (1929).
           SOURCE: KW-55
           COMMENT: Spanish American history to 1600.
2159. Vertex, Jean. Bistrots, Reportages Parisiens, 1936,
           April.
           SOURCE: SCRBNR; KW-55
2160. Very, Pierre. M. Malbrough Est Mort, 1938, Mar.
           SOURCE: SCRBNR; KW-55
2161. Vespa, Amleto. Secret Agent of Japan, (1938).
           SOURCE: KW-55
           COMMENT: Japanese Secret Service.
2162. Vicaire, Georges. Bibliographie Gastronomique,
           (1890).
           SOURCE: KW-55
2163. Vieira, Antonio. Sermao e Carta, (1800).
           SOURCE: KW-55
2164. Villard, Henry. The Past and Present of the Pike's
           Peak Gold Regions, (1932).
           SOURCE: KW-40
           COMMENT: Princeton U.Press reprint of 1860
               original.

2165.   Villehardouin and DeJoinville. Chronicles of
        Crusaders, 1929,Mar.
        SOURCE: EH-MP; KW-40
        COMMENT: Prob. Everyman's Library ed.
2166.   Villiers, Alan John. Grain Race, (1933).
        SOURCE: KW-40
2167.   Villiers, Alan John. Stormalong, (1937).
        SOURCE: KW-55
        COMMENT: World voyage: ship "Joseph Conrad".
2168.   Villon, Francois. Oeuvres,
        SOURCE: KW-40
        COMMENT: 15th century.
2169.   Vindel, Pedro. Estampas de Toros, (1931).
        SOURCE: KW-40
2170.   Viollet-Le-Duc, Eugene Emmanuel. Annals of a
        Fortress, (1875).
        SOURCE: KW-40
2171.   Vollard, Ambroise. Paul Cezanne, 1926,Sept.
        SOURCE: SB
2172.   Voltaire. History of Charles the Twelfth, King of
        Sweden, (1760).
        SOURCE: KW-40
        COMMENT: 1925 edition trans. by Winifred
             Todhunter.
2173.   Voltaire. Zadig, (1749).
        SOURCE: KW-40
        COMMENT: Engl. trans. publ. 1929.
2174.   Vos, Bert John. Essentials of German, (1903).
        SOURCE: KW-55
2175.   Wagner, Richard. The Twilight of the Gods, (1911).
        SOURCE: KW-55
        COMMENT: Trans. by Margaret Armour.
2176.   Wahlen, Auguste. Moeurs, (1843).
        SOURCE: KW-55
        COMMENT: Usages et costumes de tous les peuples du
             monde.
2177.   Walker, Edith B. Tales of the First Animals, (1930).
        SOURCE: KW-55
        COMMENT: Juv. lit.: paleontology.
2178.   Wallace, Edgar. The Double, (1928).
        SOURCE: KW-55
2179.   Wallace, Edgar. The Green Archer **, 1924,Aug.
        SOURCE: EH-GS
        COMMENT: Probably this one.
2180.   Wallmsley, Leo. Three Fevers, 1932,Aug.
        SOURCE: EH-MP; KW-40
        COMMENT: About a family of fishermen.
2181.   Walpole, Hugh. The Dark Forest, (1916).
        SOURCE: KW-55
2182.   Walpole, Hugh. Fortitude, (1913).
        SOURCE: KW-40
        COMMENT: Probably read in HS or soon after.

2183.   Walpole, Hugh. <u>Rogue Herries</u>, 1930,April.
       SOURCE: EH-MP
       COMMENT: EH requests copy; receives May 22, 1930.
2184.   Walsh, Ernest. <u>Poems and Sonnets</u>, (1934).
       SOURCE: KW-40
2185.   Walsh, Maurice. <u>The Dark Rose</u>, 1938,Mar.
       SOURCE: SCRBNR
       COMMENT: Historical fiction, 17th,C.
2186.   Walsh, Maurice. <u>Green Rushes</u>, (1935).
       SOURCE: KW-55
       COMMENT: Sinn Fein,1916.
2187.   Walsh, Maurice. <u>The Hill Is Mine</u>, 1940, Nov.
       SOURCE: EH-MP
       COMMENT: Ordered by EH.
2188.   Walsh, Maurice. <u>The Road to Nowhere</u>, 1934,Oct.
       SOURCE: EH-MP; <u>KW-40</u>; KW-55
       COMMENT: EH ordered.
2189.   Walsh, Maurice. <u>The Small Dark Man</u>, (1929).
       SOURCE: KW-40
2190.   Walshe, Douglas. <u>Close-up</u>, (1934).
       SOURCE: KW-40
2191.   Walsingham, Thomas De Grey. <u>Shooting</u>, (1900).
       SOURCE: KW-40
       COMMENT: Badminton Library of Sports, Vol.2.
2192.   Ward, Alfred Charles. <u>American Literature 1880-1930</u>,
       (1932).
       SOURCE: KW-40
2193.   Ward, Rowland. <u>The Sportsman's Hand Book</u>, (1906).
       SOURCE: KW-40
       COMMENT: Taxidermy and hunting.
2194.   Ware, Joseph E. <u>The Emigrants Guide to California</u>,
       (1932).
       SOURCE: KW-40
       COMMENT: Reprinted by Princeton U.Press in 1932
         from 1849 original.
2195.   Warner, Sylvia Townsend. <u>Summer Will Show</u>,
       1936,June.
       SOURCE: SCRBNR
2196.   Warren, Samuel. <u>Ten Thousand a Year, parts 1 & 2</u>,
       (1840).
       SOURCE: KW-55
2197.   Wassermann, Jakob. <u>The World's Illusion</u>, 1928,Feb.
       SOURCE: SB
       COMMENT: Feb.13-28.
2198.   Wassermann, Jakob. <u>The World's Illusion</u>, 1921.
       SOURCE: GH-EH; EH-CH; KL
       COMMENT: GH recommended to EH, who later sent copy
       back to his father.
2199.   Waters, Helena L. <u>From Dolomites to Stelvio</u>, (1926).
       SOURCE: KW-40
       COMMENT: 4 maps and 26 pictures.
2200.   Waugh, Evelyn. <u>A Handful of Dust</u>, 1934, Oct.
       SOURCE: EH-MP; KW-55
       COMMENT: Ordered by EH.

2201. Waugh, Evelyn.   Labels: A Mediterranean Journey,
       (1930).
            SOURCE: KW-55
2202. Waugh, Evelyn.   Scoop, (1938).
            SOURCE: KW-55
2203. Waugh, Evelyn.   Vile Bodies, 1930,Apr.
            SOURCE: EH-MP
            COMMENT: EH ordered. Arrives May 22, 1930.
2204. Waugh, Evelyn.   Waugh in Abyssinia, 1937,Apr.
            SOURCE: SCRBNR; KW-40
            COMMENT: Italo-Ethopian War, 1935-1936.
2205. Webb, Mary.   Precious Bane, (1924).
            SOURCE: KW-55
2206. Webb, Sidney and Beatrice Potter.   Soviet Communism:
       A New Civilization? 1936.
            SOURCE: MP-EH; KW-55
            COMMENT: 2 vol. work.
2207. Weidman, Jerome.   The Horse that Could Whistle
       "Dixie," (1939).
            SOURCE: KW-55
2208. Weidman, Jerome.   I Can Get It For You Wholesale,
       (1937).
            SOURCE: KW-55
2209. Wells, Herbert George.   Bealby, (1915).
            SOURCE: KW-55
2210. Wells, Herbert George.   The Bulpington of Blup,
       (1933).
            SOURCE: KW-40
2211. Wells, Herbert George.   The Mind of the Race, (1915).
            SOURCE: KW-55
            COMMENT: Pub. under pseud. Reginald Bliss.
2212. Wells, Herbert George.   The Outline of History,
       (1921).
            SOURCE: KW-55
            COMMENT: Third ed. 1921 rev. First ed. 1920 (2
                vols.).
2213. Wells, Linton.   Blood on the Moon, 1937.
            SOURCE: SCRBNR
            COMMENT: "Autobiography of Linton Wells".
2214. Wells, Wells.   Wilson the Unknown, 1931,Feb.
            SOURCE: MP-EH; KW-55
            COMMENT: MP sent copy. Woodrow Wilson. Wells Wells
                pseud.
2215. Wendell, Barrett.   English Composition, 1916.
            SOURCE: OPHS
            COMMENT: HS text.
2216. Werfel, Franz.   The Forty Days of Musa Dagh, (1934).
            SOURCE: KW-55
2217. Wertenbaker, Charles.   To My Father, 1935.
            SOURCE: KL:Farrar and Rinehart
2218. Werth, Leon.   Clavel Soldat, (1919).
            SOURCE: KW-55
2219. Wertheim, Barbara.   The Lost British Policy, (1938).
            SOURCE: KW-55

2220. Wescott, Glenway. Fear and Trembling, (1932).
           SOURCE: KW-40
2221. Wescott, Glenway. Good-bye, Wisconsin, (1928).
           SOURCE: KW-40
2222. Wescott, Glenway. The Grandmothers, 1927,Sept.
           SOURCE: SB; Paris Tribune
           COMMENT: EH: Problem is every word written for
              immortality.
2223. Wescott, Glenway. " Miss Moore's Observations,"
           (1923).
           SOURCE: KL:EH Collection
           COMMENT: With Marianne Moore's poem "Marriage".
2224. West, Rebecca. The Thinking Reed, 1936,Mar.
           SOURCE: SCRBNR; KW-55
           COMMENT: Pseud.
2225. West, Willis Mason. American History and Government,
           1916.
           SOURCE: OPHS
           COMMENT: HS text.
2226. Westermarck, Edvard Alexander. The History of Human
           Marriage, (1921).
           SOURCE: KW-40
           COMMENT: 3 vols.
2227. Weyman, Stanley John. Historical Romances, (1933).
           SOURCE: KW-40
2228. Wharton, Edith. The Age of Innocence, (1920).
           SOURCE: KW-55
2229. Wharton, Edith. A Backward Glance, 1934.
           SOURCE: EH-MP; SCRBNR; KW-55
           COMMENT: Ordered by EH.
2230. Wharton, Edith. Ethan Frome, (1911).
           SOURCE: KW-55
2231. Wharton, Edith. The House of Mirth, (1905).
           SOURCE: KW-55
2232. Whelen, Townsend. Wilderness Hunting and Wildcraft,
           (1927).
           SOURCE: KW-55
2233. Whistler, James Abbott McNeill. The Gentle Art of
           Making Enemies, (1890).
           SOURCE: KW-40
2234. White, Edward L. Lukundoo, (1927).
           SOURCE: KW-55
2235. White, Gilbert. The Natural History and Antiquities
           of Selborne, (1789).
           SOURCE: KW-40
2236. White, William Chapman. These Russians, 1931,Jan.
           SOURCE: MP-EH
           COMMENT: MP sent copy.
2237. Whitman, Lawrence. The Road to Happiness, 1913,Dec.
           SOURCE: KL
           COMMENT: EH saw play.
2238. Whitman, Walt. Leaves of Grass, (1855).
           SOURCE: KW-55

2239. Whitman, Walt. " O Captain, My Captain," 1915,Feb.
           SOURCE: OPHS
           COMMENT: Memorized for HS.
2240. Whitman, Walt. Poems and Prose of Walt Whitman.
           SOURCE: KW-55
2241. Whitney, Parkhurst. Not Tonight, 1937, June.
           SOURCE: SCRBNR
2242. Wilde, Oscar. Poems of Oscar Wilde.
           SOURCE: KW-55
2243. Wilder, Thornton. The Bridge of San Luis Rey, 1927,
           Nov.
           SOURCE: SB; EH-MP
           COMMENT: EH thought it was a fine book of short
               stories. EH-MP May 31,1928.
2244. Wilder, Thornton. The Woman of Andros, 1930.
           SOURCE: EH-Thornton Wilder
           COMMENT: EH in close correspondence with Wilder
               1929-1931.
2245. Wilkins, George H. Undiscovered Australia, (1929).
           SOURCE: KW-55
2246. Williams, William Carlos. Life Along the Passaic
           River, (1938).
           SOURCE: KW-55
2247. Williams, William Carlos. Spring and All, 1923,Aug.
           SOURCE: SB
2248. Williams, William Carlos. A Voyage to Pagany,
           (1928).
           SOURCE: KW-55
2249. Williams, William Carlos. White Mule, (1937).
           SOURCE: KW-55
2250. Williamson, Henry. Salar the Salmon, 1936,June.
           SOURCE: KW-40; KW-55
           COMMENT: Two copies.
2251. Wilson, Edmund. The American Jitters, 1932.
           SOURCE: EH-Samuel Putnam; KW-55
           COMMENT: EH: one of the best books published in
               1932.
2252. Wilson, Edmund. Axel's Castle, (1931).
           SOURCE: KW-40
           COMMENT: "study in the imaginative lit. of
               1870-1930."
2253. Wilson, Edmund. I Thought of Daisy, (1929).
           SOURCE: KW-40
           COMMENT: EH probably read it year pub.
2254. Wilson, Edmund. To the Finland Station, 1940,Nov.
           SOURCE: EH-MP
           COMMENT: EH ordered.
2255. Wilson, Edmund. Travels in Two Democracies,
           1936,June.
           SOURCE: SCRBNR; KW-55
2256. Wilson, Harry Leon. Ruggles, Bunker, and Merton:
           Three Masterpieces of Humor, (1935).
           SOURCE: KW-40

2257. Wilstach, Paul. Islands of the Mediterranean,
          (1926).
          SOURCE: KW-40
2258. Winegate **. Fire and Sword in India **.
          SOURCE: KW-40
          COMMENT: May be Fire and Sword in the Sudan by
          F.R.Wingate (1896).
2259. Winkler, John K. W. R. Hearst, (1928).
          SOURCE: KW-55
          COMMENT: Journalism.
2260. Winz, Claud **. Le Port du Feu**.
          SOURCE: KW-40
2261. Wister, Owen. "A Gift Horse," 1929,Dec.
          SOURCE: EH-MP
          COMMENT: EH:one of three or four best stories OW
          has written.
2262. Wister, Owen. "The Honorable Strawberries,"
          1929,Dec.
          SOURCE: EH-MP
          COMMENT: EH: damn fine story.
2263. Wister, Owen. " Philosophy 4," 1929,Dec.
          SOURCE: EH-MP
          COMMENT: EH: badly written. Feel ashamed even to
          read it.
2264. Wister, Owen. " Pilgrim on the Gila," 1929,Dec.
          SOURCE: EH-MP
          COMMENT: EH: one of the three or four damn fine
          stories O.W. has written.
2265. Wister, Owen. Roosevelt, the Story of a Friendship,
          1880-1919, 1930,April.
          SOURCE: EH-MP; KW-40
          COMMENT: EH requests copy, arrives May 22, 1930.
2266. Wister, Owen. The Virginian, 1916.
          SOURCE: KW-40; Fenton
          COMMENT: HS reading.
2267. Wister, Owen. Works of Owen Wister, 9 vols. **.
          SOURCE: KW-40
          COMMENT: No 9 vol. edition of Wister.
2268. Wittmer, Felix. Floodlight on Europe, (1937).
          SOURCE: KW-55
2269. Wodehouse, P. G. Young Men in Spats, (1936).
          SOURCE: KW-55
2270. Wolf, Robert. Springboard, (1927).
          SOURCE: KW-55
2271. Wolfe, Thomas. Look Homeward, Angel, (1929).
          SOURCE: KW-55
2272. Wolfe, Thomas. Of Time and the River, 1935, Mar.
          SOURCE: EH-MP; KW-40
2273. Wolfe, Thomas. The Web and the Rock, 1939,July.
          SOURCE: EH-MP
          COMMENT: EH: home town stuff marvelous. N.Y. stuff
          very poor. Negro narrative best he's done.

2274.   Wolfe, Thomas. You Can't Go Home Again, 1940,Nov.
        SOURCE: EH-MP
        COMMENT: EH ordered. EH: home town stuff wonderful
           and unsurpassable. Other stuff over-inflated
           journalese.
2275.   Wolff, Jetta S. Les Pierres qui Parlent, (1923).
        SOURCE: KW-55
2276.   Woodbury, David O. The Glass Giant of Palomar,
           (1939).
        SOURCE: KW-55
        COMMENT: Telescopes and astronomy.
2277.   Woodrooffe, Thomas. Yangtze Skipper, 1937,July.
        SOURCE: SCRBNR; KW-55
2278.   Woodward, William E. Lafayette, (1938).
        SOURCE: KW-55
2279.   Woolf, Leonard and Virginia, eds. The Hogarth
           Letters, 1934,Mar.
        SOURCE: SB; KW-40
        COMMENT: Collection of letters by British authors.
2280.   Woolf, Viginia. The Voyage Out, 1934,Mar.
        SOURCE: SB; KW-40
2281.   Woolf, Virginia. The Common Reader, 1927,Feb.
        SOURCE: SB; KW-40
        COMMENT: Purchased copy Mar.,1934.
2282.   Woolf, Virginia. The Common Reader, second series,
           1934,Mar.
        SOURCE: SB
2283.   Woolf, Virginia. Flush, 1934,Mar.
        SOURCE: SB; KW-55
2284.   Woolf, Virginia. Jacob's Room, 1934,Mar.
        SOURCE: SB; KW-55
2285.   Woolf, Virginia. The Second Common Reader, (1932).
        SOURCE: KW-40
2286.   Woolf, Virginia. Three Guineas, (1938).
        SOURCE: KW-55
2287.   Woolf, Virginia. To the Lighthouse, 1934,Mar.
        SOURCE: SB; KW-40
        COMMENT: Purchased two copies.
2288.   Woollcott, Alexander H., ed. Woollcott's Second
           Reader, 1936,Mar.
        SOURCE: SCRBNR; KW-40
        COMMENT: Includes: EH, Dorothy Parker, Wm.Bolitho,
           Stephen Crane (Whilomville), R.L.Stevenson,
           D.H.Lawrence, and others.
2289.   Wordsworth, William. " Daffodils," 1914,Jan.
        SOURCE: OPHS
        COMMENT: EH memorized for HS.
2290.   Wordsworth, William. "The World is Too Much With
           Us," 1917,Apr.
        SOURCE: OPHS
        COMMENT: Memorized for HS.

2291. Work,Burr & Thompson. Prison Life and Reflections,
         (1849).
         SOURCE: KW-40
         COMMENT: Memoirs of three Abolitionists imprisoned
            in Missouri.
2292. Wylie, Elinor. Jennifer Lorn, (1923).
         SOURCE: KW-55
2293. Wylie, Elinor. The Orphan Angel, (1926).
         SOURCE: KW-55
2294. Wyss, Johan David. The Swiss Family Robinson,
         1929,Nov.
         SOURCE: SB
         COMMENT: Purchased a copy.
2295. Yeats, William Butler. Autobiographies, (1926).
         SOURCE: KW-40
2296. Yeats, William Butler. Dramatis Personae, 1936,May.
         SOURCE: SCRBNR; KW-40
2297. Yeats, William Butler. Early Poems and Stories,
         1926,Apr.
         SOURCE: SB
2298. Yeats, William Butler. Poems, (1901).
         SOURCE: KW-40
2299. Yeats-Brown, Francis Charles Claypon. The Lives of a
         Bengal Lancer, 1930, Dec.
         SOURCE: EH-MP
         COMMENT: India.
2300. Yormolinsky, A. Dostoevsky, A Life, 1934, Nov.
         SOURCE: EH-MP
         COMMENT: Ordered by EH.
2301. Young, Francis. They Seek a Country, (1937).
         SOURCE: KW-55
2302. Zangwill, Israel. Dreamers of the Ghetto
         (vols.I&II), (1898).
         SOURCE: KW-55
2303. Zweig, Arnold. The Case of Sergeant Grischa, 1929.
         SOURCE: EH-MP; KW-55
2304. Zweig, Arnold. Education Before Verdun, 1929,June.
         SOURCE: EH-MP; SCRBNR; KW-40
         COMMENT: Trans. Eric Sutton. First of trilogy:
            Sergeant Grischa, Crowning of a King.

Subject and Title Indexes

We have tried to subject code as many of the entries as possible. However, most of the novels are not coded, for their subject matter was not usually available in the NUC. Other entries may not be complete. Some, I am sure, are altogether wrong. Computers make few errors; human beings make many. Do not, therefore, take the index as an absolute. Call it, rather, partial. The precise user will still have much work to do.

SUBJECT INDEX

Title Index

Numbers refer to *Hemingway's List of Reading* and the absence of accents follows the usage of that list

Library of Congress Cataloging in Publication Data

Reynolds, Michael S   1937-
    Hemingway's reading, 1901-1940.
    Includes indexes.
    1.   Hemingway, Ernest, 1899-1961—Books and reading.
I.   Title.
PS3515.E37Z7548   813'.52   80-7549
ISBN 0-691-06447-4